DIAMOND
DAYS

DIAMOND DAYS

Life in Minor League Baseball

To Ted –
Best Wishes
Jeff Klein

Jeff Klein

To order additional copies of this book, contact:
Xlibris Corporation
1-888-795-4274
www.Xlibris.com
Orders@Xlibris.com
21897

CONTENTS

CHAPTER 1

Opening Day

We were all young and goggle-eyed.
We were fulfilling our dream.

—*Al Rosen, third baseman*

Winter is over. The hot-stove leagues have been laid to rest. The trades, the contract negotiations, the injury rehabs; all are left behind for now. What remains is pure—the game itself on the field. A new season means new hope. Hot prospects are out to quickly climb the ladder in their farm system. Fringe players are out to show they are prospects. For those hobbled by injuries in the past and burdened with questions of the present, this is their time for resurrection. For the minor league journeymen, this may be the year they finally get called to The Show. And for the veterans who were big leaguers in seasons past, this is a chance for another taste of the dream.

The 2000 season begins. The contract and signing bonus hassles are over for nineteen-year-old Rick Asadoorian, the top draft pick of the Boston Red Sox in 1999. Having missed the Rookie and Short-Season Class-A seasons last year, this season will mark his first as a professional. Joe Strong, at age thirty-seven, reports to the Calgary Cannons, the Triple-A affiliate of the Florida Marlins after spending last season with the Double-A and Triple-A teams in the Devil Rays organization as well as Mexico City. He is still waiting to throw a pitch in a major league game.

Ed Yarnall is returning to the Columbus Clippers after an extended period in Spring Training. He was thought by many to be the number five starting pitcher for the Yankees after an excellent 1999 campaign in Triple-A Columbus and appearances in five games for the world champions. Back problems and some weak outings changed his travel destination from the Big Apple to central Ohio. At twenty-four, the future is still wide open as he begins his attempt to retake his place in the majors. One of his teammates, thirty-year-old outfielder Jon Zuber, knows the struggle well, having spent the last few seasons bouncing between Triple-A and major league ball. He is looking forward to another run at the big leagues, this time with a new team after eight years in the Phillies system.

The future was wide open for Adam Hydzu in 1990 when the San Francisco Giants selected him the first round of the draft; the fifteenth pick overall among all teams. In the 1990s he made it as far as Triple-A in several organizations. Now he begins his eleventh professional season in Altoona, home of Pittsburgh's Double-A team, the Curve.

After being cut by the Braves in minor league Spring Training, Chris Poulsen spent a great deal of time on the road to attend independent league tryouts for the Northern, Atlantic, and Frontier Leagues. He finds a roster spot with the Chillicothe Paints of the Frontier League, one of six veterans of affiliated baseball on the team. Elsewhere around the Frontier League, former Yankee farmhand Alejandro Bracho is once again playing in North America, this time for the Richmond Roosters, after pitching in Taiwan the previous year. In Dubois County, Fran Riordan begins his season playing first base, unaware what the season has in store for his baseball resume.

The teams themselves may be in transition. Affiliations with major league clubs will change. A team may find itself in a new league, playing at a new level, perhaps with a new name. Many cities and towns can trace their minor league roots back over a century, covering many different leagues. Some places are welcoming baseball back after years or even decades since the last pro team was there. What is most important to the majority of fans is that a professional baseball team is calling their town home.

And visitors are welcome. Take the time to chat with an usher in Nashville, a fan in Appleton, or a concession worker in Johnstown, and one will walk away with a story or two from the local baseball lore. Cliff Fralick has been working the gate at Everett Memorial Stadium for twelve years since his retirement. Happy to talk to first-time visitors, he's sure to point out the plaque that marks the spot where seventeen-year-old Ken Griffey, Junior's first professional home run, landed.

Although the season may not begin until May or June for some independent and lower level minor leagues, a springlike optimism pervades in every park at the season's start, be it in April or beyond. Regardless of the month, the die-hard fans scan the rosters to see if the local favorites have returned and to discuss the merits or pitfalls of the new players. They speculate on the careers of those who have moved on. The signs on the outfield walls advertising everything from insurance to pizza to lube jobs are touched up. The new paint continues to the grandstands and scoreboards. The intermingling smells of fresh-cut grass and barbecued regional specialties hover over the field. Red, white, and blue bunting is hung around the park for the first game. Fixtures are polished; the souvenir stands are restocked. Everything old is new again.

These are the rituals played out across the country in the factory towns of the Midwest, along the rivers in the Carolinas, high in the mountains of northern California whose dry winds carry line drives well beyond the outfield fences, and in the hundreds of other places in the United States and Canada which now, or once, called themselves home to pro ball. The city names speak of the diversity of locales from Akron to Zebulon. In 2000, there were two Columbuses, two Charlestons, two Charlottes, two Greenvilles, two Portlands, two Richmonds, a Salem, a Salem-Keizer, and a Winston-Salem. Or one could catch a game in the more uniquely named Kissimmee, Medicine Hat, or Rancho Cucamonga.

If the city names are colorful, then the team names add to the flavor of the game. Some teams proudly carry the same name as their major league parent club. Others go by monikers like the Boll Weevils and the Express. Animal lovers can root for the Muckdogs, Alley Cats, and Crawdads. For those inclined to the nobility, the Lumber Kings of the Midwest League hold court in Clinton, Iowa. Want some music? Try the Nashville Sounds, Greenville (Misssissippi) Bluesmen, and the New Britain Rock Cats. And for a few years, fans of singer Warren Zevon once could find the Werewolves of London north of the U.S.-Canadian border in London, Ontario.

In Albuquerque, life imitated art (cartoon art, that is) when the city's new team was christened the Isotopes. Although the name can in part be attributed to New Mexico's history in the development of atomic power, it was largely inspired by a television episode of *The Simpsons* in which Homer's beloved Isotopes are almost moved to Albuquerque. Although the fictional Isotopes remained in the fictional Springfield of *The Simpsons*, the idea for the team's name moved to the Southwest when professional baseball returned to Albuquerque after a two-year absence.

Minor and independent league baseball is more than just a professional sport played during the hot months of the year. It becomes part of the community in culture and identity, in friendship and in family. The park is where you go on summer evenings to catch up with friends you haven't seen for a while, as well as to catch a game. Attending a game is like attending church or a concert on the village green. Players and fans get to know each other on a first name basis. Lifelong friendships are formed. In some cases, a player may settle in a minor league town he once played in when his career is over.

Players are not isolated to the field. Before the game, they may be found stretching in the stands or in the open walkways between the clubhouse and the field. There is usually time for an autograph or casual conversation. For wide-eyed children walking in proudly wearing their oversized baseball gloves, it is an opportunity to see their heroes without the separation of fences between them. To them, anyone wearing the uniform is a titan.

"It's a great thing," said Phil Dauphin, who played in five different minor league farm systems. "Part of the fun of being in the minor leagues is getting to be so close to the fans, to be able to interact with them."

The minor leagues have grown tremendously in popularity in the past fifteen years. Many reasons are given. As described earlier, there is a feeling that these teams truly belong to the town. With the promotions, demotions, and trades within the major league farm systems, players change teams more often than their major league counterparts. But the feeling prevails among local fans that whoever wears the uniform of their team are part of the community, however briefly.

In the simple case of economics, it is much less expensive to attend a minor league game—a family of four can get in the gate at the local park for less than the price of a single box seat ticket for the majors. The atmosphere is much more laid back as well. While there is no doubting the fire and competitiveness of the players, there is more of an allowance for them to have fun between innings, participating in team promotions and mascot antics that become less common in the majors.

In the major league world of large and small markets, where many teams are out of contention at the start of the season, springtime in the minors means that this year is *the year* for the local heroes. Anything can happen for a team, for a player. It may unfold over the season, or it may come in the course of one game—or even less. Part of the beauty of the game is that in one single pitch, one single swing, or one single play in the field or on the base paths, a legend can be born.

CHAPTER 2

This is the Life:
Welcome to the Pro's

You've got to be part of an organization, now—
where before you were playing more as an
individual.

—Harry Eisenstat, pitcher

A career in professional baseball can take many unexpected turns, but Robert Moses Grove never thought he'd begin his career by being traded for a fence. In 1920, with one year of semi-pro ball under his belt, the left-handed, flame-throwing pitcher was signed to a contract with Martinsburg, West Virginia of the Class-C Blue Ridge League. The ball club, however, was having financial difficulties. Their home field consisted of little more than a grandstand and the layout of the field. What was still lacking was an outfield fence.

News about the twenty-year-old southpaw quickly traveled around baseball. In the days when nearly all of the minor league teams were independent of any major league affiliations (Branch Rickey was just beginning his revolutionary "farm system expcriment" with the St. Louis Cardinals), competing offers from clubs of all levels were arriving in Martinsburg. Accounts vary on the exact sum paid, but Grove's contract was sold to the Baltimore Orioles (then belonging to the Double-A International League) for approximately $3,500. The funds received by Martinsburg were used to construct the outfield fence in their home park.

A few years later, Baltimore would turn a handsome profit by selling Grove to Connie Mack's Philadelphia A's for $105,000. In the course of his seventeen years in the major leagues, Robert Moses "Lefty" Grove would win three hundred games and be elected to the Hall of Fame in 1947. The outfield wall in Martinsburg never saw the hallowed halls of Cooperstown.

Before the farm system of affiliations to major league clubs became widespread, minor league teams were free to sign nearly anyone they wished. Team officials of the Worcester Boosters in the Eastern League got to know the motorman on the trolley line that ran from their town to Woonsocket, Rhode Island. This motorman had a son who was a catcher on a nearby semi-pro team. Largely as a favor to the father, the team signed his son to a professional contract.

The following year, the trolley motorman's son, Charles Leo Hartnett, made his major league debut with the Chicago Cubs at age twenty-one. Nicknamed "Gabby" by his teammates in his rookie year because he rarely spoke, he went on to play in the majors until 1941. He was regarded as the best catcher of his era in the National League, a sentiment that earned him induction into the Hall of Fame in 1955.

In 1934, Hal Doerr was catching for the Portland Beavers of the Pacific Coast League. When the team was in his hometown of Los Angeles, his younger brother, Bobby, who was still in high school, would take fielding practice with his older brother's team. The younger brother was soon noticed by another local PCL team, the Hollywood Stars and, at age sixteen, was signed by the team with the stipulation that he return to high school in the fall to attend his senior year.

Two years later, Hal would join Bobby in San Diego, where the Stars had since moved and been renamed the Padres. Also during that season, the team's owner invited "some skinny local kid" to take batting practice with the team. The players on the Padres, many of whom had major league experience, took exception to their practice time be taken up by some unknown. As the kid began hitting balls deep into the outfield, though, the grumbling died down. Doerr overheard one of his veteran teammates remark that this kid would have a contract by the time the team left for its next road trip, a prediction which proved to be true. On the team's next travel day, the kid showed up at the train depot with his suitcase in one hand and a newly signed contract in his pocket. The kid's name was Ted Williams.

In those years, scouts for major league teams were rare on the West Coast. One of those few scouts, Harry Johnson, recommended to Boston's general manager, Eddie Collins, that the Red Sox sign Doerr. Collins traveled West to see Johnson's player and was suitably impressed. Between games of a double header in Portland, Collins informed Doerr that the Red Sox were going to purchase his contract. Doerr played his first major league season in 1937.

During that same trip, he saw Ted Williams taking batting practice. Although the newly signed Williams was not playing much at the time, Collins saw enough to make an agreement with Padres owner Bill Lane that Boston would have the first chance to buy Williams' contract. The Red Sox purchased Williams' contract during the Winter Meetings following the season.

In 1938, the Red Sox decided to give Williams a closer look in Spring Training. Eddie Collins contacted Doerr and asked him to have Williams meet him in Los Angeles so that Doerr could make sure he got to Spring Training without any problems. That spring, however, Nature had other plans. The day before they were scheduled to leave, a severe rainstorm made the roads, bridges, and railroad tracks between San Diego and Los Angeles impassable. Williams was on his own. With phone lines also downed by the storm, the two players managed to contact each other with the aid of two ham radio operators. They agreed that they would each try to get to Indio, which was as far to the west as the trains could reach after the storm, by whatever means were available.

Doerr was able to get a bus into Indio, where he met teammates Babe Herman and Max West. There was no sign of Williams. Unable to do anything more, Doerr boarded the train with Herman and West. The three had a four-hour layover after reaching El Paso, so Herman decided to make the best of it. He suggested that they cross the border into Juarez to get some dinner. When they returned to the train depot, they found Williams waiting on them, having arrived on a later train. The four players continued on together to Florida. When Doerr introduced Williams to manager Joe Cronin, the rookie Williams, in his typical, spontaneous way, greeted the baseball veteran with a hearty, "Hiya, sport!"

By the end of Spring Training, the Red Sox decided to send Williams to Minneapolis for another year of experience. In 1939, Williams joined Doerr in Boston, where their careers would continue to intertwine from Fenway Park to the Hall of Fame.

While very few careers would lead to a bronze plaque in Cooperstown, some players can look back on a career filled with Hall of Fame encounters. In 1933, Harry Eisenstat was pitching for his high school team in the Brooklyn city championship game, played in the Dodgers' Ebbets Field. Dodgers skipper Casey Stengel, early in his Hall of Fame managerial career, had his catcher, Al Lopez (who would also enter the Hall as a manager), scout the young pitcher. The Dodgers wound up signing Eisenstat, who would spend eight years in the majors, pitching in 165 games for the Dodgers, Tigers, and Indians.

Eisenstat's major league career would be peppered with Hall of Fame footnotes. While in Detroit, he roomed with the Tigers' future Hall of Fame first baseman Hank Greenberg. In one historic game, he took the mound against Cleveland's Bob Feller (another

Hall of Famer) as the Cooperstown-bound pitcher struck out eighteen Tigers to establish a new single game strikeout record. However, Eisenstat got the better of Feller in the game as the Tigers prevailed against the Indians, 4-1. In 1939, Eisenstat joined the Indians in a trade that sent yet another future Hall of Famer, Earl Averill, to Detroit.

If the Boston Red Sox had some incredible results from the scouting trip to the Pacific Coast League that netted them Bobby Doerr and Ted Williams, they let another future star slip through their fingers the next decade. The team released Al Rosen after he tried out for a Class C farm team in 1942. Fortunately, Rosen's baseball career was saved by the friend of a friend of a friend.

His roommate knew a scout who knew Jim Gruzdis, the manager of the Thomasville Tommies in the North Carolina League. Gruzdis was in need of a third baseman after the team's starter at third broke his leg. Rosen went to Thomasville and, shortly thereafter, signed his first professional contract for ninety dollars a month. Eleven years later, Rosen was voted the American League's Most Valuable Player.

During his twenty years as a major league outfielder, Jay Johnstone earned a reputation as a major league flake. It's a small wonder, then, that he signed his first professional contract to avoid legal problems with the NCAA.

A high school standout in football as well as baseball, Johnstone was heavily recruited by major universities all over the country who were eager to have him grace their gridirons. He was so impressed on several of his visits that he wound up signing letters of intent to seven different schools, which created a huge problem with NCAA regulations, although he wasn't aware of the havoc he was creating at the time.

"They said, 'If you like this place so much, just sign this piece of paper.' So I did," recalled Johnstone.

His multiple commitments resulted in numerous universities

fighting over who had the legal rights to him. Tired of the hassle and seeking to avoid all of the entanglements with college football, he signed a professional baseball contract with the California Angels instead.

In 1944, Cal Hogue was part of a team of high school players assembled by St. Louis Browns scout Curt Hammenback. Hammenback brought the team to Newark, Ohio to play against the Browns' farm club there. Hogue pitched well, despite losing the game, 2-1, and received an invitation for a tryout the following spring where he was signed to his first professional contract.

That same year, sixteen-year-old Jim Greengrass began playing baseball in the Yankees farm system, making $110.00 a month with a $1.50 per day in meal money. In his eyes, life couldn't be any finer. (He still has his first contract framed and mounted on a wall in his home.) When Greengrass returned to school for his senior year, he was ineligible to play any sports because he had been paid to play baseball. But giving up school athletics for professional baseball was a trade he was willing to make.

"I was something of a celebrity in town," he said of his return from his first summer in pro ball.

Guy Morton, Jr. was only four years old in 1934 when his father, who spent eleven seasons pitching for the Cleveland Indians, passed away. He was sent to Mississippi to be raised by his grandparents. With no other children close by, he began throwing rocks to pass the time, often using the insulators on nearby telephone poles as targets. As the years passed, he developed a strong throwing arm through this unorthodox pitching practice, and it appeared that he might follow in his father's professional footsteps.

Guy Morton, Sr. had a career total of ninety-eight wins and eighty-five losses. To this day, he remains on the top twenty lists of several of Cleveland's all-time pitching records. Despite losing his father at such an early age, the younger Morton held on to what few memories he had of him.

"My dad had scrapbooks and I would read through them. He was my idol even though I knew him just a little bit. People were always asking me if I was going to be a baseball player like my daddy."

At age fourteen, he moved to Alabama, where his American Legion coach took an interest in his throwing ability. While he had the strength, the refined skill and knowledge of the game was still missing.

"I hardly knew how to get on the mound," Morton joked.

However, he soon mastered the art of pitching and was attracting scouts during his sophomore year in high school. During his junior and senior years, he was already playing semi-pro ball. At this time, the area around Birmingham, Alabama was a hotbed of young talent including future major leaguers Frank Lary, Frank House, and Willie Mays.

In his senior year of high school, his career took an unexpected turn when he hurt his arm playing football. Unable to regain the extra zip he had once had on his fastball, he opted to move to the receiving end of the pitches and became a catcher.

After attending the University of Alabama on a baseball scholarship, he was signed to a professional contract by Johnny Murphy, a scout for the Red Sox. The signing bonus for the prized prospect was six thousand dollars. (In accordance with the rules of that time, any player receiving a signing bonus of more than six thousand had to go directly to the major league team.) He began his pro career close to home, in Birmingham, where he played for Boston's Double-A club.

Like Morton, Jeff Heaverlo was the son of a major league pitcher. His father, Dave, spent seven years in the big leagues pitching for the Giants, Athletics, and Mariners. Fortunately for the younger Heaverlo, his father was there to give him advice before he turned pro. At first, though, like the sons of many ballplayers who are away from home, he learned to throw from his mother. When he was in high school, his father began quizzing him on the mental aspects of the game—anticipating what strategy should be employed and why.

In his senior year of high school, he was drafted in the thirteenth round. He was ready to sign a contract, but his father felt he would benefit more from college experience before joining the professional ranks. In 1999, after three years of college, the Seattle Mariners drafted him as a supplemental pick between the first and second rounds. Heaverlo greatly appreciated having the opportunity of learning from his father.

"I felt fortunate, being able to grow up with my dad. Even going into college it was a big help because I knew more about the game. It's incredible how much more you can pick up when your father has played the game."

Reid Ryan knew where he stood when he became a professional. The son of Nolan Ryan, he keenly understood how far his last name would take him—and where it would stop.

"I think it's whatever the person makes it out to be," the younger Ryan explained. "Being a son might get you on the field, but it's not going to get people out for you."

Ben Grieve also grew up in baseball while his father, Tom, was playing for the Rangers, Mets, and Cardinals. When Ben was drafted by the Oakland Athletics, Tom Grieve knew that this would give him a mental edge, having seen the game from the inside.

"He had the benefit of being a bat boy and not being in awe of major league players. So that when he went to the minor leagues, it was pretty much what he expected he was going to be doing ever since he was a sophomore in high school."

Grieve believed this edge also carried onto the big leagues, where Ben was the American League Rookie of the Year in 1998. He described how Ben's perspective was different than his own had been as a rookie.

"I expected that the ball was going to be thrown so fast that I couldn't even see it. Or that a player would hit it so hard that I couldn't even catch it. These are stupid things that you think because they are major league players. These kids realize that the major leagues are a higher level of play, but they don't go in there in awe, not knowing what to expect."

In 1948, John Romonosky was pitching for a local team on weekends in Harrisburg, Illinois, a small coal-mining town of nine thousand residents. One of the local businessmen arranged to have a scout for the St. Louis Cardinals watch the team one day in the hopes of getting Romonosky and perhaps others signed to a professional contract.

On the day the scout arrived, Romonosky was scheduled to pitch the first game of a double-header. Any concerns the scout may have had were erased by the nineteen strikeouts that Romonosky racked up in the game. As usual, he was planning to play in the field during the second game, but the scout would have no part of it; wanting instead to get back to Romonosky's house and get his signature on a contract before anyone else discovered his find.

With high school one year behind him, Romonosky went west to Fresno, California to pitch for a C-League team in the Cardinals system. He discovered how fierce and talented the competition was in his first game as he allowed just one run in ten innings—and lost 1-0.

In the early days of Major League Baseball's amateur draft, which began in 1965, players often learned which team had selected them several days after the fact. In contrast, Rick Asadoorian got the news almost instantly with the aid of modern technology in 1999. His family received the news while he was away on a class trip. They paged him with a message to call home, which he did by using a cell phone.

The Boston Red Sox had told him that he was "their guy" prior to the draft, which was pretty exciting for someone who grew up in New England. Getting the actual news, however, made the pre-draft speculation quickly pale in comparison.

Pre-draft predictions are fluid in nature. A player's status can rise or fall depending on health concerns or perceptions about their signability. Even the players themselves can't rely on what they are told by team scouts.

"The people you're talking to aren't usually the ones that make the call," explained John Stewart, the seventh round pick of the Texas Rangers in 1998.

The Kansas City Royals wanted to make sure they would get their selection with the thirty-second overall pick in the 1999 Draft, a supplemental pick in the first round. With signing bonuses for top draft picks soaring, they didn't want to risk selecting a player they could not sign. Their caution also saved pitcher Jay Gehrke a great deal of waiting and speculation.

After the draft was already underway, Gehrke received a call from a Kansas City scout, asking him if he would sign with the Royals if chosen in this high spot. Gehrke confirmed that he would, and was subsequently drafted and signed by the team.

In the years before independent baseball returned in force, going unselected in the draft usually meant the end of a player's hopes for a pro career. Bryan Eversgerd saw the rounds pass him by in 1989, but was not about to give up the dream. As a last-ditch effort, he attended a tryout in St. Louis' Busch Stadium. The next time he set foot in the park came five years later when he was wearing the major league uniform of the Cardinals.

The transition from high school or college ball to the professional ranks can be overwhelming. "Living in hotels and out of suitcases were a change of life," recalled Mark Eichhorn, a former major-league pitcher. For many players, life in pro ball marks their first time away from home or a college campus.

"It was a very maturing experience," says Jim Pankovits, describing the adjustment to life in the minors. "I was playing on a college scholarship, living in the dorm, eating at the training table. Then I was on my own."

Added to this is the grind of playing nearly every day. Gone are the two, three, or four-game weeks of school ball. Gone, also, are the days of being the top player on one's team. The talent level takes a dramatic jump as the professional ranks are filled with players who were all top players on their respective school or other amateur teams.

"I went from being the best on a team of twenty-five players to being on a team with twenty-five of the best players and playing against another team with twenty-five of the best," recalled ex-Pirate pitcher Ron Neccai.

J. M. Gold, the top draft pick of the Milwaukee Brewers in 1998, quickly discovered the jump in talent level from his high school days, but also understood that the best course was to concentrate on his own skills. "You don't want to worry about what talent the other people have. You want to take care of your own business."

"It's a different kind of game when you're playing in amateur compared to professional ball," Harry Eisenstat pointed out. The hometown comforts and familiarity vanish quickly. "Just getting acclimated to the people you're playing with—your teammates—and getting acclimated to the fields that you're playing on; it's entirely different."

Paul Splittorff's biggest adjustment during his first season came when he was promoted from rookie-level ball in the New York-Penn all the way to the Royals' Triple-A club in Omaha in one leap.

"All my teammates had been high school or college players, but so many of the guys at Omaha had spent some time in the major leagues. Many were over thirty, and for the first time I was in a men's league."

Granted, the amount of culture shock will vary depending on the player's background and outlook. When the Phillies signed him in 1959, John Herrnstein still had a leg in a cast due to an injury suffered while playing football for the University of Michigan. After he reported to his first minor league stop in Des Moines, he was surprised at the lack of training regimen and discipline he found in pro ball. Although he knew he had plenty to learn before making it to the majors, four years of playing football at a major university had seemed like more of a professional environment to him.

Not that all changes are for the worst. David Dalton remembered many positives from his first season in pro ball after graduating from college.

"Not worrying when my next thirty-page paper is due was great," he said. "I got to stay up late, sleep in late, sign autographs, and play for a good team."

. . . in a Strange Land

For players from abroad, there are the added dimensions of dealing with a new language and culture. When players from Latin America first began playing in the United States, they were left to their own devices in trying to communicate with their manager and teammates and to find their way around in new, strange cities. Unfortunately, they also dealt with prejudice in these early years. Some American players, unable to understand the language and customs, would label their Latin teammates as lazy and dishonest.

"My greatest surprise was interacting with the Latin players," said John Stewart of his first year in pro ball. My college coach told me of stories about them stealing things from your locker or trying to undermine you in some way. I couldn't have found that to be any further from the truth."

As the number of Latin players has grown tremendously, so have the efforts of the teams to ease their transition. There are classes to learn English as well as to learn about the cuisine and other cultural differences that these young players will encounter. It is typical for teams to now have at least one coach who is bilingual in English and Spanish to help with communications. Manager Jim Saul would sometimes sit in on these classes to pick up on Spanish so that he could communicate with his Latin players better.

In the past few years, the number of players from Taiwan, Japan, and South Korea has also begun to increase. With this trend comes the demand for translators to work with multiple nationalities. During the 2000 season, the Pawtucket Red Sox had one translator, Chang Lee, who could speak both Korean and Japanese, in addition to English, to help pitching coach Rich Bombard work with his imported prospects.

Rick Asadoorian's professional debut was delayed by contract negotiations that lasted through the summer of 1999. By the time all the papers were signed, he began playing in the Gulf Coast Rookie League that fall. In the short amount of time that comprises the GCL season, he had already picked up some of the Spanish, Korean, and Japanese languages.

When he played for New Zealand in the International Fast-Pitch Softball World Series in Michigan in 1996, eighteen-year-old Travis Wilson had no thoughts of a career in baseball. After all, the game wasn't even played in his country. The closest sport was fast-pitch softball, which he began playing when he was nine.

However, a year later, he was back in the United States; this time in West Palm Beach to attend minor league Spring Training after being scouted in the tournament and signed by the Atlanta Braves. Accent and slang notwithstanding, he was at least able to speak the same language, but dealing with the on-field changes from softball to baseball nearly proved to be his undoing. In his first year, he hit a mere .215, with very little power for Danville in the Appalachian League.

Determined to succeed in his new sport, Wilson continued to hone his baseball craft. Over the next two seasons he batted over .300 in Rookie and low-A ball, followed by a respectable 2000 season in high Class-A Myrtle Beach. A hot start in Double-A in 2001 earned him a promotion to Triple-A Richmond where he returned to play in 2002 and 2003, remaining one step away from becoming the first New Zealander to play major league baseball.

It's a long way from Taiwan to Asheville, North Carolina, but Tourists pitcher Chin-hui Tsao dealt with the transition fairly well in 2000. In every city in the South Atlantic League, he would attempt to find a good Chinese restaurant to deal with some of his homesickness. Not that he completely ignored the local fare. " . . . I'm also starting to like fried chicken," he explained to a local reporter.

CHAPTER 3

This is the Life: Day by Day

The minor leagues were so much fun because it was
something you dreamed about doing . . . you were a
professional.

—*Jack DiLauro, pitcher*

Tom Lawless has seen a great deal of life both on and off the field during his career. From 1982 to 1990, he played in the major leagues. Following his playing days he became a minor league manager. He has yet to become bored with it all.

"Many stories and experiences come out year after year in the minor leagues," explained Lawless. "You see different things in this game. What we like to tell our players every year is that the experience you gain and the friends you meet in your years in the minor or major leagues are priceless. Enjoy, relax, have fun while you're in the game."

Home Away from Home

For minor leaguers, like their major league counterparts, "home" during baseball season is only lived in for approximately half of the time. With the low pay, particularly in the lower minors, and need for only a short-term lease, the accommodations for those who are out on their own are usually quite basic—and often cramped. Former Yankee shortstop and broadcaster Tony Kubek once shared an attic with five teammates in Owensboro, Kentucky during his minor league days.

Don Gutteridge's first year in professional was 1932, when he played for the Lincoln Links of the Nebraska State League. After arriving in Lincoln one afternoon to join the team, Gutteridge had no idea as to where he would be living. With nowhere else to go, he found his way to the ballpark and arrived as the team was warming up for a game. It wasn't until after the game that he found a place to stay when a teammate offered to share a room.

Phil Dauphin soon learned where minor leaguers stood in Reds owner Marge Schott's world. During Spring Training in 1994, players were two and three-deep in each hotel room while Schott's St. Bernard, Schottzie, had its own room.

When Tom Grieve arrived in Burlington, North Carolina for his first season in 1967, he was the last of four players sharing a two-bedroom trailer. The only place left for him to sleep was a cheap, Naugahyde couch on which he had to keep a sheet to keep from sticking to the upholstery.

"Looking back, I could never sleep there now," Grieve said. "But at the time, that's what we had, that's what you did, and it was no problem."

Furnishings are often as sparse as the rooms themselves. Braves farmhand Chris Poulsen slept on an air mattress in the kitchen of a shared apartment while in Jamestown, New York. While the kitchen's linoleum was better for his sinuses than the carpet in the living room, he still had to deal with a slight slope in the floor.

Sanitation was another issue.

"Four guys and no cleaning lady," said Rex Hudler of his minor league living arrangements. "You could imagine how dirty the places would get."

Then there are the misadventures in cooking. For many

players, the pro experience also means it's their first experience in having to fend for themselves in the vast wilds of the kitchen.

George Virgilio began playing baseball in the Braves farm system after graduating from high school in 1989. During his first season away from home cooking, he lost around fifteen pounds.

Some meals work out well, especially if someone else is doing the cooking. While playing for the Midwest League's Waterloo Hawks in 1968, Bill Lee roomed with six teammates (including Carlton Fisk) above a restaurant that had a promotion that if a pitcher threw a shutout, he won a steak dinner. Lee only played in Waterloo for one month, but was able to cash in on one dinner.

By most standards, frozen waffles should be easy to prepare. But Pat Ahearne recalled a teammate (whom he chose not to name) who knocked on his roommate's door, complaining that there was something wrong with the waffles—they weren't cooking properly. Bleary-eyed, the roommate went into the kitchen only to find the waffles sitting on top of the toaster instead of being inserted into the slots.

"I wasn't actually there," said Ahearne. "But I believe it."

Ahearne went on to explain that his belief in the story stems from his own first-hand experiences with the rookie chef. Such as the time the team had him convinced that there was a real-life Jurassic Park in Miami. The teammate was awestruck and kept insisting that the team visit the park.

In 1938, seventeen-year-old Hal Newhouser signed with the Detroit Tigers out of high school. His first assignment in the minors was in Alexandria, Louisiana of the Evangeline League, a long way from a future pitching career that would net him two MVP awards and an induction in Cooperstown. He was met at the Alexandria bus station by a team official at four o'clock in the morning and driven to a boarding house that had seen better days. His tiny room contained a small chest of drawers, a folding, military-issue cot, and a single bare light bulb for illumination. The room also lacked a door, which allowed the symphony of snoring from about a dozen of his teammates also residing in the house come through loud and clear. He chose to spend the night at the ballpark instead, sleeping on a pair of benches in the clubhouse.

Sleeping in clubhouses was elevated to complete residence for three Pacific Coast League managers by the early 1980s. Moose Stubing (Salt Lake City), Rocky Bridges (Phoenix), and Ken Pope (Spokane) each spent the season living in their respective teams' clubhouses during the season.

"It saves me three hundred dollars a month," explained Stubing at the time.

And Bridges couldn't see the point in paying rent just to hang up his clothes.

"I don't have that many clothes, anyway. All I need is my uniform," said Bridges.

Other attempts to save money had mixed results. Johnny Pesky, who would go on to play for ten years in the majors, recalled the horrific results when one minor league teammate gave another one a haircut to avoid the barber's bill.

"Not too well done," he described in an understatement.

Teams often provide assistance to the players in finding apartments or perhaps a spare room for rent. However, in the case of the Lehigh Valley Black Diamonds of the Atlantic League, the team had too many distractions in 2000 to help its players. The team owner declared bankruptcy while the team's stadium was still under construction. The team was able to find a place to play—a six hundred-seat amateur ballfield in Quakertown, Pennsylvania—but could provide no help for the players.

With area rental properties scarce and hotels too expensive for frequent residence, several players, the pitching coach, and some family members began camping in a state park nearby for slightly over a dollar per night. While agreeing that the area was beautiful, Black Diamonds manager Wayne Krenchiki opted not to rough it for the season. "I need a bed," he said. Due to the conflicting schedules with amateur teams at the park, the Black Diamonds often played their games at noon. The players would then return to the campground to fish and have their nightly cookouts.

From 1968 to 1971, the players for one Carolina league team had two "home" towns. The cities of Raleigh and Durham shared the same team, with half of the season's home games played in each town. Unfortunately for the players, this made it nearly impossible to find a place to live.

"You would live out of the bus and your suitcase on the road and out of your car when you were at home," explained Jon Matlack, a member of the 1968 Raleigh-Durham squad.

There are situations that work out better for players. Jim Pankovits spent his first year sharing a trailer with a teammate, George Ploucher, in Covington, Virginia. While space inside the trailer may have been tight, there was the outdoor attraction of a nearby pond beneath a covered bridge to cool off in. A few years later came a significant upgrade when he was playing Triple-A ball for the Padres in Hawaii and sharing an apartment with Rick Lancellotti just three blocks from Waikiki Beach. Dick Phillips, who was managing Vancouver in the same league, had an apartment in Hawaii and wanted someone to stay in it during the season. In addition to it being fully furnished, he also had a car there for the tenants to use.

Having managed in minor league baseball for thirty years, Jim Saul is well traveled. For him, it is the game itself that is important—the location will take care of itself.

"I'm here in Jamestown, New York," said Saul during a 2000 interview. "A lot of people wouldn't like it—I enjoy it. It's a small town; you get to know the people. They're good people and lucky to have baseball. They know it, and I know it."

Adopted Families

In some cases, particularly in the lower minors, local fans

and booster clubs offer players a place to stay, rent-free. For the players, their hosts may become like a second family to them. San Diego Padres pitcher Brian Tollberg recalled his host family in Chillicothe, Ohio from his 1994 season in the Frontier League. "I loved it . . . I lived on a four hundred-acre farm, came and went as I pleased, and got to work around the farm on our off-days."

Before one game in Chillicothe, Kathy Robson, Steve and Leah Deffenbaugh, Bryan Joseph, and Mike Climer swapped stories about having players in their homes. The player often becomes part of the family, and the family takes pride in the player's accomplishments. "When he hits a homerun, it's like, 'That's my kid!'" said one host family mother.

Hosting players gives the families a unique look inside the game as they learn about life in baseball. "As old as I am, I see these players on the field, and I look up to them," said one host. "But at the same time, I get to know them and realize that they are just kids. In baseball, they're men, they're heroes, but when they're in your home you realize how inexperienced they are in the game of life."

For both the players and fans, the hosting experience forms friendships that last long after that particular season ends. During the season, the families find themselves drawn into the rollercoaster ride of a player's season.

Bryan Joseph's son, Mitch, had been a bat boy for the Paints in 1999 and was treated very well by the players. The Josephs had also heard about being a host family from friends of theirs who were currently hosting a player. They decided to fix up a room in their basement and host a player in 2000.

"I thought it would be interesting," said Joseph. "Maybe to get an inside scoop and . . . to just be part of the Paints organization in a way."

One week into Spring Training, the Josephs originally were assigned two players—a rookie from California and a returning player who had lived in an apartment the previous year and was looking forward to staying with a family. Both players thought they stood a good chance of making the team. Although they were optimistic, they caught Joseph and his wife off-guard—they hadn't counted on the possibility that they would take in a player who would be cut later on.

On the last day of cuts, the players were told the final roster would be posted in the evening. Joseph and his wife went out to run some errands. When they returned, both players' cars were in the driveway. The one-year player met the Josephs and told them that the rookie had been cut. They went down to the basement to talk to the young pitcher. He talked about how he was done with baseball and how he would start making some plans for when he returned to California. The player left the following morning before anyone else in the house was awake.

"It was a pretty emotional moment for him," Joseph recalled. And it was also tough for the Josephs' two children. "They get attached to the players . . . it was really difficult. This was *our* player."

The down times weren't done. Two weeks into the season, the remaining pitcher in their house, who had been battling some arm troubles, was also cut. He stayed with the Josephs for a few more days before leaving. But there was little the family could do for him except to lend a sympathetic ear. The day he left, the Josephs were introduced to their new player, Josh Lamberg. To their relief, he was a catcher.

"We were kind of hoping not to get another pitcher—they can really come and go," said Joseph. "When I looked at last year's rosters at the beginning and the end of the season, I saw a fifty percent turnover."

Fortunately for both the player and family, Lamberg stayed the entire season with the Paints.

Many players remain in touch with their host families long after their playing days are over. When Tom Grieve played in Salisbury, North Carolina, he had dinner every Sunday night with local fan Horace Hilton and his family (no relation to the hotel family). More than thirty years later, Grieve still exchanges Christmas cards with the family.

Tom Parsons and his wife still keep in touch with the couple, Mary and Ben Piazza, they rented an apartment from while Tom was in the minors in the late 1950s. When Parsons' wife was pregnant with their first child, Ben would not hear of her driving down to the park in the middle of the night to pick Tom up when the team came back from a road trip. Instead, Ben did the driving, regardless of the day of the week or the time.

Many minor and independent league towns have active booster clubs for their teams. Any player who has had the opportunity to be in these places leaves with fond memories of cookouts and friendships. In a profession whose nomadic nature doesn't allow one to plant roots anywhere for very long, these ties can become very important, however brief they are.

"It's really great when you're playing in a town where people recognize you and say 'hi' if you're in a store and you see people wearing the team's hats and shirts," said one Midwest League player. "You feel like you belong, even though you're only there for a few months."

Jason Baker, a veteran of five minor league seasons and one year in independent ball, sees a definite advantage to playing in the smaller towns.

"The fans come out to the park and they know everybody. I just had minor surgery on my leg, and people will come up to me in a store ask me how I'm doing, how my leg is doing."

The Chillicothe Paints Booster Club has been around nearly as long as the team itself. The boosters help coordinate volunteers to help house the players for the season. While the players are responsible for their own meals, the families often feed them at home. For road trips, the boosters stock the bus with lunch meat, soda, donuts, and the like.

The support does not stop with the players themselves. To help upgrade V.A. Memorial Stadium, the Paints Boosters rebuilt part of the stands to allow better access to aisles and installed seatbacks in the lower sections of the stands. It is not unusual to find club president Harry Chenault and others at the ballpark early on a summer morning taking care of small repairs or touching up some paint.

In Hagerstown, Maryland, there are regulars who always come out the park and supported "their" players on the Suns. On Saturday nights, they provide dinner in the clubhouse for the players. On other nights, like in many ballparks, they would sit by the dugout and chat with the players before the game. Cameron Reimers, who pitched for the Suns in 2000, remembered these fans fondly.

"You meet people from all over. It's one of the things you're going to remember for the rest of your life. Even if you don't ever see those people again, you're going to remember them. It's something I'm truly going to cherish, no matter what."

Throughout the season, many clubs hold promotions for the teams or have cookouts for the players and their families. Like the players they support, boosters will board buses to travel to other stadiums to provide a cheering section for the visiting team.

The Good Life

Despite the uncertain futures and some of the hardships that their career brings, ballplayers are, by and large, happy with their lives. This is the first taste of life away from home or college, and the world is a big place with even bigger promises waiting just around the corner. And even if the salaries and stadiums are scaled down from those of the big leagues, there are still plenty of things that make life good.

"There's a lot of things I like," said Myrtle Beach infielder David Dalton. "I made friends I'll always keep in touch with. The fact that people treat you like a big leaguer even though you're not is kind of funny, but still flattering. I don't have to get up early and go to 'work'. The little perks like discounts at clothing stores and things like that are nice too."

When Brad Lidge was playing for the Kissimmee Cobras in the Florida State League, his teammates were able to benefit from some of his signing bonus. Lidge, a first-round draft pick for the

Houston Astros in 1998, bought a ping pong table for the team's clubhouse. The manager and coaches were initially none too thrilled about the purchase, but their attitude changed when they saw that players were no longer arriving late for pre-game practices. In fact, many of them were showing up at the park hours early in order to get in a few games on the table.

With their meager salaries, some players seek ways to augment their income. While this is done mainly in the winter, some have found creative ways to earn a little extra cash during the season. George Virgilio recalled minor league teammate Turk Wendell holding an auction to sell his clothes to teammates so he would have enough money for a trip home.

Mark Eichhorn remembered another such teammate from the minors—Orval Kiser—who was more creative in his fundraising efforts. Kiser would eat any and all kinds of insects that his teammates found and brought to him. However, to actually get to see the meal consumed was strictly a pay-per-view event. Whether Kiser charged by the session, by the bug, or perhaps by the antenna is not known.

During his first year in professional baseball, 1949, John Romonosky was earning $150 a month to pitch for the Fresno Cardinals. The salary didn't leave him much after paying for his room and meals, but he had no complaints. By season's end, he had posted an 18-9 record, earning Rookie of the Year and All-Star honors. For his accomplishments, the Cardinals doubled his salary to three hundred a month.

"I said, 'Man, I'm on my way,'" recalled Romonosky, reliving the early days of his career when nothing seemed out of reach.

Later in his career, he returned to California while playing in the Pacific Coast League and found another attraction there in Hollywood, which was, literally, the home to the Stars—the Triple-A baseball team.

"Hollywood was the best town in California, especially if you were a single man," he explained. "All of the beautiful gals that were trying to get into movies went to Hollywood. You would see some interesting sights."

Chuck Connors, formerly of the Brooklyn Dodgers and Chicago Cubs, was playing first base for the Cubs' Pacific Coast League affiliate in Los Angeles when he decided to leave baseball in favor of a full-time acting career in February of 1953. He had appeared in his first movie a year earlier. Although he was cast in more movies, Connors' claim to fame came in the television series, *The Rifleman*, which lasted longer than his playing career would have.

Trades

The July 31 trading deadline is quickly approaching in the major leagues. Playoff contenders are scrambling to fill in the last few holes on their rosters, while the remaining teams are looking to the future to see what prospects they can get. The line in the newspaper or on television will state that the desperately needed left-handed reliever was obtained for "two minor leaguers." End of story—bring on the pennant race.

Meanwhile, down in the bush leagues, belongings are being tossed in bags, lease terminations are negotiated, quick parting handshakes between best friends are made, airline tickets passed out or gas tanks are filled, and life goes on. This creates a domino effect as other players are promoted or demoted to balance out the minor league rosters within the farm system. The scene is repeated several times over.

Even the rumors of a trade can trickle through the farm system. While Jeff Heaverlo was pitching for the Mariners organization in Single-A ball, he would get calls from his brother, who lived in Seattle, reporting about possible trades to at least three different teams.

"Today I'm a Mariner," said Heaverlo. "Tomorrow I may be something else. You can't dwell on it—not in this business."

There are those instances, though, when a trade comes complete with several conveniences. During Spring Training of 1996, pitcher Pat Ahearne, who was trying to make the Tigers' major league roster, was traded to the Mets for another minor leaguer, Steve Lackey.

The Tigers gave Ahearne a rental car to help move his belongings. Ahearne drove from Lakeland to Port St. Lucie, where he met Lackey in his hotel room. After shaking hands, bags were unloaded and loaded, with Ahearne moving into Lackey's old room and Lackey taking Ahearne's rental car. Lackey then drove to Lakeland to join the Tigers in their camp. So in a matter of hours, two players, two rooms, and one car were traded in one deal.

In 1993, Phil Dauphin was playing for the Cubs' Triple-A team in Iowa. During a road trip in Buffalo, he received a phone call in the middle of the night from Cincinnati General Manager Jim Bowden congratulating and welcoming him to the Reds and telling him a travel agent would be calling him to make arrangements.

"I went along with this, but I thought it was one of my teammates messing with me," Dauphin recalled. "I had grown up a huge Reds fan. After I hung up, I thought it was weird because all of the guys were probably asleep."

As it turned out, the Reds had claimed him on waivers. He called his agent to find out if any of this was true. The agent checked and called him back to tell him that the Cubs placed him on waivers, at which time the Reds did indeed claim him.

After flying back to Des Moines, he drove to Indianapolis, which was home to the Reds' top farm team. By the time he got to Indianapolis, he figured the game would be over, but then he caught the game broadcast on the radio and learned that the game was going into extra innings. So after a long day of travel, he made it to the stadium to suit up and join the team.

While trades are obviously made for the benefit of the major league team, they can also provide a boost to a player's career. After spending five seasons in the Reds organization, including four at-bats in nine major league games, Jim Bolger received a phone call in the winter of 1954-55 from the Chicago Cubs informing him that his contract now belonged to them. Bolger, an outfielder, knew his chances of making the Reds were slim with players like Ted Kluszewski, Gus Bell, and Jim Greengrass patrolling the outfield in Cincinnati. He made it to the Cubs roster to stay in 1955.

Family Life

The wives and children of the players often share in the nomadic existence of baseball. Jamie Keefe has spent ten seasons in professional baseball, playing in the Padres and Pirates farm systems followed by three seasons in independent ball, the last two spent mostly as a coach with the Paints. After the 2000 season, he and his wife, Kelly, decided to remain in the off-season. At the time they were interviewed by the author, they had spent ten consecutive months living in Chillicothe. It was their longest stay in any one location in the past ten years.

When the team leaves for the road, the families are left behind in a strange town, away from their own friends and relatives. In many cases among the wives, close-knit ties are formed as they are all together in the same situation, wondering how long their stay in this town will be, and what the near future will hold for their husbands.

"You become a family in a short amount of time," said Kelly.

The nature of the business can be difficult for these friendships, though. A family may find itself uprooted again as a player is demoted or released while another family benefits; their husband and father is given a better opportunity or more playing time. Clubhouse rumors about demotions and releases that are commonplace for players can be tough for the wives to handle.

Kelly was well aware of the anxiety caused by these rumors. "There are things I don't want to know. I don't want to hear about it."

"For example," Jamie elaborated. "Kelly may be best friends with Joe Blow's wife. Then he is released so I can take his spot."

A player movement, regardless of whether it is up or down

in the system, means more hurried packing and moving for the household. As the player reports to his new assignment, his wife is left to do most of the packing and transportation. "We should have bought stock in U-Haul," joked Kelly.

Major league teams employ personnel to help coordinate the moves by providing information on housing, helping with leases, etc. The Keefes noted that the Padres did an excellent job in assisting them in their frequent moves.

Despite the help, problems still arise. When Jamie was assigned to play in Clinton, Iowa in 1996, he and his wife arrived in the evening and spent the night in a hotel. The next morning, they found that all of their belongings had been stolen from the trailer—two weeks before his next payday. New teammates and their families immediately pitched in to help the couple out.

"You find out who your friends are pretty quick," said Jamie.

During the 1969 season, Joe Nossek's family had to move four times as he was traded from the Athletics to the Cardinals, playing at Triple-A and in the majors for both teams.

When they settled in with their three children in Des Moines, Iowa, the home of Oakland's Triple-A team, Nossek gave his wife his last twenty dollars, which had to last until the next paycheck, before leaving on a road trip. The next day, he arrived in Tulsa and received a phone call from his distraught wife. Their two-year-old daughter, who was just discovering the wonders of flushing toilets, had taken the twenty-dollar bill and flushed it away. In response to the crisis, his wife's parents drove to Iowa from Ohio that same day to help the family.

Despite the hardships of family life in the minor leagues, the family can also be a tremendous source of support in the bleakest of times in a player's career. In 1952, Jim Greengrass was ready to quit baseball, but his wife persuaded him to try one more season.

The Yankees had tried to convert Greengrass from a third baseman into a pitcher, but the experiment wasn't working very well. He was sent to the Beaumont Roughnecks of the Texas

League. Manager Harry Craft saw his potential with a bat and patiently taught him how to be an outfielder, explaining the nuances of positioning against different hitters and reading how the ball came off the bat. In September of that year, he made his major league debut—in the outfield.

Lights, Camera . . .

When asked if any movie accurately depicts minor league baseball, the players are almost unanimous in their answer—*Bull Durham*. Much of the camaraderie, the joking around, and the antics are true. The film's writer and director, Ron Shelton, was a former minor league ballplayer.

The scene where Kevin Costner set off the water sprinklers at night to make the field unplayable for the next day's game is an act seen many times in real life by ballplayers, including Tom Grieve. Grieve saw players so worn out near the season's end that they hosed down the home plate area at two in the morning so that the game wouldn't be played the next day.

In one instance during the 1952 Longhorn League season, the players didn't have to lift a finger to wash out the field. The groundskeeper for the Lamesa Lobos turned the sprinklers on at eleven at night, got drunk, and forgot to turn the water off. It wasn't until the team's owner arrived at the ballpark twelve hours later that the sprinklers were finally stopped.

The most realistic part in the movie for Grieve was when the manager would call the player into his office and what he would say to him when he was released. "That conversation has taken place thousands of times."

John Romonosky figured that he would be spending Spring Training of 1954 doing little else but playing baseball for the St. Louis Cardinals in the hope of making the major league squad. For a short time, however, he got to experience a taste of Hollywood during the making of the movie *Strategic Air Command.*

Jimmy Stewart played the lead role of a baseball player who was called back into service with the air force during a Cold War crisis. For three days, Stewart arrived at the Cardinals camp early in the morning for his baseball scenes. Stewart's co-star and the film's leading lady, June Allyson, was also on hand for some of the baseball scenes.

But wearing the uniform didn't make a ballplayer out of the famous actor. For long-range shots, a Cardinal player of roughly the same size and build as Stewart was used to make the fielding plays. When a close-up of Stewart making the play was required, slow, easy grounders were hit to him to ensure that the scene could be done.

While the process of movie-making may have been an interesting diversion for the players, St. Louis manager Eddie Stanky thought the whole thing was a waste of his team's valuable training time. Still, the players enjoyed themselves, at times to Stanky's annoyance. During the duration of the filming, the players constantly had urgent reasons to go back and forth between the field and dugout, usually to retrieve "forgotten" gloves and to replace mysteriously broken shoelaces. By sheer "coincidence," June Allyson had a box seat right by the Cardinals' dugout.

"It was great to be able sit in the clubhouse and watch him [Stewart] put his uniform on like we did, then to go out and play catch with him," said Romonosky.

When the motion picture reached the theaters, the three days of filming with the Cardinals were compressed into three minutes of on-screen time.

"You had to look quick," explained Romonosky. "To see yourself standing out there."

Regardless of his minimal screen appearance, Romonosky still looks back on the experience as a highlight of his playing career.

Like Romonosky, Jamie and Kelly Keefe got an inside look at show business when scenes for the movie *A Little Inside* were filmed in Chillicothe in 2000. The film is about a minor league ballplayer who must raise his daughter alone after his wife dies.

Jamie was hired as an advisor, ensuring the on-field scenes were realistic, and also appeared in several scenes. Kelly was chosen to play the mother of Hallie Eisenberg's character (the daughter) after the actress who supposed to be in that role became unavailable. She was working in a department store and was caught off-guard when Jamie walked in with one of the film's casting directors.

"I wondered what he was doing, walking around with this blonde," she joked.

Although their on-screen roles were small, the Keefes did get their piece of Hollywood immortality, etched firmly in celluloid.

August

August is often the most trying month of the season. The minor league season is drawing to a close. The buses reek of a season's worth of spilled food and cigarette smoke. Nerves have become a little raw—something that was easily laughed off in April may now bring about a face-to-face confrontation. Injuries that were bearable in May and June are now a heavy burden that drags the entire body down. Players used to the twenty to thirty games played in a high school or college season now feel the effects of a 130-game schedule.

For the fortunate few who find themselves in playoff contention, there is still a high level of excitement on the team. For the rest, the focus turns toward their own performance and how the major league club will view them. In August 2000, the Oklahoma City Redhawks were below .500 and well out of the Pacific Coast League's playoff picture. R. A. Dickey was on that team.

"You're not playing for anything but your stats and pride at this point," he said. "It's hard to go to the field continually knowing that you're not going to be playing for a championship. That's when, as a professional, you've got to take over and take care of business. I'm in the 'taking care of business' mode right now. A lot of times, guys don't remember how you start, but how you finish."

Some players question themselves and their past season. Were their statistics what they should be? With less than a month left, there is little to be done to improve them. On the other hand, a late season slump brings a player's durability in question. Salaries are based on a player's performance from the previous year, and a poor showing will squeeze a paycheck that is already thin.

The younger players wonder if they will be promoted the following year or released when the new crop is scouted and drafted. In the higher levels, the chance of a September call-up looms large. Will this be the chance for a big break? Or will they be passed over only to wonder if they will forever remain in minor league limbo? The winter provides many hours to think about the season past and the possibilities of the next one coming.

As the 2000 season drew to a close, Cameron Reimers, a Blue Jays farmhand in his third year of pro ball, took time to reflect on his profession and his life.

"Everybody tends to think that playing pro baseball is the greatest thing on earth, and that there's nothing better. To tell you the truth, it is. But there's also a lot of tough things that come with it. The tough thing for me is being away from my family, my girlfriend, and my buddies back home.

"But then I think about my friends back home and how they're working nine-to-five jobs and they want to be in my shoes. You don't want to disappoint those people. You tend to get a boost thinking about how people are counting on you to do something they've never done. Especially where I'm from— there are very, very few people who have gotten to do what I'm doing.

"You learn to appreciate what you've got. You've got a dream to chase and you're going to do it as long as you can. You just have the best time of your life."

Winter

If not playing ball or attending college in the winter, many minor leaguers must find a way to make ends meet. Considering that they are trying to find a job that they know will only last a few months, they pretty much take what they can find.

Minor league manager Trey Hillman found ways to supplement his income while staying in the game during the off-season. While many winters were spent giving baseball clinics, he also managed in Hawaii, Arizona, and Venezuela.

"When you do winter ball, it's pretty much ten months out of the year," said Hillman, explaining how much of a year could be spent in the game.

Guy Morton worked in a tire manufacturing plant. Joe M. Morgan drove a snowplow, coal truck, and an oil truck when not working as a bill collector, census taker, or half a dozen other jobs. Dave Campbell tried his hand in several professions over the years, working as a substitute teacher, an insurance salesman, and attending school to be a real estate agent. Cal Hogue worked as a plumber when he wasn't playing winter ball. Al Gallagher still works as a substitute teacher. Nate Minchey dressed up as a mascot at business conventions. Blake Stein officiated basketball games.

Eric Wedge, a manager in the Indians organization before getting promoted to Cleveland, keeps busy with an investment he made with money from his major league playing days. Wedge is part-owner of sports complex in Danvers, Massachusetts that includes indoor baseball and softball fields for year-round leagues in the cold Northeast.

Completing a college degree has been a more attractive option for many as it helps set them up for their post-playing career lives. Still, once a degree is obtained, the limitation of a few months' duration at a job still hinders one's off-season choices in employment.

After returning to college and finishing his degree the previous winter, Jason Baker relied on his musical talent instead of his education. A well-practiced violin player, he traveled around as a street musician, playing in front of department stores and the like. In fact, the pay wasn't bad at all around the holiday season as he would rake in fifty to sixty dollars an hour in tips playing Christmas carols. One year, during a week-long trip from Lynchburg, Virginia to Baltimore, Philadelphia, and Newark before returning home Christmas Eve, he made slightly over two thousand dollars—many times more than he had made during any one week in baseball.

Dwight Pope did even better by swapping his bat for a golf club after the 2002 season. Pope, a catcher who played in four different independent leagues in slightly more than two seasons, won a $110,000 in a golfing long drive contest. That total was more than thirty times the amount he had earned in baseball.

CHAPTER 4

This is the Life: On the Road

We are trying to make these guys millionaires,
because if you can play five years in the big leagues,
you'll be set for life. So I tell these guys if you don't
want to be a millionaire, go somewhere else and
punch a clock.

—*Arnie Beyeler, manager*

Another fact of life in the minor leagues is the road trips. Unlike the major leagues, travel in the minors has usually been several grades below first class. In the early years of the minors, some teams could not even afford a bus, instead resorting to a handful of leased automobiles that would make several trips each to get the team from one town to the next. It was not uncommon for games to begin with half of the visiting team in the ballpark and the other half in transit.

When the team did have a bus, there was rarely a driver that came with it. The chauffeuring duties generally fell to the manager, although in some cases a player would drive in order to earn a few extra dollars.

Depending on the geographical layout of the league, the drives would range from country drives of few hours to all-night treks.

Most distances between cities in the Midwest and Florida State Leagues were and are still easy, but a season in the Texas League will give a player thousands of miles of road experience and many nights on the road.

The buses of old offered little in the way of luxury. They were often retired school or army buses. What no longer suited the original owners was perfect for minor league owners operating on a shoestring budget. Boarding players quickly scrambled to get to the windows during the summer in order to get as much of the incoming breeze as possible. These window seats were not as prized earlier in the season for teams in the north as even the closed windows produced a chilly draft around their battered frames.

Don Gutteridge's first team bus was actually an old Ford truck with benches mounted on the sides of the open bed. This was how the Lincoln Links traveled the circuit of the Nebraska State League in the early 1930s.

"If it was raining, you just sat there and got rained on," Gutteridge said.

More than forty years after the war ended, Nate Minchey and his Burlington Braves teammates rode a World War II vintage bus. Iowa in the summer was not the most comfortable place to be riding a bus with vinyl seats and no air-conditioning.

"You had to take your clothes off to stay cool," remembered Minchey. "And then your whole body would stick to the vinyl. Getting up was like taking tape off bare skin."

During his 1968 season in the Carolina League, future Met pitcher John Matlack got to experience the thrills and chills of the "Blue Goose." The "Goose" was an old blue bus that had the peculiar habit of having its windows fall out when the bus was moving too fast.

While the amenities were scarce, there were the occasional privileges. Harry Eisenstat remembers that while most of the team tried to sleep in their seats during the night rides, the pitcher scheduled to start the next day's game had the luxury of sleeping on duffel bags in the back. Another highly sought after sleeping space was the area between the roof and the luggage racks above the seats (on buses that had them). For the players who could fit there, they offered a place to stretch out while napping.

Jay Gehrke discovered that having a larger sized body size helped him in getting comfortable on the bus. Although a smaller player may not feel as cramped in a seat, Gehrke, at six-foot-six and two hundred thirty-five pounds, rarely had to share his seat with anyone.

John Romonosky, who played in the minors from the late-1940s through the 1950s, experienced both ends of quality in buses as he worked his way up to higher levels of play. His first travels in the California League were in an old yellow school bus. When he reached the Double-A Southern Association, his team roamed in a converted Greyhound bus that had only one seat aside from the driver's seat. The rest of the bus, which was also air-conditioned (a very rare luxury in those days), was fitted with bunk beds.

In more recent years, the buses have improved, with more comfortable seats, air-conditioning as a standard, and even televisions and VCRs on board. Still, the players must pass the time. Sleep comes easier to some than others. Even with the addition of video entertainment, some time-honored activities such as card playing remain popular.

R. A. Dickey, a pitcher in the Texas Rangers farm system drafted in 1996, measured the length of the bus trips by the movies shown. "In the Florida State League, you usually didn't see the whole movie. In the Texas League, you could see two or three in one trip," he explained.

Al Rosen remembered the things players would do while trying to break up the boredom. One such activity was "Sitz," a game in which players on each side of the bus would count how many dogs they saw. Arguments would ensue as to whether one side had actually seen a dog they had just counted. If going through farm country, the focus would shift to counting cows. The prize for the player with the most heads (or, perhaps, paws and hooves) was paid in bottles of cola.

"The biggest liar always won," Rosen recalled.

There are no rules in baseball governing good taste in on-the-road entertainment. Steve Dawes remembers doing animal calls with Andres Galarraga at three or four in the morning during all-night bus rides to the dubious delight of their teammates.

David Bresnahan led his Williamsport teammates in loud, if out-of-tune sing-alongs featuring theme songs from TV sitcoms after the team's manager banned beer-drinking on the bus. The purpose of the songs wasn't for passing the time, but merely for masking the sounds of pop-tops and hissing as the contraband beer cans were opened.

Talk to a player with a few years of minor league experience about traveling and you'll usually hear a story about a breakdown. Nate Minchey's ill-fated Burlington team bus died on the road at least three times during his season in the Midwest League.

During a Southern League road trip in the late 1970s, the Columbus Astros were heading north from Savannah to Nashville when their bus broke down on the highway near Statesville, Georgia. The driver got out to investigate, checking the engine in the rear of the bus, when he found that the fan belt had caught on fire. The players were allowed to bring beer on the bus and quickly came out with their coolers to use the ice and water (not the beer itself) to extinguish the flames.

Fortunately, a minister from Statesville happened to pass by and offered to help. He sent his church's bus to bring the players into town where they spent the night while the bus was repaired. They resumed their trip the next day, arriving at the ballpark in Nashville at six in the evening—one hour before game time.

Then there was the time the Great Falls Dodgers wandered into the "Town that Time Forgot." Early into a Pioneer League-length, thirteen-hour trek from their hometown in Montana to Ogden, Utah, the bus blew a tire just short of the Montana state line. The team bus limped into a small town that consisted of a gas station, general store, and four or five houses.

As several players walked behind the gas station to use the

bathroom, they beheld a gruesome sight. Mounted on the fence post were about a dozen deer heads, swarming with flies and rotting in the open air.

Stepping into the general store, they were spared the sight of any more decapitated wildlife. However, food was not an option as the only produce was a lone bunch of withered and blackened bananas. The canned foods were little better, having expired as much as eight to ten years earlier.

"It was like we stepped into *Deliverance* or something," recalled former Great Falls pitcher Jason Baker.

During one Midwest League road trip to Kenosha Wisconsin, fate waited until the Peoria Chiefs' team bus was pulling into the hotel parking lot. Over the two hundred miles from Peoria, Illinois, to Kenosha, the bus rolled on without incident. As the bus was completing the last few feet of the journey, a loud thump was heard and felt by the team. Phil Dauphin saw a tire go sailing from the bus and strike a parked car, the result of loose lugnuts.

"The bus drivers could drive through anything," remembered Phil Dauphin. During a return trip to Peoria one rainy night, the windshield wiper stopped. Dauphin, who was sitting at the front of the bus, couldn't see anything through the window except for the hard rain beating on the glass, but the driver was undeterred. Dauphin got increasingly unnerved by the lack of view and was looking around to see if anyone else had noticed this problem. All of his nearby teammates were asleep or otherwise occupied, so Dauphin kept his fears to himself and hoped for the best. The bus eventually arrived home safely.

When Hank Sauer was playing for the Butler Yankees of the Pennsylvania State Association in 1937, it was routine for the team to push the bus uphill on some occasions.

At the time, they chalked it up as part of the minor league experience.

"We just thought it was the normal thing," said Sauer.

Jay Johnstone had his fill of adventure on the road in the California League during the 1964 season. On one trip from Reno, the team bus broke down in Donner Pass, the infamous site where a pioneer wagon train was snowbound, eventually forcing its members to resort to cannibalism in order to survive.

"That was fun," Johnstone commented. "Guys were going, 'We've gotta get out of here! Who's gonna eat who?'"

The teams were not the only victims of mishaps on the road. Eastern League president Tommy Richardson was growing increasingly concerned after umpires Harry King and John Stevens failed to show up for a game in Utica, New York on May 29, 1946. Heavy rains had caused the Susquehanna River to overflow its banks in Williamsport, Pennsylvania where King and Stevens had been working. Richardson began to fear the worst after the pair were not heard from. The roads were impassable, and the telephone lines were down.

Two days later, he received word that King and Stevens were fine, just a little hungry. The floodwaters had stranded the two in their hotel room for twenty-three hours with no access to food. Their hotel was only two miles away from Richardson's home.

In 1952, Bill Valentine took a train to Abilene, Texas for a Longhorn League umpires' meeting prior to the start of the season. Following the meeting Valentine and his umpiring crew drove to Big Springs in the pouring rain for the first game when they heard on the radio that all Longhorn League games had been postponed due to the weather.

The crew decided to stop in Sweetwater for the day to relax and enjoy a rare break. When they got back on the road the following day, they were surprised to hear the score on the radio for the game they were supposed to have been officiating. Valentine and his partners were fined twenty-five dollars apiece, ten percent of their monthly salary, for missing the game.

The higher a player rises in the minors, the better the traveling conditions are. In the higher minor leagues, airliners (or trains in earlier decades) become more commonplace. The early years of the Pacific Coast League saw travel accommodations on par with the major leagues. The league itself was sometimes referred as "the third major league" due to the level of talent there. It was not uncommon to find team rosters stocked with quite a few former major leaguers, not to mention up-and-coming future stars.

Trains were the mode of transportation for these teams. With the favorable weather on the West Coast, seasons began in early April, while the major league teams were still in Spring Training. Over the course of the year, when the major leagues were still playing around 150, PCL teams played from 170 to 200 games. This was also achieved by efficient travel schedules. In a typical week, a series between two teams would begin on Tuesday, with single games played between the same teams from Tuesday to Saturday. Doubleheaders were played on Sundays. Monday was set aside as a travel day. With the travel done by train, visiting teams could arrive in the next city with their players well rested and ready for the next seven-game series.

With the growth of commercial air travel, the sky became an option in the higher-level leagues, although this was sometimes a mixed blessing in the earlier years. In 1962, the Buffalo Bisons, then the Triple-A team of the Philadelphia Phillies, leased a DC-3 from the Holiday Inn Corporation. The plane was still painted in the green and gold company colors. Outfielder John Herrnstein described it as looking "hilarious . . . like a big canary."

The color schemes aside, the problem with the DC-3 as a team plane was that it could not carry the entire team. Pitchers who were not scheduled to pitch in the first game would travel by some other means. With the remaining team members, along with their luggage and equipment, still presented a weight problem for the aircraft. To prevent the plane from exceeding its maximum safe weight, the gas tanks were only partially filled. This meant that the plane could only fly for approximately two hundred miles at a time before landing for more fuel, often in rural airports with little more than a dirt landing strip and a shack.

"It was almost like being on a bus," said Herrnstein. "Because it would take us maybe twelve hours to fly from Little Rock to Rochester."

R. A. Dickey's first experience with flying came in 1997 when he played in the Hawaiian Winter Baseball League. The flights weren't limited to between Hawaii and the mainland; the games were played on four different islands, and the teams flew from one to another.

The hotels, particularly in the lower minors, were rarely something to speak of. Older veterans of the New York-Penn League remember The Kirkwood in Auburn, New York.

The building was a combination of a hotel, a bus station, candy store, and a home for the aged. The rooms had no light switches, and the beds had mattresses that sagged to the floor. Depending on the vacancies in the hotel, as many as five or six players might be crammed into a room. The quality of the construction left much to be desired.

"I don't think there was a right angle in the whole building," recalled Jack DiLauro. "To walk down the hallways straight, without banging into the walls—you had to be drunk."

There was one night at The Kirkwood in particular that DiLauro will not soon forget. It involved a teammate of his whom everyone called "Teddy Twilight." He wore his hat with a bent brim pulled low over his eyes and would play with it in that position. During the game, a huge wad of tobacco was constantly in his mouth. He refused to spit. Consequently, the juice would dribble out of his mouth and onto his jersey, creating stains that no laundry detergent could remove.

Fortunately for the rest of the team, no one was rooming with Teddy that night. He also had the habit of taking his bat with him wherever he went, taking practice swings in his spare time. "He wasn't a bad hitter," explained DiLauro. "He was just crazy."

At around one or two o'clock in the morning, his teammates in the adjoining rooms were awakened to the sounds of tremendous booms and smashes from Teddy's room. Three or four teammates ran to Teddy's door, frantically pounding on the door. Teddy flung open the door in his underwear, with his eyes bulging out and his ever-present bat in his hand. When his teammates asked what was going on, he replied by holding up his bat and screaming, "Bat! Bat! Bat!"

Every following question was answered the same way, with Teddy shaking his bat and yelling, "Bat! Bat! Bat!" The room inside looked like a war zone. Every piece of glass and furniture was in pieces. His teammates tried to sit him down on the remains of his bed to calm him down, but he quickly leaped up with his bat and began his chant again.

As far as his teammates were concerned, it was the end of Teddy Twilight's last remnants of sanity. There was no one in his batter's box. He had gone way out in left field and was over the wall. His next uniform jersey would be a straightjacket.

Teddy went running toward the bathroom and stopped at the doorway, resuming his yelling, but refusing to go any further. Slowly, his teammates peered over his shoulder. There, perched atop the rubble that had once been a sink, was a huge flying bat, which had earlier flown into the room and was the target of Teddy's rampage.

Someone tossed a towel over the bat and carried the bundle over to the window to let it go. While the room was a shambles, the bat was apparently unscathed. "Teddy struck out a lot," DiLauro explained.

Joe Short discovered a shortfall in his accommodations in Pulaski, Virginia while playing in the Appalachian League in 1958. After dropping his suitcase off in his room, he opened the window to let the place cool down. What he didn't take into account was the train depot about four hundred feet from the hotel. Upon returning to the room after dinner, he found his bed covered with a thick layer of coal dust from the nearby trains.

CHAPTER 5

Strange Innings, Part 1

*The beauty about baseball is that the more you
know about it, the more you don't know about it.*

—*Al Gallagher, ex-player, manager*

During the 1996 American Association championship series,
the Oklahoma City 89ers second baseman caught an Indianapolis
base runner with a hidden ball trick. Faking that the ball was
tossed back to the pitcher, he waited until the runner took a
slight lead off of the bag and quickly tagged him out with the
ball he still had hidden in his glove. It turned out to be a key play
in a game that Oklahoma City won by a run. The 89ers went on
to win the series as well.

Although the art of the hidden ball is performed most often
by infielders, it is not their exclusive domain, as proven by Al
Schact in 1913. Schacht was pitching for the Jersey City Skeeters
in an International League game against the Buffalo Bisons. Like
most pitchers, Schacht was a poor hitter, but managed to reach
base that game on a walk.

The Buffalo pitcher, likely unnerved by the rare sight of
Schacht on base, tried to pick him off, but threw wildly. As
Schacht dove for the bag, the ball struck him and wound up

beneath him when he landed in the dirt. The ball's unintentional path went unseen by the first baseman, who was desperately searching for the missing sphere. Schacht, taking advantage of the confusion, tucked the ball into a pocket in his pants and proceeded to run the bases as the Bisons went on a madcap hunt for the very same object.

Schacht, deciding to end with a little flair, slid across home plate, only to have the ball roll out of his pocket in the process. The umpire immediately called Schacht out, ignoring the prankster's protests that he had only been pulling a joke. The umpire, who was clearly not amused, reported Schacht to the league president, who fined the player fifty dollars. It is small wonder that Schacht returned to the baseball field after his playing days were over, performing comedy routines for the fans.

While the hidden ball trick has been a part of baseball's legendary history of sneaky tricks long before the turn of the century, it was greatly outdone by the piece of "magic" performed by David Bresnahan on August 31, 1987. The ensuing chaos that resulted from that included an unearned run that was scored after the runner was tagged out at home plate, the end of a professional baseball career, and a controversial vegetable.

A long, frustrating season was coming to a close for the Williamsport Bills, the Double-A Eastern League affiliate of the Cleveland Indians. They were in second-to-last place in their division, twenty-eight games out of first, and everyone just wanted the season to be over with. But Bresnahan, or "Brez" as he was called, had an idea to make the season a memorable one.

For over a month, he had brought up the idea of bringing a potato into the game, substituting it for a ball in the middle of a play. His teammates loved the idea, although some preferred that it just remain an idea—not a reality. For those in favor of the spud play, it had become a challenge to hold their teammate to his proposal.

One of Bresnahan's teammates checked with a friend who

was umpiring in the major leagues to determine whether a run would count during a play involving a potato. Baseball had no rules governing the use of fresh produce in a game, so it was assumed that the play would be nullified, with the guilty party getting an early exit from the game, at worst. With the risk of a potentially costly run seemingly done away with, the potato scheme got the green light.

The fateful day dawned on a Monday. The Bills were scheduled to play a doubleheader against the Reading Phillies, and manager Orlando Gomez had Bresnahan behind the plate during the first game. Bresnahan brought a small arsenal of carved and peeled potatoes to his locker in preparation. All that was needed was the right situation. Although the season was long lost for the Bills, the game was crucial for the Phillies, who were vying for home field advantage in the playoffs.

In the top of the fifth inning, Reading catcher Rick Lundblade singled and reached third on two consecutive sacrifices. With two out and a runner on third, Fame beckoned to David Bresnahan.

As the next batter approached the plate, Bresanahan turned to the umpire, Scott Potter, and told him that the webbing on his mitt was broken. Potter allowed him to fetch his replacement from the dugout. While Potter, Gomez, and the Phillies were unaware of what was about to unfold, most of the Williamsport players could barely contain their laughter. Some just stared incredulously as Bresnahan nonchalantly picked up his mitt with the potato hidden inside, unwilling to believe that their long-standing joke was about to become reality.

Bresnahan returned to the field with his new mitt and stealth spud. As he crouched behind the plate, he carefully removed the potato from the mitt and kept it in his right hand. The pitch came in low and away for ball one. Bresnahan nabbed the ball and quickly stood up and wheeled toward third base, arm cocked. Seeing Lundblade with a slight lead off the bag, he fired the potato wildly to third base, an apparent attempt to pick off the runner.

The Bill's third baseman, Rob Swain, was in on the gag and made sure he missed the errant throw despite a wild lunge, allowing the potato to sail into left field. Lundblade took off for home for a seemingly easy run. Before he could reach the plate, however, Bresnahan tagged him with his mitt, which was still holding the real ball.

With the "third out" accomplished, Bresnahan rolled the ball toward the pitcher's mound. Potter, still unaware of the substitution, confronted Bresnahan, stating that a second ball was not allowed on the play. Bresnahan explained in a reasonable tone to the exasperated umpire that no rule concerning multiple baseballs had been broken.

At this time, the left fielder came jogging in with the spud, much to the amazement of Reading coach George Culver, who had been standing by third base.

"Here comes the left fielder and he's got this potato and I thought, 'What the hell?' You couldn't make a movie and come up with this scenario," Culver recalled.

Then the field umpire returned with the potato he took from the left fielder and gave to it Potter. The plate umpire went from annoyed to furious. Unwilling to let any stunts like this pass through his game, he allowed the run to count, much to the protest of the Williamsport team.

After the real third out was made, a fuming Orlando Gomez removed Bresnahan from the game. But the Bills, apparently inspired by their wayward spud (not to mention their wayward teammate), later rallied to win the game.

The next day, Gomez called Bresnahan into his office and told him to pack his bags—he was fired. Bresnahan was stunned.

"I didn't think I'd get fired over it," he recalled. "But I think a .150 batting average had something to do with it, too."

After a long phone conversation with his father, his sense of humor had recovered, enough for him to make another trip to the local supermarket. On Wednesday, each of his teammates found a potato sitting in their lockers. Gomez found one waiting for him on his desk with the following note attached:

Orlando—

This spud's for you!

—Brez

This would not be the end of the story. A writer for the *Chicago Tribune* named Bresnahan Sports Person of the Year for "attempting to have a little fun with life, to inject some lost levity into sports." During the following season, the Bills invited Bresnahan back to the stadium for ceremonies to retire his jersey number, where he signed baseballs and, of course, potatoes for the fans. His notoriety earned him an invitation to Japan to appear on a television show there. Bresnahan was taken aback by all of the attention he received over the incident.

"That was overwhelming. It was almost embarrassing. I got so much press, it continued to snowball. I had a lot of good experiences because of it and I'm thankful for it. I got a lot more out of it than I ever imagined. I didn't do it for any notoriety— I did it for my teammates.

"A lot of people thought I disgraced the game and I get offended by that. It wasn't my intention. The game is important to me, played right. And I guess throwing a potato is not right. But if you understood, and were on my team at the time, I think it was right."

Even the potato lasted far beyond its only game. After the inning, it was unceremoniously tossed into a trashcan by one of the umpires. A teenaged fan, recognizing the importance of the spud on the long, storied history of the country's national pastime (OK—it was on a whim), retrieved it from the can and preserved it in a jar of alcohol. Twelve years later, the fan donated it to the Baseball Reliquary, an institution devoted to the study of baseball and its interaction with American society.

CHAPTER 6

Coaches and Managers

*You've got to be who you are and work off of that to
become better.*

—Eric Wedge, manager

*Wanted: Personnel with experience for seven month-long position
of leader, teacher, counselor, interpreter, and evaluator. Must be
willing to travel 50% of the time. Pay is low, conditions will vary,
expect to lose top-performing personnel during the season.*

As tough as the job of a minor manager or coach may be, it's
a position that has former players lining up to fill. For some, it is
a way to continue their baseball careers; careers that were
sometimes cut short by injuries or careers that may have stalled
out in the minor leagues. For those who had a taste of the majors
and are still hungry for more, coaching and managing in the
minors presents a path back to The Show. Still, others are content
to go wherever the game takes them.

Like their major league counterparts, they are aware that their
contracts offer little in the way of job stability. A good season
means that one has lasted from Spring Training to the final
game. Hopefully, it will carry over into another season with
the team or perhaps a position at a higher level in the minors.

And for a very few, it means that they will get the promotion to the majors.

Unlike the jobs of their major league brethren, it's not a profession that will put food on the table all year round. Except for those who have money in the bank from a decent major league career, the approach of the off-season means it's time to search for another temporary job. Few are the winter jobs that have gone untouched by minor leaguers. Like their players, coaches and managers can be found selling insurance and used cars, driving snow plows and back hoes, substitute teaching, house building, and oil drilling. Some stay in the game by conducting baseball clinics or managing in the winter leagues of the Caribbean, South America, and Australia.

Over the years, it's a job that has evolved. Up until the 1970s, there was often only a manager on the team. It was largely up to the players to improve their play through repeated practices and games. Little was offered in instruction beyond what the manager could provide for the twenty-odd players playing nine different positions. Additionally, the manager often assumed the responsibilities of being the team trainer and bus driver.

In the present, a minor league team will usually have a pitching coach and another coach to assist the manager. Additionally, major league organizations have roving instructors to provide additional teaching in specific areas. A trainer who is usually a physical therapist covers physical conditioning and rehabilitation. And to the relief of many managers, their seat on the team bus no longer comes with a steering wheel directly in front of it.

There are two primary reasons for the increase in coaching support in the minors. One is financial. Millions of dollars are now being paid to draft picks, giving teams the added incentive to provide all of the possible resources to help their investments pay off at the major league level.

Secondly, the players of today play less ball as amateurs than the players of earlier generations. They may play more games in a structured setting such as little league and school athletics, but the many hours spent on the sandlots simply playing have largely been replaced by other sports, video games, the Internet, and other activities that weren't available in the past.

The Transition

The day finally arrives when the glove and bat go from being the tools of one's playing trade to being the tools of one's teaching trade. Rick Burleson spent fourteen years in the major leagues, making the All-Star team four times. By the end of his playing days, he had not tired of the daily routine. In fact, his love of being on the field influenced his decision to become a coach. Burleson, who managed the San Antonio Missions in 2000, explained the transition from player to coach succinctly. "As a player, you just do it. As a coach, you have to explain how to do it."

Like Burleson, Sixto Lezcano had a full major league playing career under his belt when he returned to the minors as a coach. Despite his years in baseball, he knew that coaching would bring him more new experiences.

"I thought about giving back to the game and the young players what I've learned and am still learning," he explained. "I knew I can be patient and with gray hair, I can inspire respect."

At age twenty-two, Ben Crowley was still looking forward to many more years of playing, but was also looking well beyond that in 2000. An outfielder with experience in both affiliated and independent league baseball, he was already returning to his college in the off-season to coach until he had to report to professional Spring Training.

"I have a coaching bug—I definitely want to do that," said Crowley. "I don't know what level I'll do it at. Time will tell. But I'll keep playing until I can't play anymore."

Rangers farmhand John Stewart was also looking ahead while still early in his pro career.

"Coaching would be a consideration. If I come up short of my ultimate goal to play in the majors, I'd like to help someone get as far as they possibly can."

By 1987, four years had passed since Jon Matlack had finished his thirteen-year pitching career with the Mets and Rangers. He hadn't considered coaching while still playing, but a few years out of the game altered his perspective.

"It took all that time for it to call me back," explained Matlack. "I was sort of disgruntled with the world I was in. The more I looked at baseball, the more I saw that maybe I could be of some use. Things were going on at the big league level that I was taught not to do in A-ball."

Matlack also returned to the mound in the winter of 1989-90 during the brief lifespan of the Senior League, which was made up of retired big leaguers.

"I played the first year in that thing and that was a blessing. It got you back in touch with the emotions and the feelings you dealt with during the ballgame and the reality that it isn't really as easy as you think it is. That was very beneficial in terms of relating to the kids I was coaching. After that, I was able to look at things a little more philosophically."

Nick Fiala signed with the St. Louis Cardinals in 1977. After progressing steadily through the minor leagues, he was called up to St. Louis in September of 1981. A week later, he was traded to the Cincinnati Reds. He spent the 1982 season in Triple-A. During Spring Training the following year, he retired after learning that he would be returning again to the minors, this time in a diminished role.

"I was going to end up being a utility guy and decided to move on after starting every day for three and a half years in Triple-A," he explained.

From 1983 through 1989, he worked primarily in the real estate business, but also coached baseball part-time at his old high school and junior college. He also coached a summer collegiate team for several years, sending about thirty of his players into the professional ranks, four of whom made it to the majors. As the decade drew to a close, Fiala decided to go into coaching full time.

In the fall of 1989, he joined the Yankees as a coach on their instructional league team and coached for them again in 1990. By the end of the season, though, the Yankees organization was in chaos due to the suspension of owner George Steinbrenner by the commissioner. With assignments in the farm system being up in the air at best, Fiala left the organization to become a coach at the University of Illinois. Due to new restrictions on the number of full-time coaches a college was allowed, Fiala left the university to coach junior college ball in 1994.

After the college season was over in 2000, he became the manager of the River City Rascals of the Frontier League. Since the independent league started later in the year, its schedule was a good fit around Fiala's continuing college duties. Additionally, the Rascals were close to his home, which meant he could stay with his family. As for his long-term future in coaching pro ball, he was well aware of the uncertainty of his profession.

"Who knows what's going to happen over the course of the next few years? I could still be here and stay at home—not be gone for six months. My youngest daughter is going to be a freshman in high school and the middle one is a senior.

"If the right opportunity is there, who knows? I've got to keep my options open. For the immediate future, my plans are to do this again next summer."

Often times, a retiring player will seek help from his agent in pursuing a coaching job in professional or college ball. The decision to become a coach is theirs alone, not the agent's.

"We can't make their decisions for them," explained Tommy Tanzer, an agent with over twenty years of experience.

A former player is not obligated to stay with an agent, but many remain with the people they have worked with throughout their playing careers.

"If a player makes a commitment to me, I look at that as a commitment we make to each other for as long as they want that commitment to be there," Joe Bick explained. Bick also has over twenty years of experience and spent six years working for the Cleveland Indians.

In Spring Training of 1988, the Cleveland Indians approached twenty-five-year-old farmhand Trey Hillman about taking a scouting job. Realizing he was a long shot to make it to the major leagues as a player, Hillman accepted the Indians offer in hopes of remaining in the game. The following year, the Yankees hired him away from the Cleveland organization as a coach. In 1990, at the age of twenty-seven, Hillman became a minor league manager.

"I never allowed myself to second guess," said Hillman, who was managing the Yankees top farm team in Columbus nine years later. "I spent a lot of time soul-searching and thinking about what my long-range goals were. Those were to make it to the big leagues. I felt that I had a better chance in some other avenue than as a player."

Tom Lawless was an extra player on several talented St. Louis teams in the mid-1980s. His bench time gave him the opportunity to observe manager Whitey Herzog and the coaches. This led him to decide to go into coaching when he retired in 1990.

Eric Wedge always had an interest in managing, but never figured on it coming so soon. At age twenty-nine and after seven surgeries on his knees and elbow, the ex-catcher for the Red Sox and Rockies found himself looking at a premature retirement from playing in 1997. He and his agent got together to start working on possible contacts for a coaching position. In 1998, he began his new career in baseball as manager of the Indians' Class-A South Atlantic League farm team in Columbus, Georgia.

Jim Pankovits was first approached about being a coach in 1980, when a farm director told him that it was unlikely that he would ever see any time in the majors as a player. The director thought he would make a fine coach and told him to consider making the change. However, Pankovits did make the major leagues in 1984 and played there for much of the next seven years.

During this time, he did keep the idea of coaching in the back of his head. His father had managed professionally. Additionally, Pankovits was reluctant to completely leave the game he loved. He played his final major league season with Boston in 1990 and, after an injury-plagued season with Pawtucket in 1991, knew it was time to move on. That off-season, the Red Sox offered him a managerial position with their Double-A club in New Britain.

Pankovits described some of the bigger elements involved in becoming a manager. "Leading, organizing, disciplining twenty-five to thirty people, holding them accountable for their actions. Also, trying to figure out what management wanted and how to achieve success when it really isn't in black and white in the minor leagues. It's a strange business because there is no measure of success down here. It's a balance of development and winning. No one ever gives you the formula or the grading scale."

In 1975, manager Clint Courtney of the Richmond Braves suffered a fatal heart attack. Veteran player Al Gallagher was asked to fill in as manager until Bob Lemon could be brought in to take over the team. Following his short managerial stint, Gallagher began to look at coaching as the next step in his career. For Gallagher, the biggest adjustment was having to consider the game from all positions, not just the one he had played.

(It should also be noted that Gallagher holds the unofficial record for having the longest name in professional baseball history. His given name, Alan Mitchell Edward George Patrick Henry Gallagher, came when his parents, who had waited years to have a child, gave their newborn son all of the names they had been considering for him.)

George Culver's first venture into coaching came in 1978, when he became a player-manager for a co-op team (a team with multiple affiliations) in Bakersfield of the California League. After finally retiring from playing, Culver had to keep reminding himself that he was a coach and no longer a player.

"I don't think you ever lose the desire to play," he said.

The other big adjustment has been the nature of how pitching is handled now that the pitch count and specialized relief pitching are a part of the game. Culver never even heard of these things while he was still pitching. As a coach, he doesn't like to see young pitchers immediately stuffed into a specific part of the staff.

"It would kill me when a pitcher reported to the team and asked, 'What's my role here?' I would say, 'What's your role? Your role is to show up and play! What's the difference if you're pitching in the seventh inning or the first inning? Just get the job done.'"

The balance between player development and winning in the minors is definitely tipped toward player development. A first place finish for a team in the Texas League will have no bearing on the major league club's performance, but the development of a couple of prospects on that farm team may be what puts the parent team in the playoffs a few years later. No one will argue that the first priority of a farm system team exists to develop players. At the same time, there are also the intangibles in the experience of playing on a championship-caliber team and learning how to win as a professional team. Rick Burleson had this basic rule of thumb—"Try to win the game from the seventh inning on."

"It's a fine line," said Eric Wedge, explaining the manager's balance between player development and winning ballgames. "At lower levels, it's primarily one hundred percent development. As you move up from level to level in the minor leagues, it becomes a little bit more about winning at each level. Development is always first and foremost when it comes to minor league baseball, but winning and understanding what it takes to win or to be a winner is part of development."

As former players themselves, managers are acutely aware of

their influence on their players' careers, many of which are short, and nearly all of which have their disappointments.

"If the player believes that you are putting their career in front of your own as a manager or as a coach, then there is no real problem with the adjustment," said Trey Hillman of helping players along in their careers.

"I have them be the best that they can be and not have any regrets in what they did," said Jim Pankovits.

Part of being a manager is being a mentor to these young players, many of whom are away from home for the first time. The addition of players from outside of North America also means extra duties in helping these players adjust to a strange language and culture. Jim Pankovits credits his experience of playing winter ball in Puerto Rico and South America in relating to what his foreign players are dealing with as well as picking up some of the Spanish language.

In the winter of 1995, Trey Hillman found himself managing some young Japanese prospects in Hawaii. Although he was experienced in managing Latin players, this situation meant dealing with yet another culture and language. However, he found that the game itself quickly overcame many of the barriers he faced.

"The Japanese typically have a great respect for the game. They don't ever question authority and they don't have any problems with who is running the club or how you want things done. The only problem every now and then is communication. But they were very bright. When the interpreter wasn't around, we'd demonstrate what we wanted done and they would make adjustments."

Handling demotions is never easy as a player, but a manager must ensure that the player quickly gets back on track in his new assignment for the sake of both the player and the team. The disappointment of a demotion is understandable, but remaining under a dark cloud because of it is unacceptable in the professional ranks. Allowing that dark cloud to remain may allow it to bring down other players. There is no set way for a manager to handle this.

"Every case is different," says Burleson. "I tell the player what is expected of him and expect him to lead by example."

"I give him a twenty-four- to forty-eight-hour cool-off period," said Trey Hillman, who, managing at Triple-A, must work with players who have just lost their spot on a major league roster. "As soon as they are here, I tell them 'Welcome back. I know you're not glad to be here but we're glad to have you. And my objective is to get you back as soon as possible.'

"Then I give them their twenty-four or forty-eight hours to get the bad feelings out of their system. If they haven't gotten it out of themselves in forty-eight hours, we sit down and have a talk. I get them redirected and tell them exactly what I think they need to work on. Then we get a course of action on how to attack it. I tell them I can't help them unless they're ready to help themselves."

As the manager of an independent team, Roger Hanners had to deal with a mix of players who were either passed over in the draft or released by another organization. He briefly described what the mind sets are for his newly acquired players.

On the released, ex-affiliated player:

"He's been hurt by being released. It's tough to get him back to where he needs to be."

On undrafted college players:

"They were stars, All-American, and figure they will have no problem here. By the time the beginning of the season rolls around, they know differently."

However, Hanners also understood that no player could be neatly fit into any stereotype. "You're trying to work with twenty-four different personalities," he explained.

The Catcher Has Left the Building

Part of the manager's job at all levels is dealing with players for whom the game has no longer become top priority. This may be as a result of attitude problems or something more serious such as a death or illness in the family. Then there was the death of the King.

While managing in Texas City in 1977, Al Gallagher had a catcher, Gary Rump, who was also a devoted Elvis impersonator. When Presley died that year, Gallagher found Rump at the ballpark the following day, packing his belongings. When asked what he was doing, Rump simply replied, "The King is dead. I have to go."

This put Gallagher in a tight situation. He had two catchers on his team. One was out with a sore thumb and now his other one was going off on a pilgrimage to pay homage to his fallen king. This called for empathy and compassion. Or, failing that, a lie would do just fine.

"I went into my office and came back running to him and telling him that the colonel [Presley's manager 'Colonel' Tom Parker] had just called," said Gallagher. "I said, 'Gary, if you would play just one more game for the King and then go tomorrow to Graceland, it would be okay with the colonel.'"

Gallagher's ruse worked long enough for him to rest his injured catcher.

"He played that game and I've never seen Gary Rump again."

Remaining in the Game

The climb to the major leagues may often take even longer within the coaching ranks. And those who make it are just as likely, if not more so, as the players to find themselves back in the minors after a year or two at the top.

"It's a challenging profession," says Jim Pankovits. "After my experiences and with what I've accomplished, I'm able to pass along quite a few things to these young kids. It's really fun to see them apply some of the things that you teach them about the game and watch them progress and have success at some of the higher levels and in the big leagues."

Jon Matlack shares that sentiment.

"I get a tremendous, warm glow when somebody that you're working with grasps an idea that you're trying to get across to him and you see the light go on in their eyes. There's a tremendous amount of satisfaction derived from knowing that no matter where this guy goes, that there's a small piece of me going with him that hopefully is going to make him a better player as well as a better person."

"I'm away from my wife and two children for up to three months out of the year and that's mentally and physically draining," said Trey Hillman of the sacrifices involved with staying in the game.

Not that the game doesn't have its perks—and Hillman is just as quick to point that out. Working within the Yankees system and participating in the big league camp during Spring Training with Joe Torre were memorable both in the professional and personal sense.

And then there are those singular opportunities. While managing in Columbus, former Yankees great Don Mattingly came to town to work with the team's first base prospect, Nick Johnson.

"It's not too many people who get to go out and have dinner at Outback Steakhouse with Don Mattingly and sit and visit."

"I'm blessed," said Hillman, becoming more introspective. "God's really blessed my life with putting me in the right spot at the right time. And I just hope that one day I get an opportunity to do it at the major league level. But if I don't, then so be it; because I've had a lot of fun down here helping the guys who have made it."

Where Credit Is Due

Although their daily grind of practices and paperwork can often be thankless, the coaches and managers do not go unremembered by the players who have moved on. When asked who was the most influential helping them get to the top, many major leaguers will quickly mention a coach or a manager from the minors or from even before they turned pro.

For Jim Pankovits, the one who stands out was his manager

in Hawaii, Doug Rader. "He made quite an impression on me as far as his competitiveness and the ability to balance that with making his career fun."

"I'll never forget my manager in Scranton for three of my five years there—Marc Bombard," said Jon Zuber. "He's the greatest manager I've had in professional baseball. I learned a lot about the approach to the game. I'd play for that guy anytime, anywhere."

Bombard, who coached in the majors for one season (Cincinnati in 1996), has over 1,300 minor league wins as a manager.

During his first season in the minors, pitcher Nate Minchey was suffering through a long stretch of bad pitching when he was approached by his manager, Alan Bannister. Bannister, who had spent twelve years pitching in the major leagues, saw something in the young player that the player couldn't see in himself.

"He said, 'I know you are going to be a big league pitcher someday—no doubt in my mind. You just have to not worry about what's going on now and keep getting better everyday.' Those encouraging words kept me going through many rough spots in my career."

In 1963, Steve Demeter played for manager Darrell Johnson while with the Rochester Red Wings. Johnson would later manage the Boston Red Sox to the American League pennant in 1975.

Johnson taught Demeter not only about hitting but how to look at the game as a manager and to anticipate what may happen in any particular situation. Demeter later coached in the majors with the Pirates and later became their coordinator for minor league instruction.

"Had I played for him five or six years before [going to the majors], I believe I would have been a better big league player," said Demeter of Johnson.

Lenny Johnston was the manager of the Burlington Senators

of the Carolina League when Tom Grieve played there in 1967. He remembered Johnston as a disciplinarian who also understood the need to ease the pressure on his players from time to time.

After one game when the team played poorly, Johnston told the players' wives and girlfriends to go home as the players would be staying late. But instead of chewing out his players, Johnston got a couple of cases of beer from the concession stand and brought it to the clubhouse. Everybody had to drink at least one beer, whether they usually drank or not. Johnston's aim was not to get anyone drunk, but to give his young players some perspective about who and where they were. For hours, the manager and players sat, drank, and talked about baseball.

"That was his way of getting his thoughts across," recalled Grieve.

Chris Nichting was pitching for the Albuquerque Duke in the early 1990s when, frustrated with his career, he was ready to quit. Albuquerque pitching coach Bud Black was aware of this while watching a game with Nichting.

Black asked Nichting why he thought he couldn't stay in the majors. Nichting told him and Black agreed, then proceeded to give him the advice that kept Nichting in the game, even through a five-year gap between major league appearances.

"He said, 'The key to anything is assessing your abilities fairly. You're never as bad as you think you are and you're never as good as you think you are,'" Nichting recounted.

David Dalton credits his success in his senior year at college for allowing him to make it into pro ball. A self-described "late bloomer," he acknowledges that without the help he received, his playing days would have ended in college. Coach Jeff Edwards arrived at Liberty that year and was told by manager Dave Pastors that Dalton was to be Edwards' "project."

"He worked with me every day, teaching some mechanical techniques that changed my game one hundred eighty degrees offensively and defensively."

George Staller, the manager of the York White Roses in the Piedmont League was Brooks Robinson's first professional manager and later coached in Baltimore when Robinson was playing there. He was instrumental in having Robinson moved from second base to third.

"It was the best thing that could have happened to me," Robinson said.

Hagerstown pitching coach Hector Berrios would don full catching gear to work with his pitchers to get a better perspective of the pitches. Cameron Reimers was one of many players who greatly appreciated the extra effort his coach gave.

"He would do this day in and day out," explained Reimers. "He's one of the guys who have helped me out the most."

Jon Matlack fondly recalled Johnny Murphy, the general manager of the Mets. In St. Petersburg, Florida, Murphy, wearing a suit and tie and wingtip shoes, spent hours in the bullpen with the young hurler.

"He laid his suit coat and tie on the ground," recalled Matlack. "And he was on the mound, demonstrating the delivery he wanted me to try and use—in his wingtips, for crying out loud. It was actually the beginnings of the delivery I wound up using at the big league level."

While former Braves farmhand Chris Poulsen was playing independent ball in Chillicothe, one coach, Jamie Keefe came out of retirement to play shortstop when the team became shorthanded. Like Poulsen, Keefe had played several years in affiliated ball before going to the Frontier League. Although only apart in age by a few years, Poulsen clearly looked up to Keefe as a mentor.

"He's seen it all—playing in affiliated ball, then playing here, then becoming a coach. He's always a step ahead of you—a step ahead of things mentally, a step ahead of you in the game. He's someone you can learn from easily—you can talk to him about certain situations and he isn't going to talk down to you."

Jim Saul is frequently mentioned by former players as a huge influence in handling themselves as professionals, yet still ensuring that they enjoyed and appreciated their time in baseball, no matter how long or short. After retiring from playing, the former Triple-A catcher went immediately into coaching. In 1973, he managed the Salinas Packers in the California League. In the following years, he managed teams in eight different leagues as well as serving two major league coaching stints with the Cubs and Athletics.

"I pretty well knew that I wanted to continue in baseball as a young man," said Saul. "Even after my playing days. I think I've got the knowledge and I think that I can communicate with kids in a way that would be beneficial to them—and to myself, also."

Play It Again

The transition from player to coach is not always a one-way trip. Sacramento River Cats manager Bob Geren discovered this while managing the Pacific Coast League team in 2000. Geren, a former big league catcher who spent most of his major career with the Yankees found himself down to one catcher after Danny Ardoin was traded by the parent club, Oakland, to the Minnesota Twins. With no backup to warm up relief pitchers in the bullpen, Geren spent several games splitting time between the dugout and bullpen as he worked to get his relievers loosened up for the game.

During the same year, Chillicothe coach Jamie Keefe returned to the infield as the Paints found themselves in need of a shortstop following the loss of several players to affiliation contracts and injuries. Keefe enjoyed his few weeks back on the diamond, but knew that it was coaching that lay in his baseball future. He became a full-time coach again after a suitable infielder was found to replace him.

Character Issues

However important their job is, not only to the their own careers but to those of their players, managers and coaches like to have their fun as well. Granted, they must uphold the discipline on the team, but they still know that life can't always be taken too seriously. After all, they were once players, too.

Jim Saul, or "Big Jim" as he is known to his players, has seen a lot in his forty-plus years of baseball. Standing well over six feet tall at around 240 pounds, he could appear to be a menacing presence—until one speaks to him.

All those years of bus rides and bad food have not diminished his sense of humor—but may have warped it a bit. Many an unsuspecting player, seeing his manager in some public place like a supermarket, would go up to say hello.

"What's up, Big Jim?" was the typical greeting.

In a booming voice loud enough for bystanders to hear, Saul's response would be something like, "Wup! Wup! Woooooooop!" Then he would walk off, leaving his player to deal with the stares from the crowd.

"He's a super guy to play for," said Chris Poulsen, who played for him in Jamestown. "He never put any pressure on you. He threatened to kick all of our butts if we didn't have fun. That's one thing he tried to stress—have a good time."

Mickey Hatcher had a well-deserved reputation as both a team leader and goofball as a player. He never let up once he became a manager. Jason Baker, who played for him in Great Falls of the Pioneer League, explained:

"He loved to win, but he was also a crazy guy. He loved the game and he loved to get guys out there who wanted to work hard.

"But off the field, he wanted to be the first one in the shower and he wanted to be the first one out to the nearest happening place. He had the crowds. He'd wear a cowboy hat and everybody knew as soon as he came—everybody would yell, 'Mickey!' He was something else."

Long before his glory years when he led the New York Yankees to seven World Series titles, Casey Stengel was managing the Eastern League's Worcester Panthers in 1925. In his double duty as a bus driver, he noticed that his players were prone to jumping out of their seats and racing to open windows on one side of the bus or the other. He was confused and a little unnerved until he discovered the cause of this behavior—the sight of virtually any young woman.

"Gee, you guys sure can see a skirt," Casey grumbled. "I wish you could see my signs as well—or half as well. I'll put on a kimono out there on the coaching lines if you think it will do any good."

Jersey City manager Bruno Betzel unknowingly read one of his players the riot act after a game in 1946, with the player just inches away. Bobby Thomson had muffed a bunt play while playing third base in the game. After the game, the players got into waiting taxicabs to return to their hotel. As was the norm in those days of meager baseball salaries, they crammed as many people as they could inside each cab in order to split the fare among more passengers.

As luck would have it, Thomson wound up crammed in the same cab as Betzel. Thomson was actually stuffed under another player, and went unnoticed by his irate skipper. Betzel, still fuming over Thomson's error, ranted on about Thomson to the other, more visible players. When the cab arrived at the hotel, Thomson made sure Betzel had already walked away before venturing out of the car.

"It was funny how he chewed me out but never knew I was in the cab with him," laughed Thomson, who would later hit the famous "shot heard 'round the world" home run to clinch the 1951 National League pennant for the New York Giants.

Joe Schultz, manager of the San Antonio Missions in 1956,

was a St. Louis native and a huge devotee of his hometown Anheuser-Busch product. He enjoyed teasing his third baseman, Brooks Robinson, whom he called "Arky" in reference to Robinson's home state of Arkansas, about Robinson's preference for soda pop over beer.

Robinson laughed at the memories. "He would say to me, 'Arky, you'll never make the big leagues drinking soda pop and eating ice cream. You've gotta pound down that Budweiser.'"

The hitters for the Hagerstown Suns were suffering a collective slump in July of 1982 when manager Grady Little decided it was time for a change. Having made several adjustments to the batting order to no avail, Little turned the lineup card over to his twelve-year-old son, Eric, for one game. Eric Little's line-up did the trick as the Suns downed the Alexandria Dukes 11-5.

"It helped remind everybody that the game is still fun," remarked Dave Falcone, Hagerstown's designated hitter. "Everybody was getting a little tight."

If many keep their fun-loving ways, they also keep their competitive nature long after they've played their last inning. Baker had Charlie Hough as his team's pitching coach while playing in San Bernardino. Hough, a former major league pitcher with 216 wins in The Show, would regularly throw batting practice. But if any batter started hitting his pitches *too* well, Hough would go back to his money pitch from his playing days, the knuckleball. The would-be hitting stud would quickly find himself dealing with a phenomena he had never seen before as the ball wobbled and danced its way to the plate, seemingly defying the laws of physics.

"He could throw from behind his back, between his legs. He was a character all around. He was fun to work with, too," said Baker.

Burleigh Grimes rode his success with the spitball all the way to Cooperstown, but by the time he was managing in the minor leagues, his trademark pitch had been outlawed by professional baseball. But as Ralph Kiner, himself a future Hall of Famer at the time, found out, Grimes was not about to let a bush leaguers tee off on him at will during batting practice. Like Hough with his knuckler, Grimes would put his young charges in their place with his creatively doctored pitches.

The late Jimmy Reese, a former roommate of Babe Ruth's and a longtime coach in the minors and majors, had his own unique way of throwing batting practice. Using a bat that was sawed off at the barrel, he would hit the balls to the batters.

It is clear that those people who remain in the game to coach in the minors have a deep love for the National Pastime. So it shouldn't come as a surprise that they are prepared to overcome many obstacles to stay close to their chosen sport. Not even an ejection by the umpire can keep some away from the game.

When Kinston Eagles manager Dennis Holmberg was thrown out of a Carolina League game against Winston-Salem in 1980, he was not about to retire to the locker room and sulk. However, retiring to the locker room in order to sneak back into the game was another matter altogether.

Several minutes later, the Kinston team was surprised to find their mascot in their dugout. The umpires ignored the costumed creature who, unbeknown to them, was now Holmberg in disguise. With his new persona in place, Holmberg safely remained in the Eagles' dugout to manage the rest of the game.

Tacoma Tigers skipper Ed Nottle was known as the singing manager. He had recorded an album, and his music would be played between innings in Tacoma to help sell records. After an ejection in one game, Nottle shifted from singing to acting.

After getting tossed, Nottle was far from through with the umpire. He sought out the team mascot and shortly thereafter returned to the field in the tiger's costume. Upon approaching the umpire, he began making a scene, kicking dirt on the umpire's shoes.

The umpire just laughed it off as a mascot's prank, unaware that Nottle was getting his revenge.

It was September of 1986. One had to wonder what Branch B. Rickey, the farm director of the Pittsburgh Pirates, was thinking as he received the manager's report from the organization's affiliate in Prince William. Rickey was the scion of a great line of baseball executives and would himself later become the president of the Pacific Coast League. Rickey's grandfather was a baseball pioneer who helped create the farm system and ushered in major league baseball's integration by signing Jackie Robinson. Rickey's father (Branch Jr.) was a farm director for the Dodgers and Pirates.

In 1986, the end-of-season report on each player from the Prince William Pirates was not in the usual written form but on tape. Prince William's manager Rocky Bridges borrowed team broadcaster Dave Collins' tape recorder and gave a monologue on the entire team. In closing, he borrowed a phrase from Reds' color commentator Joe Nuxhall and said, "This Rocky Bridges, rounding third and heading for home." Then he finished off by warbling "Happy Trails" onto the tape.

This Would Have To Be Called "On-The-Job Training"

Although midseason managerial replacements are not uncommon in the minors, they do not happen nearly as often as in the major leagues. During the 2000 season, two manager's positions were unexpectedly vacated, putting two men into a spotlight that neither had counted on.

Marty Dunn has seen plenty of baseball, both as a high school coach and an independent team coach. After playing college baseball at Alabama State University, he became a chemistry teacher and baseball coach. In 1993, after five years of coaching at Chillicothe High School in Ohio, he was asked by Chris and Roger Hanners if he would coach their team in the newly formed Frontier League. While still staying with his teaching job, he took the Paints' offer to coach the team under manager Roger Hanners.

About midway though the 2000 season, his eighth with the Paints, Dunn was thrust into the manager's set when Roger Hanners suffered a heart attack. Although the Paints were considered one of the best run teams in independent ball, their roster situation was a mess. Several of their best players, including Mike Cervanek and Joe Colemeco, had been signed to farm system contracts. Other holes in the lineup were caused by injuries. Desperate for some infield relief, the Paints pressed their other coach, Jamie Keefe, back into service as a shortstop.

Faced with a shorthanded roster and a coaching staff that was back in cleats, Dunn pressed on. Hanners would spend the remainder of the season in convalescence. Now he had to fill the shoes of a manager who was very popular and well respected not only by his own players but throughout the league as well.

Dunn was able to bring the team back to its winning ways, guiding the Paints to within one victory of getting into the Frontier League's post-season. Looking back at his first few days as manager, he was quick to share the credit of his managerial success with his players.

"It was a tremendous effort on their part," said Dunn. "We have some very respectful guys. I try to be respectful of them and I had confidence in what I was doing. I don't try to be domineering over people but try to create an air of working together. It's just the same thing [as being a coach], now I have a different label by my name.

"There are some game decisions that have to be made which are my responsibility. But as far as the team goes, we try to sell the issue that we're all together in this with one objective—to win. And you get everybody pitching in."

But as successful as Dunn's managerial stint was, it was not to be a stepping stone to bigger things in baseball—by Dunn's own choice.

"If this had happened to me fifteen years ago, this is something I would have thought about," he said late in the season. "I've been teaching high school for eighteen years. I've been a baseball head coach for thirteen years. I have a wife and two kids—and Chillicothe is my home now."

Dunn was not the only Frontier manager to unexpectedly get the job in 2000. Fran Riordan was the first baseman for the Dubois County Dragons when the year began. With about a month remaining in the season, the Dragons ownership cleaned house, firing the general manger, manager, and coaches. Riordan, a .300-plus hitter a few weeks shy of his twenty-fifth birthday, was called into the team office at midnight and was offered the manager's job in addition to playing first base for the remainder of the year. He accepted the offer, although he had never considered coaching before.

"I really hadn't though of it. I've been a player all of my life. I've never even coached high school or have been an assistant coach. This [the manager's job] is just for this year. Next year, I'll be playing full time again."

Meanwhile, Riordan had to adjust to his new role while still playing.

"There's more to think about before the game, during the game, and after the game. I've actually found myself struggling some in the playing aspect because my head is so far into what's going on in the field, to who I have coming in to pitch, pinch-hit, pinch-run. So I've given away some at-bats this year from the managing aspect."

The 2000 season was Riordan's fourth year in the league and the second with Dubois County. After the season, he returned to the Richmond Roosters, for whom he had played in his first two years. Despite his initial reservations about managing, he was not only the Roosters' first baseman, but also their manager.

CHAPTER 7

Behind the Mike

To be able to watch baseball every night,
relay the excitement of baseball to others listening
and watch unexpected events occur live is the
best part of the job.

—Shane Griffin, radio announcer

Like the personnel on the field, minor radio and television announcers have become well acquainted with the trials of baseball life. A few, like Spokane's Bob Robertson, have become part of the local baseball institution. Many others find themselves in a more transient state, moving from one location to the next as team ownerships change or franchises move.

For an announcer, the minor leagues allow them to get a glimpse of some future history—watching, analyzing, and interviewing young players who may go on to be major league stars.

The career path of an announcer is not as well defined as that of a minor league player. The minors are a proving ground for them, giving them experience in sports broadcasting that may lead to jobs in the major leagues or at the top level in other sports. From that perspective, a move "up" for an announcer may mean moving from a Triple-A team to a Double-A one. However, the Double-A team may be in a larger media market area, which means more exposure for the people sitting behind the microphone. With different goals, constantly shifting circumstances, and last-minute opportunities, every announcer has a unique road to be traveled.

Wishing to start a career in broadcasting, John Miller had sent demo tapes out to teams all over the country with no success. Shortly before the season was to begin, a broadcaster in Lynchburg, Virginia had just left for another broadcasting job, creating a sudden need for the Lynchburg Hillcats. On April 1, Miller was given the job with little time to prepare for his first ever season in the booth.

Andy Young was set on becoming a broadcaster at an early age. "It's a job I started preparing for when I was about seven or eight years old and figured out how to work that radio next to my bed. When I was in high school, I was announcing baseball games in my head and occasionally in the privacy of my bedroom or behind the lawnmower where I was working."

By college, at the University of Connecticut, he began doing hockey play-by-play on the college radio station, but still wanted to do baseball. At first, he split the school's baseball schedule with six others, but was the number one broadcaster by the time he graduated. While searching for a radio job in baseball in 1981, he began substitute teaching to make ends meet.

His first job came in 1984 with the Alaska Goldpanners of the Alaskan Baseball League, a summer collegiate league, broadcasting on KFAR radio in Fairbanks. The following year, he did his first radio work in pro ball, announcing for the Carolina League's Durham Bulls.

The reality of the work conflicted with his longtime dream. The grind of doing multiple jobs for the team, including typing, running across town for photocopies, and occasionally working in the team store, wore him down. He left baseball after the season, believing at the time that his broadcasting days were over.

By 1989, he began thinking of returning to baseball, limiting himself to short-season Class-A ball to keep from burning out. In mid-season, he heard from John Brown, the general manager of the Burlington Indians in the short-season Appalachian League. The team's announcer was leaving, and Young filled in at the microphone for the last three weeks of the season with little expectation of doing any more radio work the following year. To his surprise, the three weeks were very enjoyable and he was eager for more. He credited much of that to working with the team manager, Jim Gabella and pitcher Mike Gonzalez.

He stayed on in Burlington in 1990. In 1991, at Brown's suggestion, he moved south to announce games for the Vero Beach Dodgers for two years before returning to Burlington for the 1993 season. He had two assignments in 1994. During Spring Training, he was the public address announcer and ticket salesman for the Chicago White Sox. Then he spent regular season on the radio for the Butte Copper Kings in the Pioneer League. That winter, he went to Raleigh, North Carolina to do radio work for the Raleigh Ice Caps, a minor league hockey team.

Young was hired by the Portland Sea Dogs in January, 1995, with whom he was still with in 2001. He returned to Raleigh again that winter before returning Portland on a year-round basis. In the off-season, he was the team's director of broadcasting and did minor league hockey broadcasts for the Portland Pirates.

When Dave Collins was still in high school and working at Silver Stadium in Rochester, he began doing statistics work for the broadcasters. Eventually, he began announcing over the park's public address system and later progressed to radio play-by-play work.

After graduating from college with degrees in statistics and economics, he found himself drawn to the game, working the airwaves of the minor leagues in stops that included Prince William, Lynchburg, and Elmira.

Collins was working in media relations for the Oriole's Double-A team when it was located in Hagerstown. After the franchise moved to Bowie in 1993, Collins returned to the broadcast booth. Despite a college education that could net him a comfortable position in a corporate office, Collins preferred the seating on the long bus rides and in the ballparks. Collins explained the reason he stays involved in the game.

"A love for the game and a love for what I call the baseball family, which to me is everybody from other broadcasters, media people, players, coaches, umpires, front office, and fans."

In 1983, college students Jim Lucas and Don Wardlow began their careers in the booth by broadcasting baseball games for their school, Glassboro State College. Lucas called the play-by-play action while Wardlow did the color commentary. What made the situation unique was that Wardlow was blind. But Wardlow's lack of physical vision did not prevent him from having other insight into the game.

After a one-game stint for Mike Veeck's Miami Miracle, the duo became the team's full-time broadcasters in 1991. Through the years, they followed the team to Fort Myers and also broadcasted for the New Britain Rock Cats as well as two more teams owned by Veeck in St. Paul and Charleston, South Carolina.

After twelve seasons, Wardlow stepped away from the mike for the last time to spend more time with his family. Lucas remained with the Charleston River Dogs as assistant general manager and still does the play-by-play for the team's home games.

Shane Griffin had radio waves in his blood. The son of a career radio man who taught him much about the world of radio, he began as a disc jockey, but had already set his sights on doing baseball play-by-play. He broke into baseball part time in 1995, when he called twenty-five games for the South Atlantic League's Charleston Riverdogs. He continued part time with the Riverdogs for another three seasons while also becoming the play-by-play man for The Citadel.

After two years broadcasting college sports, he sought to return to pro baseball. As luck would have it, he was the only person in a group of about two hundred people attending a South Atlantic League job seminar who was looking for radio work. After several interviews, he became the announcer for the Delmarva Shorebirds.

Although he had worked steadily in radio to get the job he wanted, he still appreciated the unique circumstances in which he had to get his foot in the door.

"My case is a rarity," he said two years after landing the Delmarva job. "There are guys that have been contacting me for two years looking for openings and have been unable to hook on with a team."

Bob Robertson grew up with the desire to play professional baseball. The son of a professional ballplayer, Robertson had played some semi-pro ball before signing a minor league contract. He quickly became aware of his limitations as a player and chose to become a broadcaster instead. In 1949, he landed his first radio job with the Wenatchee Chiefs of the Western International League. In the following years, he did broadcast work for the Tacoma Tigers and then the Spokane Indians, for whom he still broadcasts games.

Minor league baseball wasn't his only radio work. Much of his work involved college football, broadcasting for Notre Dame and Washington State University. Robertson has also worked three major league games at the microphone for the Seattle Mariners when their regular announcer had days off.

Despite his taste of the big leagues, Robertson is happy to be working in Spokane, which is part of the Short-Season Single-A Northwest League. In short-season leagues, the players are usually in only the first or second years of their careers.

"It's fun to work with the young kids," Robertson explained. "There's no bitterness there. They haven't been sent down and they haven't been overlooked by the organization for five years."

Working college football and minor league baseball has

allowed Robertson to get a glimpse of many future stars including football's Jim Plunkett and Drew Bledsoe and baseball's Mark McGwire and Alex Rodriguez. Robertson was immediately impressed when he saw eighteen-year-old Alex Rodriguez.

"The day you saw him walk onto the field, you knew he was going to be a superstar," he recalled.

Robertson's broadcasting career has also seen the transformation of radio technology. In his early days, broadcast equipment was too large and too heavy to take on the road, which led to broadcasters recreating road games in their hometown studios. Robertson was reportedly the last broadcaster to do these re-creations.

The broadcaster would have someone at the game send him the play-by-play information through various means of communication that evolved over time. At first, Robertson received his information came by Morse code tickertape, then later teletype or "page printers" as they were then called. In the final days of studio re-creation, reports were sent by phone.

The broadcasts then occurred about a half hour behind the actual play of the game. The delay would allow for times when the connection to the park was lost. They might fill a little time with an imaginary conference on the mound or by slowing down the pace of the game. The key was not to get too far fetched with the delay.

At the studio, someone would take down the information, then the broadcaster would call the game while adding sound effects, taped sounds of a bat striking the ball, crowds cheering or booing at different levels, rain falling on the grandstand roof, or an overhead airplane. Robertson's wife and son often assisted him in the studio.

"Most of the people thought they were listening to the real thing," said Robertson of his broadcasts.

People would wonder, though, when they saw Robertson in the grocery store in Washington shortly after an away game in Vancouver or Edmonton.

For teams that carry a full-season schedule on the radio (some only broadcast home games), the broadcasters spend as much time on the road as the players and coaches. Portland's Andy Young travels on the bus with the team and gets his own seat.

"That might not seem like much, but it's a biggie," Young explained.

In a concession to middle age, he also brings his own food on the road to avoid the endless stream of greasy fast food that the young players seem to thrive on.

Announcers go into every game knowing that there is a chance, however slight, to see some small piece of baseball lore created on the field. For Houston Buffaloes television announcers Dick Gottlieb and Bruce Layer, the night of June 12, 1950 made history in a tragic way.

With television still in its infancy, the announcers' area for the Texas League team was in an open area rather than being inside a broadcast booth to accommodate the large amount and size of the broadcasting equipment. During the sixth inning, fifty-year-old Sanford Twente, who had been drinking heavily and was apparently distressed about his family problems, worked his way into the broadcast area and tried to speak to Gottlieb. Gottlieb pushed the man away twice, thinking he was just a drunken fan.

As the camera was focused on the field while the visiting Tulsa Oilers took up their positions, a loud explosion was heard. Cameraman Gorman Erickson swung his camera back to the announcers and caught Twente's body on film as it was slumping to the floor next to Gottlieb.

Gottlieb quickly reacted as best as circumstances would allow, turning to the camera and saying, "Ladies and gentlemen, a tremendous thing has just happened. A gentleman has just shot himself. I return you now to the studio."

After some delay, the game resumed both on the field and on television. A shaken Gottlieb informed his wife on the air that he was all right, and then he went on to complete his broadcast.

Shane Griffin is keenly aware that each game holds the

potential for something dramatic. In the winter he sells advertising and tickets for the Shorebirds. In the summer, like the on-field personnel of his Delmarva team, he too must endure a long season of endless bus rides and fastfood meals. But when he settles inside of the radio booth at the park with his notebooks and binoculars, the excitement of the game begins to kick in.

"Every game has a storyline, and every night there is a chance to see events occur that you would not have expected—no hitter, four homers in a game by one player, perfect game, etc.," he said.

The most memorable of unexpected events in Griffin's broadcasting career came on September 12, 2000. The Shorebirds were facing off against the Columbus Red Stixx in the South Atlantic League Championship Series. The Shorebirds had taken the first two games in the best of five series, but the Red Stixx fought them to a 6-6 tie going into the ninth inning of Game Three.

In the bottom of the ninth, Delmarva had the bases loaded with two out. The task of driving in the run to win both the game and series fell to an unlikely hero—back-up catcher Mike Seestedt. Seestedt quickly fell behind in the count, one and two. As he swung at the next pitch, he caught nothing but air with his bat; strike three.

However, the ball proved to be as elusive to Columbus' catcher as it was to Delmarva's hitter, slipping past his glove to remain in play. Seestedt, seeing the ball heading to the backstop, bolted for first base as the runner on third, Raymond Cabrera, sprinted toward the plate. The catcher scrambled to recover the ball, but had to wait for a split second as the first baseman was late to cover the bag. Cabrera approached home as the catcher threw, but the run would only count if Seestedt safely made it to first to avoid the third out.

As he crossed home plate, Cabrera was looking down the first base line to see the outcome of the play. Seestedt reached the base just ahead of the throw, making Cabrera's run count. The crowd at the stadium erupted, having seen their team win the league championship on a run-scoring strikeout.

While broadcasting in Butte, Montana, Andy Young saw plenty of topsy-turvy baseball. The Copper Kings were playing the Billings Mustangs, the defending league champions who had won the last thirteen games against the Copper Kings over a three-year stretch. Billings' winning streak continued as the Mustangs scored ten runs in the top of the fourth inning. By the end of that half-inning, Young thought he had seen enough.

"I made the mistake of saying, 'Boy, fans, it doesn't get much worse than this.'"

It did get worse. In the next inning, Billings poured on another twelve runs en route to a 25-5 pasting of Butte.

Jason Robbins, the league ERA leader, was on the mound for the Mustangs the following day after the Billings landslide. The Mustangs quickly picked up where they left off, slamming four home runs in the first to stake Robbins to a 6-0 lead. Robbins' comfort zone quickly evaporated as the Copper Kings responded with nine runs in the bottom of the inning.

Both teams continued to pummel each other's pitchers, with Billings holding a 20-18 lead going into the bottom of the ninth. The Copper Kings evened the score to send the game into extra innings. The Mustangs promptly added another run in the top of the tenth, but finally fell after Butte answered with two runs in the bottom half.

The game was indicative of Copper Kings' season. Butte had a .306 team batting average, but also owned a 7.16 team ERA, the highest in organized baseball history up to that time.

The unexpected or unusual sometimes reaches to the location of the broadcaster's booth. Andy Young was almost beheaded by the unexpected during a game in Portland when the Sea Dogs' Josh Booty fouled a ball back through the open window in the broadcast booth in Portland's Hadlock Field. Young quickly ducked out of the way. When he cautiously rose up again, he discovered a baseball-sized hole in the wall behind his head.

Other broadcasting events that fall beyond the norm involve team promotions. The Altoona Curve's radio voice, Rob Egan, was once heard from the roller coaster just beyond the right field fence at Altoona's Blair County Ballpark.

Canio Costanzo, the Hickory Crawdads' broadcaster, will not soon forget the team's promotion of "PJ" night. He did the broadcast from a bed located on the lower concourse behind home plate in L.P. Frans Stadium.

"It was a neat promotion, but we picked the worst night to do it," Costanzo said. "It must have been a hundred and ten degrees."

This didn't make it very comfortable for Costanzo, who was wearing a cotton bathrobe in bed. The heat also led to another problem.

"I was sweating like crazy and drinking a lot of water. That was a mistake."

Between calling the game and doing commentary before the start of the next half inning, radio announcers have virtually no time to take a break. To compound the problem, Costanzo worked his broadcasts alone and had no one to cover for him on the air if he was in the men's room. However, to his relief, the game only lasted two hours.

For a select few, a broadcasting job in the major leagues becomes a reality. Some are happy where they are in the minors, but others share the same dream as the players. Andy Young is one of the latter.

"Part of it is ego," said Young. "Part of it is goal. You want to realize that goal. I'd like to be heard by the maximum number of people and do it at the highest level available."

Marty Brennaman reached that level after three years of minor league broadcasting. While growing up, he loved all sports, especially baseball. In college, he originally studied drama, but lost the desire to make that his profession when he saw how few actors actually made a living at it. Brennaman then switched majors to communications with the intent of becoming a play-by-play announcer, a choice that was affected by his childhood.

"Listening to baseball on the radio back in the fifties was a magical time," Brennaman explained. "Especially because TV hadn't impacted this country like it later would."

In 1971, Brennaman began broadcasting for the Virginia Squires of the American Basketball Association. That same year, the radio job for the Triple-A Tidewater Tides became available and he took on a second gig. Over the next three years, Brennaman was happy covering the Squires and Tides, but outside circumstances offered him an unexpected opportunity.

After the 1973 season, Reds broadcaster Al Michaels left to work for the San Francisco Giants. During baseball's annual winter meeting, Tidewater General Manager Dave Rosenfield heard about the open position and recommended Brennaman to the Reds' assistant general manager, Dick Wagner. At Wagner's request, Brennaman sent them a tape of one of his broadcasts.

"I actually sent the tape more as a courtesy to Dave, who thought enough of my work to recommend me, then anything else," said Brennaman. "I was not actively pursuing a big league job."

A big league club, though, began pursuing him. Brennaman was one of three finalists for the job that two hundred and twenty-one people had applied for. After two days of interviews in Cincinnati, the Reds offered Brennaman the job. In 1974, Brennaman began broadcasting Spring Training games, which helped him get settled with the team and begin to develop a comfort level. Despite the time with the Reds in Florida, Opening Day for the regular season was the true major league experience.

At the time, baseball still always held the first game of its regular season in Cincinnati as a salute to the Reds being professional baseball's oldest team. In the city, a huge parade was held and children were excused from school to attend the game if they were lucky enough to have a ticket. With the ears of the baseball world tuned in, Brennaman made his debut in 1974 with the Atlanta Braves in town.

"I was nervous. I was awed by the crowd and the hoopla of Opening Day."

History didn't wait long, as Hank Aaron was on the verge of tying Babe Ruth's home run record. In the first inning of that game, the airwaves lit up as Brennaman called Aaron's seven hundred and fourteenth home run.

Signing off

Their names are not known outside their minor league cities. As faceless voices on the radio, they go unrecognized on the streets in those cities. While fame is elusive, the job has given them a view inside the game that few people get to see. For Andy Young, the experience has altered his view of the sport.

"The reason I went into baseball might be one hundred and eighty degrees from the reason I'm still in it. I started off as a baseball fan or as a fan of baseball players. What I am now is a fan of human beings involved with baseball."

CHAPTER 8

Behind the Scenes

I just like being around the ballpark. Selling
advertising, talking with the fans, everything.

—Reid Ryan, chairman, president, and co-owner,
Round Rock Express

It is not uncommon for young baseball fans to dream of playing the game in the professional ranks as they grow older. Statements like "I want to pitch for the Yankees" or "I want to play third base for the Cardinals" are often heard. What is doubtfully ever heard from children are wishes to become an assistant general manager or public relations director for their hometown team. With the passage into adulthood come pragmatism and the need to earn a living. For some people, be it by choice or by circumstance, this brings them back to the ballpark.

"Like most kids, I always wanted to get into baseball as a player," recalled Joel White, who works for the Provo Angels. "When I was about thirteen years old, I came to the realization that I just didn't have enough talent to make it to the majors as a player, so I decided to try to work in a front office somewhere."

Professionally, they come from all walks of life. Columbus

Clippers General Manager Ken Schnacke was a mechanical engineer. Media Relations Director John Miller joined the Albuquerque Dukes for what was to be their final season after starting in the baseball business as a radio broadcaster for a team in the Carolina League.

In the past decade, sports management has become an increasingly popular major offered by some universities. In 1994, their second season of existence, the Chillicothe Paints hired Bryan Wickline, a sports administration major at Ohio University, as an intern. He returned to the Paints after his graduation the following year, and he has been with the team ever since.

The lines to get a job with a major sports franchise or college sports program, be it baseball, football, or others, are long. Baseball, more than any other sport, provides a larger opportunity for starting a sports management career due to the sheer numbers of minor and independent league teams. However, some people who start in a minor league office find themselves content to stay there.

After graduating from college and going to work as an engineer, Ken Schnacke began moonlighting as a broadcaster for minor league games in Columbus, Ohio, mostly because of his love for the game. At that point, he hadn't considered the possibility of there really being any careers in minor league baseball aside from those people on the field. He did attend the minor leagues' winter meetings in 1975, but came away initially unimpressed and feeling like an outsider.

Bobby Bragan helped to break down some barriers for Schnacke. In February, 1976, he received an offer to be the business manager for the Rio Grande Valley White Wings in the newly created Gulf States League. He gave his notice and left his engineering job to give baseball a try. After ten days on the job, the team's owners decided he had enough experience to be the general manager and team president.

After the expenses of creating the ballclub were paid, Schnacke was given his budget for the season—eight hundred dollars in cash—and the warning that the amount was all there would be. He went to Harlingen, Texas and proceeded to get started, living in a hotel and working out of the trunk of his car.

Following the season, he returned home to Columbus and was hired onto the staff of a new club that was to bring pro baseball back to the city after a six-year absence. He has remained with the team since, becoming general manager in 1989.

Like Schnacke, Pawtucket Red Sox President Mike Tamburro has been with the same International League team since 1977. He first worked for Pawtucket as an intern, while working on a master's degree in sports administration at the University of Massachusetts. After graduation, he ran a New York-Penn League farm team in Elmira, New York. Tamburro returned to Pawtucket as general manager in 1977 after Ben Mondor bought the club. He worked with Mondor as the team was raised from the ashes of bankruptcy to become one of the premier clubs in the minors. Later, he was named team president.

The Red Sox were aided by two events that helped generate publicity for the team, the longest game in professional baseball history in 1981 (see Chapter 26) and the July 1, 1982 match-up between former American League Rookies of the Year Dave Righetti (R.O.Y. in 1981) and Mark Fidrych (1976). The game was the first time two former Rookies of the Year pitched against each other in a minor league park. Righetti had been sent down to Columbus from the Yankees, while Fidrych was trying to come back from injuries. When Pawtucket manager Joe Morgan learned that Righetti was going to pitch in Pawtucket, he scheduled Fidrych against him. Adding fuel to the fire was that the game involved the top farm clubs of two major league archrivals.

"The reaction from the community was absolute mayhem," Tamburro said.

After five years in the front offices of the minor leagues, David Barnes has racked up plenty of frequent traveler points. Like many kids growing up in New England, he dreamed of playing for the Red Sox. By the time he was in high school, realized that his dream would remain just that—a dream. However, his desire to get to the majors was still there, so he began to research the business side of the game.

After graduating from Springfield College in 1996 with a degree in Sports Management, he interned with the Clearwater Phillies, Idaho Falls Braves, and the Hudson Valley Renegades. In 1998, he joined the Kissimmee Cobras as the assistant general manager. With the team closing shop after the 2000 season as part of the Florida State League contraction, Barnes was once again packing his bags.

"I hope to stay in sports," he said in late August of 2000. "Preferably baseball. I have already started to look for another job, and hopefully it will be with a major league club. I have also looked at other sports such as football, and maybe something will become of that."

A specific job title in a minor league office doesn't limit the titleholder's tasks to just that area, particularly in the lower minors. Provo's Joel White used himself to describe working in the front office.

"Technically, I'm director of Media Relations, but in minor league baseball, everybody does everything. Along with media relations, I am a sales executive and I do a lot of marketing. You can't make it in minor league baseball without being able to sell. Like I said, we all do a little of everything."

The job of a general manager in the minor leagues differs from the same position in the majors. "The title of general manager at the Triple-A level probably is more in line with the title of president on the major league club," explained Ken Schnacke. Both are involved with the business concerns of the ball club, the operation of the facility.

At the Triple-A level, the general manager has some influence in the placement of players, although the major league team always makes the final decision. His or her input is taken into account during discussions with the major league front office. While the manager and coaches focus on the players' on-field performance, the front office keeps an eye on the off-the-field aspects such as how he conducts himself away from the park and how he handles himself as a professional.

The contrast in the general manager's position between the various levels of minor league ball can be seen within an hour's drive in Central Ohio. The pre-game preparation at Columbus' Cooper Stadium runs like clockwork with the concession vendors, ushers, and other personnel going about their business. Also walking about are staff personnel from the front office, many of whom have been with the club for years. Dressed in polo shirts and khaki slacks, they move with a somewhat casual ease, but also carry two-way radios to quickly take care of any problem that may crop up. Also in the mix is Ken Schnacke, moving about the stadium while chatting with employees, media, VIPs and fans alike. Unlike his staffers, he does not carry a radio, but there are always some of his front people nearby to take care of anything he may notice or need.

State Route 104 runs south from Columbus. It's a two-lane road winding its way past silos and cornfields to Chillicothe. Forty-five miles south of Cooper Stadium, along Route 104, is V.A. Memorial Stadium, a small ballpark built on the grounds of a Veterans' Administration facility north of Chillicothe. It's home to the Chillicothe Paints of the independent Frontier League, roughly equivalent to a Class-A league. Like the Clippers' employees to the north, the Paints off-field team is also preparing for a game under the summer sky. Coming at the end of a full day in the Paints office, these preparations are no cool-down period for Paints G.M. Bryan Wickline.

With a smaller budget comes a smaller staff, but the desire to present a quality evening at the ballpark remains the same. For Wickline, it's time to be many different people and be in many different places at once. After dropping off rolls of coins for change at the concession stand, he stops to fix the radar gun at the speed-pitch booth. Then he's needed at the souvenir store. A reporter from out of town catches up with him for a few questions. He answers a few before politely steering the reporter on to his media relations director, John Wend, who is manning the public address microphone in the press box. He speaks to the clubhouse manager—a new pitcher has been signed that day and still needs some uniform pants that fit. Then it's back to the speed pitch booth to fix the radar gun again and to show the kid working the booth how *not* to damage the gun's power cord. A cashier from the ticket window walks up to him—they are out of one-dollar bills for giving change . . .

Be it in a Triple-A stadium or an independent league park, the overall goals of the staff are the same—to draw a good crowd, hopefully have a winning team on the field, and to give them some quality entertainment in a relaxed setting. The fans aren't aware of the behind-the-scene efforts, just the results.

One important job of the front office is to track roster changes and player movements. This starts at Triple-A. They check to see if the major league team has twenty-five healthy and productive players on their roster. If that is the case, that task is pretty much done for the day. If not, then the phone calls begin the major league front office to determine who will get the call to the majors. This begins a chain reaction throughout the farm system as players are moved up (or down, depending on the roster change at the major league level) to fill holes at higher levels. One player added or removed from the major league roster can affect as many as seven other players and their families in the minors.

Front office life is never the same from one day to the next. There are new people to meet, new challenges and sudden crises. Every once in a while, a more unique assignment will be added to the front office's duties.

In August 2000, Ken Schnacke and his staff were also involved in assisting with the filming of a movie, *A Little Inside*, at Columbus' Cooper Stadium. The main purpose of the filming at this park was to get crowd shots, which meant extra advertising and publicity to ensure a large turnout. Although the numbers weren't quite what Schnacke was hoping for, both he and the filmmakers were pleased with the enthusiasm, as evidenced by the forty thousand feet of film shot in the park. The crew returned after the season to do more filming, this time of the individual actors on the field. For Schnacke, this experience gave him a small peek inside the magic of moviemaking; one of the intangible bonuses of being in baseball.

As general manager of an independent team, Bryan Wickline has other duties that his affiliated counterparts do not. More along the lines of a major league general manager, he is also responsible for scouting and signing players as well as arranging trades and, as part of the business, player releases. All of this goes hand in hand with the more typical business duties such as promotions planning and marketing.

"You wear one thousand different hats," he explains. "That's just the way it has to be in independent baseball and minor league baseball. You've got to do it all [but] it's fun. I enjoy it. We have gotten to the point where we have five full-time staff in the Paints office. That has increased over the past few years from three."

With all of the responsibilities and all of the hours, what does he like best?

"The traveling. The camaraderie of the different general managers of the different teams. I've met *a lot* of people—I've met Pete Rose, Marty Brennaman, and Ken Griffey, Sr. at different events that the Paints have had. I enjoy meeting the different people in baseball and making a network."

Like the Clippers to the north, the Paints also got a taste of Hollywood when their stadium was used as a second location for *A Little Inside*. Not only was the front office involved behind the scenes, but several players, a coach, and the coach's wife got to appear on-screen.

There are essentially two seasons in the minor league baseball front office. The off-season is a little shorter, but no less the busier. From mid-September to February, the focus shifts to sales. Corporate sponsorships and ticket sales are a constant chore. Other efforts are made toward souvenirs, promotions, and other advertising. In some years, affiliated teams must work on renewing their professional association with the major league team or look around for other organizations. The independent teams review scouting reports, agent contacts, and release notices in search of hidden gems of talent.

When the Pioneer League's franchise in Helena, Montana was moved to Provo, Utah, Joel White had the additional challenge of establishing the team in a new town. For the first two months in Provo, he didn't even have an office. Although there was a high level of interest in the new team, winter is not the time when most of the public is thinking about baseball. Yet this was the time that White and his colleagues had to make people aware that they now had a local professional baseball team.

"Having seen it start from virtually nothing into what it is now has been awesome," said White.

There is no set progression up the minor league ladder to get to the big leagues for front office people. While front office staffs tend to be larger at the higher levels, there is still a significant gulf between the offices of Triple-A and the majors. Ken Schnacke has seen some of his people get hired from the Clippers to the New York Yankees, but points out a fundamental difference between the two levels as far as working one's way up.

"If you come to Triple-A and like the fact that you do a lot of different things and you have a lot of different plates that you're trying to balance at one time, this is a great spot for you. If your ultimate aim is to get into a major league organization, then you're probably better off getting a job in the mailroom of the New York Yankees."

Schnacke is content to remain in Columbus with the Clippers for both personal and professional reasons. "We love Columbus. We find it a comfortable place to raise a family. The Clippers have been a wonderful organization to work for. It's a wonderful working relationship with the most fabulous sports enterprise in the world, the New York Yankees. We've had some great teams here and have won eleven divisional pennants and seven Governor's Cups. We've had great young players come through like Mattingly, Jeter, and Bernie Williams."

The parade of talent going from Columbus to New York is evident in the Yankee line-ups. In each of the three World Series they won from 1996 to 1999; fourteen of the twenty-five players on the post-season roster were former Clippers.

"You're proud to be a part of that," said Schnacke.

Many teams have people like Schnacke who have stayed with the club for decades. Like other professions, a minor league position can be either a perfect lifetime fit or a stepping stone to other jobs.

For many sports management professionals, the lower minors and independents are a good place to start, even for those moving on to other sports. In a small organization, they will be exposed to much more in a short period of time, making a more impressive resume if they decide to move on. A woman who worked as an intern for the Chillicothe Paints three years ago now works in the NFL's Washington Redskins ticket office.

"It's been rewarding to see some of the people move on to bigger and better things," says Wickline.

Not all front office people begin their careers in sports. With a deep voice that seemingly could carry for miles on a summer evening, John Wend is a natural choice to be a ballpark announcer. He was working for a newspaper when the newly formed Chillicothe Paints asked him to be an announcer at their home games in 1993.

In the early years of the Frontier League, the seasons lasted two months, which meant twenty-six home games. Wend considered how much time he would have to spend at the ballpark along with his regular job and countered the offer by requesting that he only do thirteen of the home games. By season's end, though, he had done a majority of the games.

He continued his moonlighting job in the announcer's booth at V.A. Memorial Stadium until 1998. After retiring from the newspaper business, he joined the Paints in a full-time capacity as sales and marketing director as well as handling other media and public relations duties.

While Matt McLaughlin was working for several radio stations in the Chicago area, he hadn't considered working for a sports franchise until he began reading articles about the plans for a baseball team in Schaumburg, located in the northwest suburbs of Chicago. The Schaumburg Flyers were to be one of the Northern League's expansion teams. After making inquiries and getting interviewed, he became the Flyers' media relations director prior to their inaugural season in 1999.

McLaughlin was interested in not only starting something new, but to see it evolve over time. "It's been very beneficial for me in the long term and very educational. It's created a lot of new friendships for me and a lot of new opportunities. It's just a wonderful industry."

Although they are more like part of the uniformed team members with whom they spend virtually all their time, trainers on minor league teams often use their positions to gain experience before moving on to bigger jobs. These specialists work with the players to help prevent future injuries as well as rehabilitating them from past ones. As the fields of sports medicine and physical therapy have grown in size, complexity, and specialization, the importance of a team having a well-trained and highly skilled trainer has grown as well.

Holly Hill joined the Johnstown Johnnies as the team trainer while working on her master's degree in exercise physiology. She already had experience working with athletes in high school and college as well as serving her internship with a professional hockey team when the Johnnies radio announcer, whom she knew, told her about an opening with the team. She readily took the trainer's job, recognizing it as an excellent opportunity to get her career in higher gear.

"I really enjoy working in professional sports," she explained. "There's a lot of competition. The players are really dedicated and they really want to get back after an injury, so there's a lot more pressure on the athletic trainer and the medical staff. I enjoy that more than where it's a high school setting—there's not as much pressure and you have to deal with parents."

Hill is one of a handful of female trainers in baseball. However, she has not experienced any problems with being the only woman in a group of over twenty men.

"The guys are very respectful. As long as you keep the lines drawn, they're fine. You can have a good relationship with them."

The addition of team trainers and on-call doctors for the minor leagues is a relatively recent development in baseball, not becoming common until the late 1970s and early 1980s. During a road game in the New York-Penn League in 1968, Geneva Senators outfielder Tom Grieve was hit in the eye with a pitch. No one could tell if there were any broken bones in his face, but his eye soon swelled shut. After the game, Grieve boarded the team bus for the trip back to Geneva. It wasn't until the following afternoon that he was able to see a doctor.

One aspect of working for a minor league team is the risk to job security due to the transient nature of major league affiliations. The Albuquerque Dukes had been the Triple-A franchise of the Los Angeles Dodgers since joining the Pacific Coast League in 1972. The city itself had been home to a pro team since 1915, with a continuous presence of a team for all but four years since 1937. However, the Dodgers announced that they would be moving their franchise agreement to Portland after the 2000 season, and no affiliation could be found to replace them in Albuquerque.

The Albuquerque Dukes have had their share of successful seasons, winning over half a dozen league titles including three straight from 1980 to 1982. Future Dodgers stars from Ron Cey to Mike Piazza spent a season or more there.

John Miller joined the Dukes as Media Relations Director

for their final season, but was well aware of their history as the team closed out its run in the city. "It's something that has so much tradition and has been around for so long, it's just really unfortunate to see it end this way."

Despite the long working hours and the uncertainty of where he would be or what he would be doing after the Dukes disbanded, Miller has no regrets. When asked what he liked best about his job shortly after the end of Albuquerque's final season, he focused on one unique aspect of working in baseball. "I go to work at a ballpark. And when I was broadcasting, I was getting paid to watch every pitch of every game."

Like Miller, David Barnes had fond memories of the Cobras even as they were disbanding. "I have worked with some great people, people that I am lucky to have met," he said. I have met some great players on the Cobras, and it is neat to watch them advance to the major leagues."

Ken Schnacke echoes much of this upside to working in baseball.

"The great thing to me about the sport and the industry is the challenge. I mean, the challenge is there every day—it's what you make of it. I've never had a day in the twenty-four years here where I haven't been ready to get up in the morning, come into the office, and tackle this baby.

"My definition of a great night at the ballpark is a crowd of ten thousand and a great Clippers victory. I don't have that nearly as many times as I would like, but the battle is how many times you can get there."

"I love every part about this business," said Mike Tamburro. Pawtucket holds four baseball clinics a year for area children, a favorite event of Tamburro's. "The biggest kick is to see the kids sitting in the grass, looking up at the players in their bright, white uniforms. That's what baseball is all about."

Matt McLaughlin's most memorable moment came when Gino Caruso, a former Oakland, Milwaukee, and Pittsburgh farmhand, pitched a no-hitter on August 19, 1999 before a huge crowd on hand for a Thursday night game. One game encapsulated everything a new team could want.

"In the late innings, it became the major-league type of atmosphere where every fan in the park knew there was a no-hitter going on. With each out, you could really feel it here in the park. Nights like that—that's what it's all about. Whether you're a player or you're working for a team, that's why you do this."

CHAPTER 9

Umpires: A Season on the Road

We took pride in our work. I walked out there,
proud as a peacock. Most of us did.

—*Durwood Merrill, umpire*

It's 5:20 p.m. on August 28, 2000; a little less than two hours before game time. The heat and humidity of the Midwest summer still blankets the air as Max McLeary arrives at V.A. Memorial Stadium in Chillicothe, Ohio for a Frontier League game between the Richmond Roosters and the home team Paints. With two games remaining in the Frontier League schedule, the Paints are fighting for the final spot in the league playoffs, which are scheduled to begin in three days. Long seasons and last-minute playoff schedules are nothing new to McLeary, a veteran of over twenty-five years in the umpiring profession.

The stadium was built in 1954, when amenities for umpires such as locker rooms were rarely considered. Although the park is well maintained and nearly sparkling clean, the umpire's room is a little more than a long, narrow storage room with no showers and no ventilation aside from the small oscillating fan sitting on a table. The clubhouse manager is quick with the offer to bring a pre-game meal and beverage. As he leaves, McLeary begins his pre-game work on the baseballs, work that has become automatic to his hands after years of repetition.

Unlike the major league umpire crews, the crews in the minors and independents consist of as few as two umpires instead of four. Whoever is to work behind the plate (referred to in umpire's parlance as the "plate man") in that day's game is also responsible for "rubbing" the balls prior to the first pitch; a job that is usually done by clubhouse personnel in the majors. (At the Triple-A level, the clubhouse people sometimes do this task, but the umpires are still responsible for ensuring that the balls are properly "rubbed.")

The new balls, referred to as "pearls," are rubbed with mud to take the shine off the ball—just enough to take away the glare and make it easier to handle. There is even an "official" mud used by most, if not all, professional leagues. This mud is taken from the bottom of the Delaware River.

About four to six balls are used in minor league games (even more in the richer majors). McLeary opens a plastic container containing a mixture of Delaware River mud and tobacco juice and begins to rub the contents of a fresh box of baseballs. The tobacco juice gives the balls a certain finish that McLeary prefers. Since he doesn't chew tobacco, he relies on his umpiring partner to provide the juice.

McLeary grew up with sports officiating. His father was a football referee and was president of the Eastern Collegiate Football Officials. McLeary himself had been a ballplayer in high school and at Penn State, but knew he didn't have the talent to make it as a professional. A neighbor of his in his hometown of Johnstown, Pennsylvania, Augie Donatelli, had been a National League umpire and encouraged Max to try it.

He began umpiring pro ball in the early 1970s, but became a college coach after he had had enough of living out of a suitcase. Still, he sometimes reflected on his umpiring days. "I always wondered 'what if?'" he recalled. Finally, he returned to umpiring in 1994, the second year of the Frontier League's existence.

It wasn't until he was serving in the military that John Kibler gave much thought to umpiring. During his enlistment, he played ball with players who had Triple-A and major league experience. It was these players who suggested to Kibler that, given his love for the game, he should consider becoming an umpire. Upon completing umpiring school in 1958, he began his officiating career.

While growing up during the 1940s Bill Valentine worked at a ballpark in Little Rock, Arkansas. He took care of the visiting team's clubhouse and attended to the umpires. During this time, he was also umpiring games for elementary school children. The umpires would talk to him about their craft and would occasionally give him some of their old equipment like masks, chest protectors, and counters. One night, when he was fourteen, one of the umpires didn't show up for a men's game, so he was asked to fill in. From there he began officiating in more games for pay.

American League umpire Bill McGowan had a school in Florida that the umpires recommended that he attend. When he graduated from high school in 1950, he had a journalism scholarship to Arkansas Teacher's College (now the University of Central Arkansas). The following January, he attended the school and then went to work in the Ohio-Indiana League.

Scott Nelson, who spent the 2000 season as his first in Triple-A, described his entrance into umpiring as "by accident." In the eighth grade, he began working a summer for the city recreation department in Coshocton, Ohio; a job he would stay with each summer through high school as well. His duties consisted of preparing the baseball and softball fields for games, getting line-ups ready, and then actually coaching and umpiring in the games themselves.

His opportunity for an umpiring "promotion" came one day when an umpire failed to show up for a Pony League game to be played at a nearby field. An official came over to the city fields and asked for someone to umpire the game that night. Since the other recreation workers were older and had dates planned for the evening, the opportunity fell to Nelson. "It was big stuff. I had to find the right uniform . . . and try to figure out what I was doing, working the bases," he recalled.

He enjoyed the experience and told the official that he would be willing to fill in again whenever the need arose. He was able to umpire in several more games that season and, by his freshman year of high school, was hooked on umpiring. A member of an American Legion team, he forfeited his last two seasons of playing in order to umpire. He continued umpiring intramural games in college for extra money before leaving school early for umpiring school.

He first attended the Brinkman-Froeming school in early 1993, but did not make the cut to go on to the minors. A disappointed Nelson was approached Jim Evans, an umpire who made it to the majors in 1971 and who also ran an umpiring school. Evans advised him to stay with the game. "If it wasn't an overnight decision to go to umpire school, then maybe it shouldn't be an overnight decision to give it up," Nelson was told.

Nelson decided not to return to Ohio and instead rented an apartment in Florida. There, he officiated any game he could find, from Little League to college ball, in order to hone his umpiring skills. In April, he received a phone call from a sportswriter in Ohio who told him about a new independent professional league, the Frontier League, which was looking for umpires for its inaugural season. Immediately, Nelson drove from Florida to Zanesville, Ohio to audition.

He worked in the Frontier League that season, with plans to return to umpiring school the following year. In 1994, he attended the Jim Evans Academy, followed by some advanced training, before landing his assignment to the New York-Penn League.

In earlier years, umpires were known to spend decades-long careers officiating in the minors. There was even a father-son team in 1933, when Ulysses E. Welch, Sr., a seventeen-year veteran and rookie arbiter Ulysses E. Welch, Jr. worked together for a week in the Dixie League before being sent to separate assignments. As a general rule, umpires today are given a maximum of two years at each level, with Class-A ball subdivided into the three levels of Short-Season, Low A, and Advanced A.

The quality of locker rooms for minor league umpires has come a long way. "There are a lot of them today that are phenomenal," says Scott Nelson. In older parks, facilities were often Spartan at best, although many of these have since been upgraded. When some of these parks were built, there no were changing rooms and showers at all for the umpires, and other arrangements had to be made. In some instances, the umpires would change at their hotel before reporting to the park. The ground crew equipment storage sheds were also utilized. In these shacks, devoid of showers, the umpires could change their clothes amid battered wheelbarrows and sacks of fertilizer.

There is no home field advantage for the umpire. While the teams have at least a town they can call home for a few months, the umpires' season is but one long road trip. Their uniforms carry no city name or team logo, only the emblem of their league; they are always the outsiders in every park. Their suitcases are their offices, and the hotel phones are their link to families who may still be months away from being seen again. While major umpires, after years of hard-fought negotiations, get some vacation time during the season, those in the minors still toil without a break.

With their travel schedules even heavier than those of the teams whose games they officiate, reliable transportation is crucial. In earlier years, minor league umpires would be paired so that one member of the crew had an automobile. John Kibler was the designated driver for his crew during the 1959 season, which he spent in the Pioneer League. During the five months of baseball, he added twenty-two thousand miles to his car as he drove the circuit that spanned from Western Idaho through Montana.

Bill Valentine saw plenty of mileage in the Texas League. A single circuit (repeated many times during the season) to the cities of San Antonio, Oklahoma City, Tulsa, Shreveport, Houston, and Dallas was over two thousand miles, and this is assuming that the game assignments took the umpires in a logical travel route. Additionally, direct routes were not always available in the days before the interstate highway system was built.

While they keep their goal in mind of umpiring in the majors, the endless days away from home take their toll. Scott Nelson described a crucial difference in daily life between working games for amateur leagues and the minor leagues. "You can miss calls and have a bad day, but you're still going to get to come home to your wife and your dog. But [in the minors], you get things done and now you get to go back to your hotel room and be by yourself. Or you get to go back to your hotel room, turn on the TV and have it rehashed all over again."

There is little support outside one's own umpiring crew. "Psychologically, you just have to prepare yourself that you're actually good at what you do," says Nelson. "A good crew can make you or break you. I see my crew more than I see my wife. I was fortunate in my first year at Triple-A because they were good guys. They were good umpires too, but more importantly, they were good people."

For Durwood Merrill, his crew partner in his first season was a parade of faces; four of them, in fact. "One got sick, one had a nervous breakdown, one said he couldn't take it anymore, and the fourth guy didn't have enough sense to quit," said Merrill of his crewmates. "You're lonely. It's just you and your partner, then your partner quits. It feels like it's you against the world."

To date, the gender barrier in umpiring for professional baseball has been crossed three times. Bernice Gera was the first, officiating a New York-Penn League game on June 24, 1972 after taking the league to court to challenge their rules for physical requirements. Gera's game was a seven-inning contest, the first game of a doubleheader. After the game, she announced her retirement.

Christine Wren made her professional debut in the Northwest League in 1975. Although she did well and had advanced to the Midwest League by 1977, she quit to take a job with better pay.

The same year that Wren quit, Pam Postema graduated seventeenth out of a class of 130 at the Al Somers Umpiring School. Postema spent thirteen years in the minors, working the Gulf Coast, Florida State, Texas, and Pacific Coast leagues before getting released in 1989. Although she worked in major league games during 1988's Spring Training, a female umpire has yet to become an official big league umpire.

When shown on television, umpires are often seen in an argument with a coach or player. Contrary to what is seen, however, umpires prefer to keep a low profile. They are on the field do their job, not to become famous (or infamous). No one wants to make the news because of a bad or controversial call.

"The best time you have is when no one knows you're there," said Max McLeary.

Like hot dogs, fastballs, and the seventh inning stretch, the verbal (and sometimes worse) abuse of umpires has become a regular part of the game. Players and managers, with whom the umpires normally have cordial relationships with, can quickly turn mean in the aftermath of a close play and disputed call. Like many umpires, Durwood Merrill was on the receiving end of tirades more times than he could count.

"The brutal frankness of the language was a shock to me," said Merrill. "They never gave you much time to learn your trade. They expected you to be good and you was in the minors just like they were and you was trying to learn your craft, too. But that didn't seem to make any difference. You were just a piece of meat to the old, veteran managers."

During a Frontier League game, Springfield coach and former big-league star Ron Le Flore got involved in a long-running dispute with the home plate umpire. It culminated after one play in which a hit ball was ruled a foul after it first bounced off the batter's foot, making it ineligible for an easy fielding play and an out. Le Flore argued that the ball never hit the batter. The umpire, finding a scrape of shoe polish from the batter's foot on the ball, rolled the ball to Le Flore to show he was correct and then resumed play. Le Flore, however, was not about to be quieted.

During the next pitch, Le Flore threw the ball at the umpire. As the umpire was making the call on the pitch, the ball struck him after it had taken one bounce in the dirt. That was quickly strike three for Le Flore, who was ejected from the game.

Merrill and his partner were officiating in a California League game in Bakersfield and made a call against the home team on a crucial play. After the game, they quickly changed clothes in their black widow-infested locker room. Then they went to the door, eager to leave the spiders behind, only to discover that they had been locked in for the night—on purpose.

Sweetwater, Texas' stadium, had a changing room for umpires that was a separate building by the left field grandstand. In 1952, Bill Valentine and Al Sample had several problems during a series in the town and wound up ejecting the Sweetwater manager twice. As he and Sample were changing on the last night, Sample paused and asked Valentine if he smelled something burning. Valentine did, and the partners wondered if something was happening to the ballpark.

Then the groundskeeper came into the building and told the pair that they had better leave immediately. A group of angry fans had started a fire on a corner on the outside of the building in an effort to smoke the umpires out.

Valentine and Sample had more adventures that year in the Longhorn League. The umpire's changing room in Big Spring, Texas was located behind the centerfield wall and could be accessed by a door in the wall. Valentine was working one memorable game behind the plate while Sample worked in the field.

In the bottom of the ninth, Big Spring was down by a run with two out and the tying run was on second. The batter singled and the runner on second attempted to score. The play was close, but Valentine called the runner out at home, sealing the loss for the Broncs. Immediately after the call, Valentine saw his partner running from second base toward center field. Then Valentine saw the fans starting to pour out of the stands and onto the field.

With speed that likely would have allowed him to score with time to spare had he been the runner on second, Valentine sprinted after Sample, passing him before reaching the centerfield wall. The umpires barricaded themselves in the locker room to change.

They had to have a police escort to safely leave town. Once they passed the city line, the police cruisers had to stop, but three cars continued to pursue the pair. Eventually, the posse was down to one car and Sample, an oil worker in the off-season, decided that he had been running long enough.

Sample had a couple of three-foot-long wrenches for working oil rigs in the back seat and was ready to use them on some heads instead of on machinery. Approaching an intersection, he pulled to a stop. Both umpires jumped out of the car and each grabbed a wrench, ready to confront their pursuers. Sample was experienced with the wrench and was ready for action. But Valentine, unaccustomed to the sheer weight of the tool, lost his balance as he jerked the other wrench from the back seat. The momentum carried him over to the side of the road, where he went tumbling down a ten-foot slope covered with sagebrush.

The other car stopped, but the passengers remained inside, prolonging the standoff. Sample, now alone, was prepared to take down one or two of his attackers, but knew he couldn't hold them all off. But the men in the chase car had seen Valentine bouncing down the slope like an overgrown tumbleweed, and they began roaring with laughter. After tossing some empty beer bottles out the window, they turned the car around and headed back to Big Spring. A relieved Sample ran down the slope to fetch his partner and said, "Shake my hand, buddy. You just saved our lives!"

Considering the easygoing atmosphere of today's minor league games, it's hard to believe that passions once ran that high, but Valentine put it in perspective.

"Fans, especially in those little ol' towns, took it seriously. It was the biggest thing going on. I'm sure some of those older guys probably bet on the games."

For umpires, making it to the big leagues is just as great a thrill as it is for the players. Durwood Merrill split the 1976 season between Triple-A and the American League, filling in for a major league umpire on occasion. In 1977, he was in the majors to stay.

"Of all the thrills you'll ever get, making it is always the greatest thrill," said Merrill. "You made it. You climbed the mountain. You *are* an American League umpire."

Even though he was at the pinnacle of his career, he never lost the nervous edge he always had before the game, always hoping that he would make the right call. For this, he felt no embarrassment.

"When you lose the butterflies. When you can say, 'I don't feel it anymore in my stomach, in my bones,' then I think it's time for you to get out. It's not a disgrace to have fear. It's a disgrace not to be able to conquer it. Fear is what makes you good."

After five years in the minors, Larry Barnett became an American League umpire in 1969. He still remembers his nerves before his first game as clearly as many other details. The game was in Oakland, with the White Sox visiting. Mahalia Jackson sang *The Star-Spangled Banner*, but Barnett wasn't able to appreciate her performance.

"I couldn't hold my knees steady during the national anthem."

August 28, 2000: It's been over an hour since the game finished in Chillicothe and the Paints' slim hope of making the playoffs has faded. The players and fans have since gone home and the last remaining ballpark personnel are finishing their nightly cleanup work, chatting with one another as they haul garbage bags away from the concession area. A light still shines beneath the door of the cramped umpires' room as Max McLeary, his partner, and a league official plan the umpiring assignments for the playoffs now that the contenders have been settled. After the season finale tomorrow, the road will continue to another Frontier League town and another away game for the crew in blue.

CHAPTER 10

Strange Innings, Part 2

When you're signing, you're thinking, 'It won't be long before I'm getting a Porsche,' then you're living in a small house with seven other guys.

—Phil Dauphin, outfielder

Leaving the Game Early

While managerial ejections are a fairly frequent occurrence, a Carolina League umpiring crew stood out with the efficient manner in which they took care of business in a game in the mid-1990s. During a contest between the Lynchburg Hillcats and the Prince William Cannons, a Cannons batter hit a line drive down the right field line that cleared the fence but was ruled foul by the first base umpire. The Prince William bench was in an uproar and manager Dave Huppert was quickly ejected while arguing the call.

The home plate umpire, after some consideration, overruled his partner and called the ball fair—a home run. This instantly lit the fuse on Hillcats manager Jeff Banister. After loudly making his case against the reverse decision, he also received the thumb. Both managers were ejected on the same play—that's efficient umpiring.

Max McLeary never let the loss of one eye affect his performance as an umpire in the Frontier League. The glass eye he wore, however, did add a twist to one occurrence.

While officiating behind home plate in 1998, he was struck in the face by a ball—a very real and dangerous hazard for umpires. McLeary was trying out a new, lightweight mask made of a plastic that did little to slow the ball down. The stadium went silent as the umpire lay sprawled on his back, unmoving.

A pair of emergency medical technicians quickly responded to the stricken McLeary. One of the technicians, unaware of the false eye, opened that eyelid and shone a light onto the eye to check for pupil response—a standard check for a head injury. When the glass eye failed to respond to the stimulus, the technician, fearing significant brain trauma, began yelling for the ambulance.

Fortunately, some fans in the crowd knew about McLeary's eye. From the stands behind home plate came some yells to check the other eye. Confused by the shouted advice but desperate to try anything, the medic checked the other eye and to his surprise got the normal, dilating response to the light. McLeary stubbornly tried to complete the game after getting back on his feet. His partner, though, refused to let him return. "He said to me, 'You don't even know what land you're in,'" McLeary recalled.

Although badly bruised and sore from the incident, he suffered no severe injury from the incident and soon returned to umpiring—wearing an old-fashioned metal mask.

Then there was Rob Stratton, who escaped injury after being struck in the head by a fastball, only to walk away from the plate with a broken hand. The Norfolk outfielder was facing Charlotte's Carlos Chantres in a 2002 International League contest when a pitch came too high and inside, striking Stratton in the chin. The ball, however, wasn't done and proceeded downward from Stratton's chin and struck his right hand, breaking the thumb.

The injury occurred with one game left before the league's

three-day break for the Triple-A All-Star Game. Less than a week earlier, the Tides had lost their first baseman, Jorge Toca, to a broken leg. When asked if the injury-plagued team could make it to the break without any more injuries, pitching coach Rick Waits did have one idea.

"Can it rain tomorrow?" he asked, hopefully.

A Cursed Game?

After a bad outing on the field, many a player has felt cursed for the game. But could an entire game be cursed? A Northwest League game in 1990 seemed to be under a voodoo spell.

The Everett Giants were in town to take on the Bellingham Mariners in a battle of Class-A teams. In the second inning, a fire broke out in an apartment complex across the street from the stadium's parking lot. Efforts to contain the flames were not enough to prevent the building from being destroyed.

By the fifth inning, the bad luck descended upon the Bellingham team itself. Shortstop Lipso Nava suffered a seizure in the team's dugout. Following that, the team's pitcher broke his arm while throwing a pitch. There was no indication of any problem until the bone snapped in the middle of the throw.

(Fortunately, Nava recovered from his seizure and was still playing professional baseball twelve years after this incident.)

Perhaps They Should Have Been Rained Out

Then there are entire series that seem to be jinxed. A set of Frontier League games in O'Fallon, Missouri (home of the River City Rascals) during the 1999 season went downhill right from the first game. The Rascals were hosting Johnstown Johnnies, but the event was no party. A bench-clearing brawl in Game One resulted in both managers, Mal Fichman (Johnstown) and Jack Clark (River City), being led from the field in handcuffs.

Game Two went along normally enough, with both teams

throwing the ball instead of punches. The crowd was treated to a tight ballgame that was tied after nine innings. However, during the extra innings, it was the ball field itself that started the next confrontation. With no warning, all of the grass sprinklers went off, sending players scurrying from the quickly saturated field.

The third game provided the third ring for this three-ring circus. Rather than waiting for extra innings, the miscues began before the first pitch. While performing the national anthem, the singer forgot the words—something that can easily be attributed to nerves or the confusing time delay and echo of the public address system. As Fate would have it, though, the microphone clearly picked up the explicative the singer muttered as she lost track of her lyrics.

The last mishap occurred in the middle of the game as the River City mascot roared out onto the field riding a three-wheeled, all-terrain vehicle to entertain the crowd with several stunts between innings. As he was wrapping up, he performed a jump over the pitcher's mound. Unfortunately, the ATV landed awkwardly on its front wheel, spilling the mascot onto the diamond and breaking his collarbone.

At Least It Wasn't Another Rain-Out

During the 1964 season, fans in Bakersfield eager to catch a game one weekend were out of luck. Torrential rains washed away Friday's game. Baseball fared no better on Saturday as more showers forced another postponement. With the promise of better weather on Sunday, a doubleheader was scheduled to make up one of the two earlier games.

By noon, the meteorologist's promise came true in magnificent splendor. The sun was out and blazing, evaporating the water from the saturated field. As the players were looking toward the outfield, they saw what they thought were waves of heat and humidity rising from the grass. Upon closer examination, it appeared that the ground itself was moving in a slow wave. As the wave approached the infield dirt, it turned out to be a horde of small green frogs whose hatching has been accelerated by the recent rains. For the first time in California League history, a game was frogged out.

The Low and the High of It

If Chris Poulsen thought he had seen it all during his years in the Braves farm system, his first year of independent ball quickly changed that. In one game while playing for the Chillicothe Paints, the catcher was involved in two of baseball's rarest and most celebrated occurrences. It was June 8, 2000—a home game against the Richmond Roosters.

His first experience was inglorious, at best. With no outs, he was the runner on first base while a teammate was leading off the bag at second. The batter hit a sharp line drive that the shortstop quickly snared for an out and then stepped on second base ahead of the lead runner to get the second out. Poulsen had broken for second base during the pitch and could only watch helplessly as the shortstop then gently tossed the ball to first for a triple play.

Fortunately for Poulsen—and the rest of the Paints—the game improved from there, particularly when he was behind the plate. He caught the entire game, which turned out to be a no-hitter by pitcher Andy Lee.

"Everybody held their breath on the last play," he recounted. "As soon as it was made, everybody was running around like crazy."

According to all known baseball records, it was the first time in professional baseball history that a triple play and a no-hitter occurred in the same game.

Which One Is the Goalie?

Fans in Kingsport, Tennessee should be forgiven if they didn't comprehend the hockey celebration on their field on July 19, 1981. For the uninitiated, when a hockey player scores three goals in one game, it is referred to as a hat trick, and fans respond by tossing their hats on the ice.

During this Appalachian League *baseball* game, members of the visiting Paintsville Yankees threw their hats onto the field to honor their teammate, Mike Reddish. Reddish, a catcher who was also an avid hockey fan, had completed his own version of the hat trick, albeit a dubious one. The Yankee hats when sailing after Reddish had hit into a double play—for the third time in one game.

CHAPTER 11

The Owners

I still am a big baseball fan. I love the game.

—Ken Brett, ex-player and current owner

There is no stereotypical description of a minor or independent league team owner. Companies and partnerships own some teams, others are owned by individuals. The owners' backgrounds are as different as the organizations themselves. Doctors, dentists, lawyers, real estate agents, and other professions have filled the ownership ranks. From the dugout to the office are ex-players like Newark's Rick Cerone. Entire baseball families, such as the Ryans (Nolan and son Reid) and the Bretts (brothers Ken, Bobby, John, and George) can be found holding the title to the teams. The Northern League had some of its ties to the long-running NBC show *Saturday Night Live* with former star Bill Murray as a part owner of the Catskill Cougars and the St. Paul Saints and the show's creator and producer, Lorne Michaels, joining in the ownership group of the Quebec Les Capitals.

In some instances, the ownership is reflected in the team's name. When the Houston Astros' Double-A franchise was moved from Jackson, Mississippi to Round Rock Texas, the former Generals became know as the Express, in honor of part owner

Nolan Ryan's major league fastball which was often called the "Ryan Express." Following his retirement from baseball as a player, baseball's Iron Man, Cal Ripken, Jr., purchased the Utica Blue Sox. When he moved his New York-Penn League team, a Baltimore Orioles affiliate, to his hometown of Aberdeen, Maryland, the team's new name reflected both his tough playing style and his lifelong career with the Orioles—the Ironbirds.

The naming even crosses the borders between different sports. After the 2000 season, part of the South Atlantic League's Piedmont Boll Weevils was sold to seven-time NASCAR Winston Cup champion Dale "The Intimidator" Earnhardt. Along with an affiliation change from the Phillies to the White Sox, the team changed its name to more accurately reflect its city location and to honor its new owner. So became the newly created identity of the Kannapolis Intimidators. Tragically, Earnhardt never got to see his namesakes take to the diamond before his fatal crash in February of 2001. That season, his son, Kerry, sported the Intimidators' logo on the hood of his racing car.

Chris Hanners grew up in baseball. His father, Roger, was a coach and former minor league player. Although the son was also had a love for the game, he was keenly aware of his limits.

"I played, but I wasn't very good," Hanners explained.

Hanners had a thriving dental practice in the early 1990s when he learned about plans for the Frontier League, one of the two new independent leagues scheduled to begin play in 1993. Seeing an opportunity to become involved with baseball, he founded the Chillicothe Paints near his home in Southern Ohio.

"I thought the Midwest was a beautiful place to have a baseball team," he said of his team and his league.

Other members of the league point to Hanners and the Paints as the standard for excellence in the league. Despite being in the league's smallest market, the team consistently draws well and has made numerous appearances in the playoffs. However, Hanners is quick to deflect the credit from himself and onto his staff instead.

His satisfaction is not limited to just the Paints, but to the entire league, whose future holds much promise.

"We haven't even started yet!" Hanners proclaimed.

The four Brett brothers involved in the ownership of two minor league teams all played professional baseball. George, the Hall of Fame third baseman of the Kansas City Royals, is the best known. Ken pitched for fourteen years in the majors and was a National League All-Star in 1974. John and Bobby both played Single-A ball.

After retiring from playing, Ken managed the Utica Blue Sox, an independent team in the New York-Penn League, in 1985. Bobby saw how the team was run, and felt he could do better. The Bretts wound up buying the Northwest League team in Spokane, Washington the following year that was in dire straits and turned it into a profitable enterprise. They would then buy a second baseball team (the California League's High Desert Mavericks) as well as a minor league hockey team.

Although the brothers share a love for the game, they are serious about the business of ownership. "We want to make a profit, of course," Ken explained. "But we want the people to have a good time and to be presentable on the field. Sure, we want to win, but you can't expect that every year."

Ken Brett does enjoy some of the perks of ownership. Chiefly among them is that his son gets to field balls and hang out with the players during batting practice.

"He's in heaven out there," said Brett.

While he was still in college, Reid Ryan knew he would become a professional ballplayer, but was making plans for the time when his playing days were finally done. With an interest in broadcasting sports, he majored in that field in college. In doing so, he was following the advice of his father, Nolan Ryan, the all-time major league strikeout king and Hall of Famer.

"My dad has said this his whole life, 'You have to prepare yourself for when you're done playing.'"

After three years of pitching in the minors, Reid Ryan was released in 1996. Although he had offers to play elsewhere, he decided it was time to move on. After his release, he did some television work for the Texas Rangers and the NCAA's Big Twelve Conference baseball season. In 1997, though, he decided that his real interest lay in the professional side of the game, where his knowledge and experience in the game would be better put to use in the front office.

He and his father assembled a group of investors to purchase the Jackson Generals of the Texas League. The Generals had been suffering from low attendance for years and faced a looming expiration on their lease. The group moved the franchise to Round Rock, Texas, in 2000, bringing professional baseball back to the Austin area for the first time since 1967. Reid Ryan became the president of the rechristened Round Rock Express.

Since the move, the team has had tremendous success on the field and at the gate. In their first three seasons, the Express made the playoffs each year and captured one league title. Their stadium, the ten thousand-seat Dell Diamond, has averaged over 665,000 fans in the seventy home games per season.

After an eighteen-year career as a catcher in the major leagues came to a close in 1992, Rick Cerone had the opportunity to become an ownership partner of the Wilmington Blue Rocks. The team was a new franchise for the Carolina League that was slated to become part of the Kansas City Royals farm system. Opening Day of the 1993 season marked the first time in forty-one years that the city of Wilmington, Delaware had a professional baseball team.

Cerone's involvement in ownership wasn't done on a whim. Rather, he had been considering this option as his playing days were winding down. Though he was also a broadcaster for the Yankees, Orioles, and the Fox network following his retirement, he had other interests in the game. By becoming an owner, he was not only able to stay in baseball, but he also reaped the financial benefits of his initial investment in the team. After several years in Wilmington, Cerone had the chance to buy a charter franchise in the newly formed independent Atlantic League and build it in his hometown of Newark, New Jersey.

"I thought it would be great for economic development in Newark," Cerone said of his franchise.

But sheer economics weren't the only impact his team would have on the city. As was with Wilmington, Newark had been without a professional team for decades ever since the lowly 1949 Bears finished last place in the International League, thirty-four and a half games out of first. In May of 1998, the baseball famine came to an end as the new Bears took to the field.

When he first became an owner, Cerone knew there would be a steep learning curve. From a player's perspective of owners, he hadn't anticipated the long hours he would have to put in to make his franchise successful. In his early days of ownership, he turned to Yankee owner George Steinbrenner, for whom he had played during his career. Discovering the fine line in the minors between profit and loss, he gained some empathy for the minor league owners he had played for in the past. One can't be sure how much he is joking when he cringes as his players throw balls to the fans in the stands.

Having shifted from owning an affiliate to an independent league, he has gained more responsibility as the Bears have direct control over their roster. With this come more headaches.

"Most times," he said, comparing affiliation versus independence, "I wish we didn't have control of the players."

His team has had some high-profile players, including big league stars Lance Johnson, Pete Incaviglia, Jamie Navarro, and Jose Canseco. Some are trying to resurrect their careers; others are just trying to hang on. While the gratification of seeing one's players make it back to the majors is nice, there is also a huge void in talent left for the team to fill with virtually no advance notice.

Despite the drawbacks, Cerone draws a great amount of pride as a team owner. He sees his team playing in stadiums that are much better than what he experienced while playing in the minors during the 1970s. But what gives him the most satisfaction at the ballpark these days?

"All the kids that show up."

CHAPTER 12

Scouts

Players are signed to be released.
Coaches are hired to be fired.

—Baseball Adage

The doctor on the Oklahoma plains didn't see much hope for the young man's mangled hand. It was winter in late 1937 when the twenty-year-old oil worker was brought to him, having caught his left hand in the machinery on a nearby rig. After giving his patient some whiskey to help dull the pain, he proceeded to amputate the hand. So ended the promising baseball career—and began the legendary scouting career—of Hugh Alexander.

In slightly less than two seasons in the minor leagues, Alexander had hit in the mid .300's and collected seventy homeruns. Late in the 1937 season, the Cleveland Indians called him up to get a brief taste of the majors with eleven at-bats in seven games. Although he only managed one hit during his stint with the big league club, he was clearly marked as being ready to move on to bigger things. With the pay from baseball being little more than enough to cover basic expenses, he, like many of his colleagues, took a winter job.

The Indians hired their former prospect as a scout the

following season. By the time of his death in 2000, Alexander had worked for the Dodgers, White Sox, Phillies, and Cubs in addition to Cleveland, signing over sixty players who would see time in the majors. The pinnacle of his career came with his years with Philadelphia in the 1970s and 1980s, when the team won four division titles, two pennants, and the first World Series championship in team history.

While few, if any, scouts begin their career in quite as dramatic fashion as Hugh Alexander did, many of them still come from ranks of former professional players. The experience in evaluating the potential in raw talent can be the ticket to a coaching job in the minors, where such evaluation continues, and perhaps on to the majors. However, for many scouts, the profession remains a lifelong one.

Jim Martz was signed to a pro contract out of high school in 1956. After an arm injury ended his career, he still stayed active in amateur and semi-pro ball. In 1967, he became an associate scout or "bird dog" for the Orioles. Three years later, he was promoted to full-time scout. It would be the beginning of a career that spanned over thirty years.

Many scouts begin their trips by following leads sent to them by their networks of "bird dogs," people who want to be associated with baseball. These people are not on a salary, but they would get a small bonus if their lead is signed to a contract. Some of these people go on to be full-time scouts themselves. Others are content to remain where they are. Still, many prove themselves to be invaluable to the organizations they've worked with over the years.

"When I took the job I have now in the front office," said Gene Bennett of the Cincinnati Reds, "I had about fifteen people who I had worked with for over twenty years."

Lindsey Diehl was an ex-ballplayer who did some bird dog scouting work. In 1955, he was tracking the play of a young second baseman named Brooks Robinson in Little Rock, Arkansas and saw something special. Diehl wrote to Baltimore Orioles manager Paul Richards, for whom Diehl had played in

Atlanta of the Southern Association, and recommended Robinson as an excellent prospect. Following Diehl's advice, Richards signed the man who would become a cornerstone of the franchise and a Hall of Famer at third base.

Gene Bennett was an outfielder in the Reds farm system from 1952 to 1958 before retiring due to shoulder problems. When the team offered him a job as a scout, he thought he'd try it for "a few years" to see how it worked out. Seventeen years later, he was promoted to scouting supervisor. In 1991, he became a special assistant to the general manager. During his tenure, he signed several players who were instrumental in three World Series titles for the Reds in 1975, 1976, and 1990. Among the players he feels were the best he signed while as a scout and supervisor are the following:

- Don Gullett—pitched for nine years in the majors, won 109 games; was part of the famed Big Red Machine that won four pennants and two World Series in the 1970s, also won another World Series with the Yankees in 1977, later became a major league pitching coach.
- Barry Larkin—a perennial All-Star Shortstop, Reds team captain, a member of the 1990 World Series champions, National League MVP in 1995.
- Chris Sabo—three-time All-Star third baseman, played on the 1990 championship team.
- Paul O'Neill—five-time All-Star outfielder, won his first World Series with the Reds in 1990; after being traded to New York, he won a batting title and four more World Series rings with the Yankees.
- Charlie Liebrandt—pitched in the majors for fourteen years, compiled 140 wins; pitched on three pennant winners, including the 1985 World Series champion Kansas City Royals.
- Jeff Russell—a two-time All-Star pitcher who won fifty-six games and saved another 186 during his fourteen years in the big leagues.

In addition to the classic "five tools" or physical skills of speed, hitting, power, fielding range, and throwing, clubs are also interested in the mental aspects and personality traits of their potential players, particularly for those who are targeted for selection in the higher rounds of the draft. It's what is often referred to as the "sixth tool"—the intangibles. Gene Bennett points to traits such as intelligence, instincts, ambition, and the amount of determination to win.

"What we want to know," explained Bennett, "is if he is teachable, if he has heart, and if he has desire." From personal observation during his forty-plus years with the Reds, he has seen minor league players with average physical skills such as Pete Rose and Chris Sabo turn themselves into major league All-Stars by willing themselves to improve.

"They will not make it if they're afraid to compete or succeed," said Jim Martz of mental and personality traits. "I'm big on a strong, quality makeup."

It's often a gut feel on the part of the scout, who may only see the player in action once or twice and perhaps work in a conversation with the player shortly before the draft. Today, these intangibles are sometimes measured by a set of written exams and questionnaires. However, according to scouts, they are no substitute for direct conversation. Regardless of the era or the method of evaluation, there has always been the concern of a player's personality and motivation.

In 1945, Dodger president Branch Rickey sent scout Clyde Sukeforth to Chicago to check on Negro League player Jackie Robinson. While Rickey was sold on Robinson's physical skills, he wanted to be sure that he was the right person to handle the stress and the attention, both good and bad, of becoming the first black player in the major leagues. When Sukeforth went to Chicago, he found that Robinson was on the bench, unable to play because of an injury. This enabled him to have several conversations with Robinson, and he became convinced that Robinson indeed had what it took both on and off the field to break the color barrier.

Like so many others in their sport, scouts spend much of their time on the road, only their season runs far beyond the start of the Grapefruit and Cactus Leagues and the close of the World Series. By February, some amateur programs begin their practices. After the school seasons are over, the summer leagues begin. In warmer climates, tournaments and other leagues literally run all year long. In northern states, indoor facilities are increasing in number, providing further opportunities for observation—and making further demands on the scouts' time.

The year-long season is also true for scouts who concentrate on minor league players for their organizations to trade for or to pick in the Rule V Draft of professionals. After the minor league season come the fall league in Arizona and the instructional league in Florida. Some will accompany their teams to the major league off-season meetings held in November and December when many trades are made.

For each success in a signing come the missed opportunities by other scouts. Hugh Alexander was on a tight schedule when he was on a trip in his home state of Oklahoma one year. Along with Yankees scout Tom Greenway, he was waiting for a player to show up for a game, but the player was late. Although initial reports raved about the player's power and speed, there were some concerns about a lingering football injury. When the player did not show up on time for the game, Alexander left to scout another athlete elsewhere in the state. This left Greenway and the Yankees to eventually sign the tardy young Mickey Mantle.

Many scouts can recount the one player they saw who stood out from the rest. These are the few who, even as amateurs, seemed to be tagged for stardom. Jim Martz was working for the Major League Scouting Bureau when he recommended one such player as the best pick to all of the clubs.

"He had the best raw tools, athletic ability, and was the biggest competitor I've seen in thirty-two years of full-time scouting," remembered Martz.

The Detroit Tigers went with Martz' judgement and signed the player as their #1 pick. That player, Kirk Gibson, would go on to become a key member of two World Series champion teams (1984 Tigers and 1988 Dodgers) as well as the National League MVP in 1988.

Conversely, Martz was not very impressed with another future All-Star while he was still with Major League Scouting. He felt the player didn't have strong tools and questioned his signability. But Don Mattingly would later prove Martz wrong.

With the advent of the amateur draft in 1965, the scout's role in actually signing players changed. Before the draft was instituted, the scout first had to convince the team to sign a particular player then try to convince the player to sign with the team. Money was still an object then, with wealthier teams like the Yankees sometimes able to outbid competing teams for a player's services.

In an effort to keep things equal between teams, Major League baseball had limits imposed on signing bonuses. Players paid beyond a certain set amount (which changed over the years) had to be placed on the major league roster. Clubs and their scouts tried to work around this, sometimes with extra money kept "under the table." In 1957, Orioles scout Frank McGowan ostensibly signed pitching phenom Steve Dalkowski for $4,000, the limit at the time of his signing. In actuality, McGowan also slipped Dalkowski an extra $6,000 that went unreported.

Gene Bennett still vividly remembers scouting and pursuing players in the years before the draft. "I would call up and say, 'Hello, this is Gene Bennett of the Cincinnati Reds. We want to come and talk to you about signing your son.'

"They would say, 'We can see you tomorrow night at nine o'clock. We'll give you one hour, because we have the Yankees coming in at ten, and Cleveland's going to be here at eight.'

"That's just the way it was. You just walked in and gave them a number. You might offer them fifty thousand. Someone else maybe offered them thirty, and another offered seventy thousand.

They'd say, 'You're not in the ballpark, but we appreciate you calling.'"

Bennett chuckled at the memory of scouts lining up in the player's home. "Sometimes, we'd see the next guy," he explained, "and we would tell them that we just offered them fifty. They might say, 'Aw, heck, we were only going to offer thirty-five.' It was kind of a fun thing then."

To avoid the bidding war, they would often scout in smaller towns where a player would not get as much exposure. This was in a time when there were fewer scouts and barely a fraction of the media coverage than there is today.

After the draft was implemented, competition for players among the teams became more equal. Still, a lack of exposure for some players meant that a team could gamble by waiting to draft a lesser known player later in the draft despite the fact that they felt that player had more potential. Also, with fewer teams in the majors at that time, there was more likelihood of a player lasting longer in the draft.

In the first year of the draft, the Cincinnati Reds were leaning toward making outfielder Bernie Carbo their first-round pick. But on a rainy day in Oklahoma, Reds scout Tony Robello was attending a high school game to observe another outfielder who also did some catching. By the seventh inning, Robello was satisfied that the outfielder was a decent enough player, but wanted to see what he could do behind the plate. Robello asked the team's manager if he would be willing to move the outfielder to catcher. The manager willingly complied, and Robello got to see future Hall of Famer Johnny Bench work his magic.

"Tony said, 'I never saw an arm like that in my life,'" remembered Bennett.

Now the question was raised as to whom the Reds would take in the first round. Scouting Director Jim McLaughlin counted on the fact that Bench had virtually no exposure and that hardly anyone had ever seen him catch and recommended going with the better known Carbo in the first round. The gamble paid off as Bench was still available in the second round and the Reds got two future major leaguers with their first two ever draft picks.

"With twenty teams, it worked. If it had been today, we would have taken Bench at number one," explained Bennett. "But we would not have gotten Carbo."

The Reds luck came through again in 1969 when they signed high school pitcher Don Gullett as their first round pick. The Washington Senators had been planning on taking Gullett with their pick, the number one overall in the draft, until they invited Jeff Burroughs to a team workout. Senators manager Ted Williams was sold on Burroughs (who would become the American League's Most Valuable Player in 1974), so the team announced that he would be their choice. The Reds now were more confident they might have a shot at Gullett.

With Gullett now available to other teams, forty-four scouts showed up to see him pitch. Unfazed by the attention, Gullett struck out the first twenty batters he faced en route to a perfect game. (Even more incredibly, the opposing team's bats were only able to *make contact* with four of his pitches.) As the story spread, the Reds now felt that their chances of getting him with their first pick, the thirteenth overall, were dead.

As the Reds anxiously watched the draft, the Senators made good on their announcement and selected Burroughs. Incredibly, all eleven of the following teams also passed on Gullett, and Cincinnati got their prized pick. Gullet pitched two months that year, made the big league club in 1970, and never looked back.

Scouts still remained involved with contract negotiations with drafted players, although the signing of high round picks are now mostly dealt with the major league team's scouting director, general manager, and other front office personnel due to the increasing dollar amount of signing bonuses.

During the draft itself, most scouts remain on the sidelines, watching as their scouted players are picked or passed upon in each round. The evaluation of talent is no exact science, and often it can be determined only years later if a team's final choice for a draft pick was foresight or folly. There are moments, though, when an inkling of the future is felt as a player's name is announced.

Gene Bennett was watching the status of a high school shortstop from Michigan in the first round of the 1992 draft when the Reds' time to choose the fifth overall pick arrived. With star shortstop Barry Larkin firmly entrenched for years to come in Cincinnati, the Reds chose outfielder Chad Mottola, who would play in thirty-five games for them in 1996. All Bennett could do was to sit and watch with a sinking feeling in his gut as the Yankees, with the next pick, chose that young shortstop, Derek Jeter.

The final payoff to all of the scouting comes when a player makes it to the majors. With a constant stream of prospects to evaluate, it's difficult for scouts to track all of their signed players. After all, once a player is signed, they are in the hands of their managers and coaches, and the scouts must turn their focus onto the next crop of players. Still, there is a sense of gratification when one of their past signees is called to The Show.

"It's the epitome of your efforts," said Jim Martz. "It makes the long days, time on the road, and hard work worthwhile. I try to keep in touch with as many as possible. Some are great, others quickly forget and 'big league' you when they make it."

For most scouts and their players who have reached the majors, there are still the occasional exchange waves at the stadium and conversations that go with belonging to the baseball fraternity. But on a professional level, the players have games to prepare for, and the scouts must concentrate on the next crop of prospects looking to prove themselves.

CHAPTER 13

Crossing the Color Line

*It may not be long before Jackie Robinson of
Montreal . . . gets a chance with the
Brooklyn Dodgers.*

—The Sporting News, *April 25, 1946*

Long before Jackie Robinson made his historic debut with
Brooklyn in 1947, black ballplayers were competing on minor
league diamonds. Going back to the late nineteenth century, a
few teams included African-Americans on their rosters, while a
handful of other teams were exclusively black, but played against
teams in with white players in their leagues. As late as 1916,
Jimmie Claxton, who was of African, Native American, and
European descent, was playing for the Oakland Oaks of the Pacific
Coast League. However, the Oaks tried to conceal part of his
racial heritage by attempting to pass him off as solely a Native
American. When his black ancestry was revealed, Claxton was
barred from the P.C.L. For the next thirty years, integrated baseball
among professionals was limited to exhibition games largely
played by off-season barnstorming teams.

A year before Robinson broke the color barrier in the major
leagues he made his minor league debut with the Dodgers' Triple-

A farm club, the Montreal Royals, on April 18, 1946 in Jersey City, New Jersey. A crowd of more than twenty-five thousand spectators was on hand to watch as Robinson first grounded out, then followed with four consecutive hits including a home run to pace the Royals to a 14-1 route over the Jersey City Jerseys.

After the game, throngs of fans of all races sought to meet Robinson, shaking his hand and requesting autographs. Although the color line had been crossed, there were still many long miles to be walked in baseball.

Although integration had begun in 1946, for many years there was an unwritten rule that there were to be no more than two minority players on a team. The prejudice against blacks extended to darker-skinned athletes from Latin America who were beginning to play in growing numbers in the 1950s and 1960s. While racial problems could be found in nearly every city in the United States, the unrest grew large enough to force the Savannah White Sox of the South Atlantic league to move to Lynchburg, Virginia during the 1962 season.

The disruption over racial rights was not only limited to teams, but to entire leagues as well. Up through 1961, the Southern Association, a Double-A league, refused to admit black players. After the 1961 season, the issue of integration was raised, with heated debates ensuing among the team owners and officials. With only half of the league's eight teams in favor of allowing blacks to play, a stalemate developed. Beset with financial troubles and unable to break the impasse, the league folded—in part a victim of its own intolerance.

Away from the headlines were the daily struggles for players in the southern states where Jim Crow laws were in effect. When stopping for meals during their endless bus rides, the black players were forced to wait on the bus or sit outside on the curb until their white teammates would return to deliver their meals. After unloading most of the team at their hotel in the cities of their away games, the bus would continue on to a separate hotel for blacks.

Players from the North were often stunned by what they encountered in the South, dealing with issues that they had heard about, but were now seeing and living with for the first time. In some ballparks, there were separate locker rooms for Blacks and Whites.

This was an eye-opening experience for Tom Grieve, who saw segregation firsthand when he began playing in the Carolina League in 1967. "In the South, the first thing that hit me that was a shock in Burlington was that when I went to the ballpark and walked to the clubhouse, there were two bathrooms—one for Whites and one for Coloreds."

Jack DiLauro, who grew up in an ethnically diverse neighborhood in the North was blunt about his reaction to seeing segregated drinking fountains for the first time in the 1960s. "What the s—t is this?" he recalled asking. "I didn't know how to handle it, so I started drinking out of the 'colored people's' fountain."

While the actual experience of segregation was strangely alien to DiLauro, the ferocity of the racial division struck home in a horrifying way after seeing the torment of an African-American teammate in Rocky Mount, North Carolina. Rufus Anderson, his team's second baseman, was easygoing and well liked by his teammates. There were people in the crowd, however, who were out for blood, trying to rile him into violence. The taunts and the threats escalated to the point where DiLauro and another teammate had to physically hold Anderson to the ground to prevent the normally mild-mannered player from going into the stands. They eventually were able to calm him down and prevent a tragedy, but the shock of what could have been would linger far past that day.

After nearly forty years, the event remains crystal clear to DiLauro.

"There's no doubt in my mind that they would have killed him. That was the thing that hurt. That was part of growing up at the time. It ain't just baseball."

When Mike Hershberger was playing in Charleston, South Carolina in 1959, a former high school classmate, Chuck McDew, from his hometown in Ohio visited the park. When McDew, who was black, tried to get to the backstop to greet Hershberger, who was white, police removed him from the area. McDew protested this treatment and was subsequently put in jail.

Unfortunately, Hershberger was unaware that his friend had even been in the park, let alone that he had been arrested. It wasn't until the two met again at a class reunion twenty-five years later that he heard about the ugly treatment that McDew had been through.

Chuck Harmon, who would become the Cincinnati Reds' first African-American player, was a two-sport star in his hometown of Washington, Indiana. Although he played on integrated baseball and basketball teams in high school, he was still subjected to the barriers of segregation outside of sports. While serving in the navy during World War II, he was barred even further as he was prohibited from playing sports with white players.

Harmon played for the University of Toledo's basketball team, which made the finals of the National Invitation Tournament, while playing baseball professionally. To keep from losing his college eligibility in basketball, he played briefly for the Indianapolis Clowns under the name Charley Fine. Harmon later signed with the St. Louis Browns, but eventually left the organization to protect his collegiate eligibility, which might have been jeopardized due to changes in the NCAA regulations.

Harmon's basketball days came to a close soon after college. After being cut by the Boston Celtics during the 1951 pre-season, he became a player-coach for the Utica, New York basketball team of the Eastern League. In doing so, he became one of the first black professional coaches in basketball.

His baseball career continued. While playing in the farm systems of the St. Louis Browns and Cincinnati Reds, Harmon experienced racial prejudice in almost every conceivable way. In 1953, while playing for the Tulsa Oilers, the Reds' top farm team, he ran afoul of the law in Dallas because of his skin color.

Following a game against the Dallas Eagles, the Tulsa team got into some taxicabs to go to the train station. Harmon shared a cab with Nino Escalera, a native of Puerto Rico. When Dallas police spotted the pair, they pulled the cab over and demanded that the driver remove his passengers from the car. Although the driver explained that they were part of the team, the police were adamant, stating that there was a law prohibiting the two from riding in the cab. Eventually, Harmon and Escalera were allowed to proceed to the train station, but only after receiving citations from the police.

At the station, Harmon's teammates were dumbfounded by what had transpired. Their worries centered on how they were hitting or pitching the ball, whereas Harmon had to deal with finding alternate means of eating, sleeping, and transportation.

But there were some bright spots amid the negativity. Harmon's wife, who was of mixed ancestry, could have passed for either white or black. With segregated seating in many minor league stadiums, the quandary of which section she should sit in arose. Team management for the Tulsa Oilers decided the best solution was to get rid of Harmon. However, Cincinnati general manager Gabe Paul stepped in and told Tulsa that Harmon wasn't going anywhere—unless the Cincinnati front office decided otherwise. Paul remained true to his word. At the start of the season the following year, 1954, Harmon was a member of the Reds.

The Reds had held off bringing up Harmon and several Tulsa teammates late in the 1953 season because of Cincinnati manager Rogers Hornsby. Hornsby had been fired, but an agreement had been reached to allow him to complete the season. There was concern about how Hornsby would treat Harmon, in particular. The front office felt it would be better to wait until the following season, when Hornsby would no longer be with the team. Harmon laughed off the concerns about how Hornsby would have treated a black player.

"He was nasty guy—he didn't like anybody," explained Harmon.

If the introduction to Jim Crow was a shock to northern ballplayers, the exposure to integration was more of a revelation to southern players, both black and white. For many of these young men, minor league baseball marked the first time that any of them got to personally know someone of the other race. After months of sharing the same long bus rides and the same highs and lows both on the field, and off, most players found that the barriers of race had long dissolved, even if only among themselves.

"Even with the white boys from the south," said Jack DiLauro, "when it came to blacks and whites playing on the same team, it wasn't an issue. You're with these guys every day and everyone has one goal—that's to get to the big leagues. And you're not going to do it on your own."

"At the beginning, they were a little on the shy side," said Gene Bennett, describing how the southern whites interacted with their black teammates. "But the fact that they [the African-Americans] were good people helped them fit in a little better. Before the year was out, we had one team."

Emmett Ashford became the first black umpire in Organized Baseball when he broke in with the Class-C Southwest International League in 1952. Bill Valentine later worked with him in the Pacific Coast League. One night, Ashford took Valentine to the Porter and Waiter's club in Seattle, which was for blacks. The club wouldn't let him in because he was white. It was an eye-opening experience for Valentine.

"I said to Emmett, 'Oh, so this is what discrimination is all about,'" he recalled.

On June 19, 1999, the Northern League's Schaumburg Flyers held a tribute for Chicago-area Negro Leaguers. As part of the celebration, their starting pitcher was former Negro League star Ted "Double Duty" Radcliffe, whom they signed to a one-game contract. Radcliffe's nickname came decades earlier from the time he played two positions—pitcher and catcher—during a double header. He pitched in the first game and caught the second one.

A few weeks shy of his ninety-seventh birthday, Radcliffe became the oldest player in the history of professional baseball. In his return, he threw one pitch as planned. That the pitch didn't land in the strike zone was immaterial. In the sixty feet from the pitcher's mound to the catcher's mitt, the ball traveled an untold number of hard, long miles.

CHAPTER 14

The Ballparks

If I have to choose how to die, I want to die in a baseball field with the smell of a baseball and the sound of a hit ball.

—*Sixto Lezcano, coach*

Minor league ballparks have come a long way from their beginnings in farmers' fields. Many of the early ones were constructed gradually as the owners' finances would allow. During the Great Depression, many more were constructed as WPA projects such as Lynchburg's Merritt Hutchinson Stadium, which is still in use today. With the boom in popularity of the minors in the 1980s came increasing numbers of stadiums built with public funds as cities sought to compete for franchises. As a result, approximately half of the ballparks in use by professional baseball today were built after 1980. However, many of the older ballparks have a very long history, some extending back to the 1920s and the oldest, Pittsfield's Wahconah Park, having an opening year of 1919.

In recent years, league guidelines have dictated the upgrade of minor league parks. Better fields and improvements to team and public facilities have become the rule. The older parks, in many cases, show little evidence of their age beyond a cornerstone marking the year the park was opened. But for the players who had to play under the old conditions, the experiences were memorable, if not always pleasant.

"They were bad," said Jack DiLauro, a veteran from the 1960s. "Compared to today, they were ridiculously bad. I remember days where we had to fight over a wire clothes hanger to hang our clothes up. Some places didn't have lockers so you hung your clothes up on the water lines. The kids in college in those days had it better than the professional minor league athletes did."

Calfee Park in Pulaski, Virginia has played host to many minor league teams since its construction in 1935. The old visitor's clubhouse beyond the left field fence once had but two showers for the entire team to use, a condition that prompted some unusual player ejections from the game.

While the Johnson City Phillies were in town to play the Pulaski Cubs in 1958, the home plate umpire became the target of some unkind remarks from the visitor's dugout around the fifth inning. The umpire went over to the dugout and demanded to know who had been shooting off his mouth.

At first, no one volunteered. Then a pitcher who was scheduled to start the next day spoke up to take credit for the verbal abuse. After getting thrown out of the game, he happily went over to the locker room to take a leisurely shower without any crowding from his teammates. The other Phillies got wise to this opportunity and for the rest of the series, players were purposely getting themselves tossed in order to get better access to the showers.

Conditions didn't improve on the field, including those at Calfee Park. At one time in the late 1950s, it had no outfield fence, just light poles. If a ball got past the outfielders, there was nothing to keep the ball from bouncing and rolling away from the diamond. Other ballparks like the old one (before the present-day Dwyer Stadium) in Batavia, New York had the outfield light posts standing inside the fence. For those who liked a little variety in their obstacles, there were the telephone poles to negotiate around in the center fields of Chattanooga and Lethbridge. To add to the fun, the overhead phone lines played havoc with fly balls.

The ball field in Big Spring, Texas, had a gravel running track from the neighboring football stadium extending into left field. During track meets, a gate in the left field fence would be opened to allow the runners to use the complete track. During baseball games, left fielders had to contend with a stretch of gravel while running down balls.

The old stadium in Durham, North Carolina had a hill in the outfield that rose toward the outfield fence. Players chasing down line drives would sometimes stumble as they suddenly started up the incline. Bristol, Virginia's DeVault Memorial Stadium also had a hilly outfield.

"You get seasick watching the outfielders chase balls," said pitcher John Stewart, a veteran of several games in the Appalachian League Park.

In the early 1940s, Kansas City's old minor league park had a sign for a local jeweler above the centerfield wall with a hole in it. According to the sign's advertisement, any player who hit a ball through the hole would win a diamond watch. It seemed like a safe gamble for the advertiser as the sign was close to five hundred feet from home plate. It was found to be all the safer one day when Ralph Kiner and his teammates checked the size of the hole and discovered that it was slightly smaller than the circumference of a baseball.

"It was pretty well protected," Kiner chuckled.

When Phil Dauphin was playing centerfield in Australia during the 1991-92 season, it was on a field normally used for soccer and rugby. The warning track was made of plywood, which had been laid down to cover a ditch along the fence. It was usually best to stop before reaching the plywood as the fence itself was made of barbed wire to keep rowdy fans off the field during soccer games.

The outfields weren't the only areas to claim oddities. During the 1958 season, a rabbit decided to make the infield in Burlington, Iowa's Community Field its home. Unwilling or unable to roust the rodent, the groundskeeper routinely placed a white chalk circle around the hole to warn players of the obstacle.

During the 1980s the New York-Penn League's Watertown Indians played at the county fairgrounds. During a road trip, the annual county fair was held and a demolition derby was staged on the ball field. After the team returned, players would find spark plugs and other small automotive parts on the field.

Even today, parks found in some overseas locations provide plenty of unique and challenging features. Nick Clark, a first baseman and outfielder of a club team in Edinburgh, Scotland had his share of troubles with the playing field. During one play in right field, he painfully found a goal post mounting square used for when the field hosted soccer games. On another field, playing first base offered no better protection, as he had to contend with a four-foot-deep trench that ran along the baseline. Although he tried to avoid the pit, an off-target throw he had to stretch for and the inexorable force of gravity eventually caused him to disappear below field level.

Ask John Romonosky about the minor league ballparks he played in, and the first thing he'll mention is not one particular stadium, but the weather patterns of the California League, circa 1949.

"You could expect anything in California," he says.

Bakersfield was home to sandstorms. As the winds shifted in the afternoon, many a game was interrupted or even canceled due to the copious amounts of sand being blown into the park.

Santa Barbara's field was on the Pacific Coast, well away from the hazardous sands of Bakersfield. Not to be outdone, though, the local weather provided its own brand of dubious entertainment—fog.

"Sometimes you'd only see half of a player in the outfield," said Romonosky.

Routine pop-ups became mystery hits as the balls disappeared into the white mass. The advantage for the batter quickly turned into trouble for the base runners as players and coaches alike would peer into the outfield fog bank, attempting to determine if and when a fielder had found the ball. When the inbound throw from the field finally appeared, a mad scramble would ensue as runners darted for the safety of the closest base while the infielders hurried to get to the ball.

Fifteen years later, Jay Johnstone experienced the joys of the league's stadiums while playing for Bakersfield. He described the Modesto's night game lighting in the California League as "six guys on poles with flashlights." It wasn't much better during the day as outfielders chasing down fly balls had to be careful not to step into the gopher holes that proliferated throughout the field.

In April, before the spring thaw arrived in the Sierra-Nevada mountains, Reno had obstacles for the players to avoid even before reaching the field. When leaving the clubhouses, they had to duck to keep from getting clubbed by the foot-long icicles hanging from the roofs.

The years pass and times change, but not nature. Jason Baker, who played in the California League almost fifty years after Romonosky, recalled the typical delays in San Bernardino. The games were usually scheduled to start at seven in the evening. However, at that hour, the sun would blaze in from centerfield, directly into the batter's eyes. This often resulted in the game being delayed a half hour to allow the sun to sink just below the outfield signs.

Many of the stadiums built in the rush of the last two decades were financed partially or entirely by public funds. In some instances, this use of tax money has become hotly debated in some communities. However, the public funding of stadiums is not a new concept, but the arguments against construction have not always been based on fiscal concerns.

In 1930, a proposal was made in Columbus, Ohio to build what would be known as Redbird Stadium using public money.

The location was to be in an area known as "The Bottoms," near several old cemeteries west of the Scioto River. At a city council meeting to discuss the issue, over 1,500 residents stormed into the building with a petition against the location. Their protest was based on the fears that all of the noise and other commotion raised during a baseball game would wake the nearby dead. Despite the efforts of the local citizenry, construction of the park went forward. Curiously enough, the ballpark, now called Cooper Stadium, is used as a haunted house attraction during the Halloween season.

When the Pioneer League's Helena Brewers moved to Provo, Utah to become the Provo Angels in 2000, the team was hoping to work out a deal for its own stadium. In the meantime, the team began playing on the campus of Brigham Young University. To comply with the school's policies, the new franchise has had to forgo beer sales and Sunday games until it got its own venue.

A ban on alcohol was not an issue in the middle of California's wine country. Sonoma County's Rohnert Park Stadium had a twenty-foot bottle in centerfield whose top would burst open in a fountain of "champagne" (actually, water) every time a Crusher would hit a home run. The park's concession stands were also indicative of the team's location.

"We have the best wine list in baseball," said Kevin Wolski, who was part of the Crushers' front office.

Whether it was for practical purposes (such as the lay of the land) or for the sake of innovation, many ballparks contain features that set them apart from the hundreds of others. Within the Cooper Stadium complex is a small area named Dysart Park, which serves as a Hall of Fame for Columbus baseball. Stone monuments are positioned like players on the field, with bronze plaques commemorating players from past ball clubs in the city, dating back to 1877.

Built in 1969, Albuquerque Sports Stadium is one of many ballparks that make the most of the surrounding landscape. The field itself is dug out of the ground. Beyond the outfield wall is a rise in the earth that serves as a drive-in area. From their cars or lawn chairs or picnic blankets, the fans can watch the action below along the perimeter of the outfield. An additional unique touch is the lava rocks on the embankment going down to the outfield fence.

The ballpark in Whytheville, Virginia, once home to an Appalachian League team, had a peculiar feature just off the field. To reach the field, players and coaches had to walk past the county jail from the visitors' clubhouse. Posted on the wall was a sign ordering people not to bother the prisoners.

Johnstown, Pennsylvania's Point Stadium has been home to professional baseball since 1923. One of the first stadiums in the country to have lights for night games, it has played host to professional baseball of all levels.

Minor league teams of the Middle Atlantic League and Pennsylvania State Association called Point Stadium home prior to World War II. In 1945, the park hosted Negro League games, showcasing such talents as Satchel Paige and Jackie Robinson. During the postwar years, the park once again was home to a Middle Atlantic franchise, followed by an Eastern League team. From 1961 to 1994, the park was used for a variety of amateur teams and tournaments until professional baseball was revived in Johnstown with the establishment of a Frontier League team.

Johnstown was also a stop for the New York Yankees as they made their way north by train from Spring Training. The famed 1927 squad, featuring the likes of Babe Ruth and Lou Gehrig, played an exhibition at Point Stadium shortly before the regular season began. According to local legend, Ruth sent the ball boy on several beer runs to the bar that was immediately across the street from the left field fence.

As the ballpark is nestled in between the Stoneycreek and Conemaugh rivers and the city's downtown area, its outfield dimensions are strangely skewed, making it a hitter's haven. The right field line runs only 250 feet to the wall. The left field line is not much longer at a mere 275 feet.

"When I first saw that on the Internet, I thought it was a typo," said Matt Sheets, a Johnstown pitcher.

The uniqueness of the outfield doesn't end with the left and right lines. The left field wall extends straight over to mid-centerfield, instead of curving around like at other parks. This creates a sharp increase in the outfield depth, culminating in a distance of 395 feet in the deepest part of center field.

With the short distance of the left field wall from home plate, it is not uncommon to see batted balls bounce off the wall for only a single. To minimize potential hazards to traffic on the street that runs parallel to the wall, a seventy-foot-high net was erected behind the wall. According to the field rules, any ball that hits the netting and bounces back onto the field is still in play, like a ball that bounced off the wall would be. If the ball hits the netting and drops in between the net and the wall, it is a ground-rule double. And if the ball does clear the net, it is a home run followed by prayers and possible insurance claims.

In most parks, the outfield lines end where the outfield wall make an approximate ninety degree turn toward centerfield. At the end of Points Stadium's right field line, the wall tapers in at a slight angle, but still continues to move more away from home plate than it does toward centerfield for another fifty feet or so before finally angling over toward center.

Another Frontier League town, Huntingburg, Indiana, can thank Hollywood for its park, Huntingburg League Stadium. The park was built in 1991 as a set for *A League of Their Own*, the movie about the women's professional baseball. Six years later, it became the home of the Dubois County Dragons of the Heartland League. In 1999, the Dragons moved to the Frontier league.

The original park consisted of an old grandstand area by a baseball diamond in the city's park. The grandstand was relocated and expanded into an entire stadium to become the celluloid home of the Rockford Peaches. Many Huntingburg residents were appropriately costumed to fill the stands during the production. (Another Frontier League stadium, Evansville's Bosse Field, was also used for other scenes in the movie.)

Although the wood planking originally used in the construction was replaced by pressure-treated lumber, much of the park's interior still bears reminders from its showbusiness days. The stadium's third base dugout was the where Tom Hanks' famous "There's no crying in baseball!" scene was filmed. The Rockfield Peaches logos can still be seen on the press box and the left field scoreboard. On the outfield wall, advertising signs from real local businesses are mingled with World War II era-style signs from the movie.

Yankee farmhands playing in the Single-A Florida State League get a taste of their possible future when playing at home in Tampa. Legends Field, which also serves as the New York club's Spring Training home, is a miniature replica of Yankee Stadium.

Hanging plants are not something usually found in ballparks, but Midway Stadium comes close. The home of the Northern League's St. Paul Saints does have goldfish bowls suspended in mid-air like hanging plants for fans to watch while waiting in line at the concession stands. Other amenities are available in the seating areas such as a barber for those needing a trip and a nun who gives back rubs.

The uniqueness of some parks is not limited by what lies beyond the fences. Johnson City, Tennessee's Howard Johnson Field has a hill in the outfield that runs from right to center field up to a height of nearly ten feet.

The fans, too, become an integral part of the park. Going back to the early years of the century, fans would stuff dollar bills into the fence or netting behind home plate to reward their hometown heroes for home runs and other feats. Many players who played in Rochester's old Silver Stadium mentioned it as one of their favorite venues because the size and enthusiasm of the crowds made it seem like they were playing in the major leagues.

The fans of the St. Paul Saints are notorious for keen baseball knowledge and their willingness to use it on opposing players. Chad Akers, who visited St. Paul for three years as a member of the Fargo-Moorhead RedHawks remembered this vividly.

"Their fans would tear you up," he said, laughing—two years after the fact. "They would let you know about every mistake you make. They'd know how many RBI's you got, how many strikeouts, what your strikeout-to-walk ratio was. There were some good fans in St. Paul. They have some knowledge of the game."

Certain local fans of the Lynchburg Cardinals in the old Piedmont League preferred to keep a little distance from the park in the 1940s and 1950s. Moonshiners would take a break from working at their stills and watch the game from the hills just beyond the park. Likewise, the smoke from their whiskey stills could be seen from the playing field.

Former Reds farmhand Tye Levy recalled one fan in Charleston, West Virginia who made his sentiments known—with toast. At each home game, he would set up a table with a toaster and a few loaves of bread behind the backstop. As the game got underway, he began making toast. Every time a Charleston pitcher would strike out a visiting batter, the fan would wave a piece of toast at the victim's dugout, screaming, "You are toast!" Then the part-time baker would hurl several pieces of his burnt offerings into the roaring crowd.

Pitcher Chris Enochs, the first round draft pick of the Oakland Athletics in 1997, summed up his feelings about the crowds in the stands.

"To me, the crowd makes a ballpark."

CHAPTER 15

Strange Innings, Part 3

*You don't want to go in intimidated, but you start
wondering, 'Do I belong here?'*

—*Chris Nichting, pitcher*

Pitching Screwballs

Whether it is born out of boredom or too much exposure to
the sun, relief pitchers have been famous throughout baseball
history as being more than just a little goofy. Sitting on a bench
somewhere beyond the outfield fence or lines, far removed from
the watchful eye of their manager, they are left to their own devices
to pass the time as their teammates play. Bill Lee spent many
long hours in the bullpen building small fires from dead grass to
help keep the mosquitoes away.

When and if the time finally arrives for them to make an
appearance, it is often in the midst of a high-pressure situation.
Some claim that the repetition of being thrust into these stressful
positions takes its toll on the pitchers' sanity. Others argue that
there was never any sanity to begin with.

Yankee pitcher Ryne Duren thrived on mind games while he

was still pitching in the minors. What made Duren stand out physically from other players in the 1950s was that he wore glasses, very thick ones, at that. While many baseball people at the time questioned the wisdom of having a player wear glasses on the field, Duren turned his spectacles into a spectacle.

When warming up on the mound for a relief appearance, he would throw the first few balls away from the catcher and up into the backstop. Then he would remove his glasses and wipe the thick lenses as if they were responsible for his poor aim. After donning them again, he would squint in the direction of home plate as if trying to find his catcher. By this point, many a batter wanted nothing to do with this misfiring menace and backed as far away from home plate as possible, only to watch helplessly as Duren would whip three strikes through the zone.

Of course, the pitcher's job isn't done once the ball leaves his pitching hand. Fielding a ball launched from a bat less than sixty feet away while one is still following through on their pitching motion is not the easiest thing to do. Jerry Don Gleaton, who pitched in the majors for twelve years, had two minor league teammates whose fielding skills were at opposite ends of the spectrum.

Jack Lazorko made defense an art form, thanks to skills from another sport. He proved to be as deft with the baseball glove as he was with a goalie's glove and stick. A hockey goaltender in high school, Lazorko was accustomed to dealing with slap shots speeding his way. In one minor league game, he caught two low line drives—from between his legs.

Bill Long, the other Gleaton teammate, was not as adept. He left one game prematurely after being hit in the face with a line drive, the type of accident that has ended careers and caused permanent damage to the victim. Fortunately, he escaped any tragic injury but still suffered a broken jaw. Six weeks later, he was back on the mound, only to be hit in the chest with another line drive.

While injuries like Long's broken jaw and worse suffered by

others are nothing to laugh about, some fielding miscues on the mound do resemble physical comedy. During a game in the late 1990s, Jimmy Haynes took a line drive high in the chest while pitching for Rochester in the International League. Haynes was still leaning forward from his pitching motion when the ball struck him at an angle and bounced through the collar of Haynes' loose-fitting jersey. Unaware of where the ball had gone, the batter scrambled down the line to first base, hoping to beat the throw from Haynes. As it turned out, there was no need to hurry as the batter was safely standing on first while Haynes was still trying to fish the ball out from under his shirt.

On March 8, 1954, Wilhelmus "Win" Abraham Remmerswaal was born in The Hague, Holland. It wasn't common for Dutch children to grow up and become major league pitchers. It wasn't common for someone to be able to sweat on only one side of his body. It wasn't common for someone to be brilliant enough to master seven languages. Then again, few, if any, of Win Remmerswaal's teammates or coaches ever considered him to be common.

"Remmerswaal marched to a different drummer. Sometimes, you wondered just who the hell this drummer was!" said Pawtucket Red Sox President Mike Tamburro, who had plenty of experience with the hurler when he played in Triple-A.

Remmerswaal, who appeared in twenty-two games for the Boston Red Sox in 1979 and 1980 was a walking and pitching collection of odd habits. Paychecks were apparently an alien concept to him—he never bothered to cash them. After being repeatedly badgered by team officials during Spring Training, he went to a bank to cash his checks so the team could balance its books. When the teller asked for a piece of photo identification, Remmerswaal, of course, did not have one. Unfazed, he went back to the ballpark, obtained a team program with his picture in it, and returned to the bank with his identification. Although it wasn't a normal form of identification, it was good enough to get his checks cashed.

Then there was the time in Spring Training when Remmerswaal, after backing out of his parking spot and putting the car in drive, continued to keep driving in reverse through the entire parking lot until he reached the street.

"It's a wonder he didn't kill anybody," said teammate Mike Smithson.

Remmerswaal made a habit of extending his road trips a little longer than those of his team. One night in Columbus, Ohio, he jumped on stage at a "gentlemen's" bar and began to do a partial striptease act. Although patrons saw a little more of the pitcher than they wanted to, it would be longer before any of his teammates caught a glimpse of him. Remmerswaal disappeared after that night in the bar but finally showed up nine days later in Pawtucket.

The often AWOL pitcher pulled another disappearing act while the team was returning from a road trip in Richmond and Norfolk, Virginia. The team flew from Norfolk to Washington, D.C., changed planes, and flew on to Providence, Rhode Island. Upon arriving in Providence, they discovered that Remmerswaal was missing. Finally, after three days, Remmerswaal casually showed up at McCoy Stadium with a big box of cigars for Pawtucket owner Ben Mondor.

During the flight change in Washington, Remmerwaal had decided to take some time to do a little sightseeing. When he spoke with Mike Tamburro to explain his absence, he was matter-of-fact about the situation.

"You know, Washington is the capital of your country," he informed Tamburro. "I figured I may never get a chance to see Washington again, so I spent a couple of days looking around."

"He had a great arm," Tamburro said. "He could have made a ton of money, but that wasn't his priority. He just wanted to see the country."

Home Run High Fives

Hitters are often at their strangest in the aftermath of a home run. The cheering crowds, the fireworks, and other special effects sometimes pale in comparison to the antics of the slugger who began the whole celebration.

Eastern League Fans in New Haven, Connecticut had extra reason to cheer when outfielder Everett Nutter hit a home run during the 1920 season. Nutter, who led the league in hits and runs that year, had a special way of circling the bases after sending a pitch beyond the fence.

Upon reaching first base, he would stop to chat with the first baseman. At second, he would pause again to inquire how the second baseman's family was doing. During his rest at third, he'd share a joke with that defenseman. As he crossed the plate, he would present the catcher or umpire with a cigar before strolling to the dugout.

Beset with injuries that eventually ended his career, 1980 American League Rookie of the Year Joe Charboneau was back in the minors in 1982, playing in Double-A Chattanooga. In one game, after a prolonged home run drought, he finally connected. In partial jubilation and partial relief, he threw his bat about thirty feet in the air before jogging away from home plate. When he crossed the plate, he repeated the toss, this time with his batting helmet. The umpire was unimpressed and tossed Charboneau from the game.

When the team boarded the bus after the game, it became clear that Charboneau's enthusiasm was unaffected by the ejection. His teammates stared as he climbed onboard carrying a pair of scissors, a razor, and a fifth of whiskey. For reasons known only to himself, he began cutting his hair, then proceeded to jump from seat to seat, inviting his teammates to join in.

"We ended up shaving that whole sucker bald," recalled teammate Kelly Gruber.

Bird Shot

Medford A's outfielder Don Harrison was in a slump in early July 1981, shortly after start of the Short-Season Class-A Northwest League's year. His bat appeared to come alive, though, when he hit a sharp line drive that sent the Eugene Emeralds' right fielder, Eric Davis, scrambling to the warning track. Suddenly, Davis reversed direction and ran forward to snare the ball. Harrison retreated back to the bench with yet another out, or so it seemed.

Umpire Tony Padilla stopped Harrison and told him to take first base. As it turned out, the ball had struck a hawk as it was flying over the field, allowing Davis to catch the ball. According to the rules, the ball could no longer be caught for an out since it had already struck another object.

This seemed to be the perfect turnaround for Harrison as, later that game, he drove in a key run with another hit (this one without fowl interference). However, the bird was not as fortunate, having died shortly after dropping to the field.

All in the Family

When the Milwaukee Brewers moved their Triple-A affiliation agreement from the Pacific Coast League's Vancouver Canadians to the Denver Zephyrs of the American Association before the 1987 season, they paved the way for a family reunion. Terry Bevington, the manager of the Brewers' top farm team, had a brother who was umpiring in the American Association. How the pair treated each other off the field is a mystery. On the field, this family tandem put the "fun" in dysfunctional.

The brothers were involved in several animated screaming matches as manager and umpire throughout the season. After getting ejected by his brother after one altercation, Terry began thinking of revenge. Storming past the dugout, he was heard to say, "At Thanksgiving at Mom's house, I'm killing him!"

If at First You Don't Succeed . . .

During an Eastern League game against the Reading Phillies in 1999, Bowie Bay Sox outfielder Wady Almonte got a base hit by hitting the ball *twice* on one play. It began when Almonte shattered his bat when he hit a ground ball to the shortstop. A piece of the bat sailed over the ball before landing in its path. When the ball hit the bat for the second time, it bounced away from the shortstop, giving Almonte time to safely reach first.

After some discussion, the umpire ruled that the hit counted since the bat had technically become part of the field by the time it made second contact with the ball.

At Least the Ball Wasn't Lost in the Lights

As a pitcher, Steve Grilli saw plenty of hit balls that should have been outs get mishandled. While playing winter ball in Puerto Rico in the 1970s, Grilli saw one such play where the fielder never stood a chance.

The batter hit a routine pop fly to the outfield. Shortly after the ball took flight, the stadium lights when out. In the sudden darkness, the ball landed harmlessly on the outfield grass. When the lights came on a few minutes later, the batter had already scored on an inside-the-park home run.

CHAPTER 16

Head Games

Baseball is 90% mental—the other half is physical.

—Yogi Berra, catcher

The Mental Edge

At whatever percentage one may derive from Mr. Berra's statement, the mental aspects of the game are just as crucial to the success of a player's career as any of his physical tools. This is where baseball knowledge, instincts, and the results of endless coaching and strategy sessions come into play.

Everything from psychology to Zen meditation has been used to mold a player's mind and to improve his on-field performance. Of course, no one approach will work for everyone. One player's mental discipline is another's voodoo beads.

Josh Lamberg credits precognition for some of his success. The Chillicothe Paints catcher had yet to hit a home run in the 2000 season when he came to bat as a pinch hitter in the bottom of the ninth inning with his team trailing powerful Johnstown 5-4. With two strikes he stepped out of the batters box to refocus his efforts and saw himself connecting with the next pitch.

"I kind of believe in ESP and that kind of stuff and I saw myself hitting a home run," said Lamberg.

The next pitch was a slider that hung over the plate. Lamberg jumped on it, blasting the ball over the fence to tie the game.

Later that year, Lamberg was in the midst of a horrific run of bad luck—both on and off the field. In the previous twenty-four hours he had dealt with problems with his car and with a would-be girl of his dreams. Prior to the game, he went fishing at a notoriously good spot, yet came up empty.

The dark cloud continued to follow him into the game. Early in the game, he dropped an easy pop-up foul ball. Two pitches later, the same batter connected for a home run. As the game progressed, his streak continued as another pop-up eluded him. With runners on first and third, he attempted to throw out the runner trying to steal second, only to throw the ball into center field and allow the runner on third to score.

Things weren't much better at the plate, as he struck out in each of his first three at-bats. After returning to the bench following his third whiff, he became convinced that his run of bad luck was over. By the time he returned the batter's box for his fourth at-bat in the bottom of the ninth, he was ready to draw blood. Lamberg recounted his feelings.

"Since the start of the game, I've got three strikeouts, I've dropped two pop-ups, and I've got a throwing error. I said, 'That's it. It can't get any lower from here. I'm ripping it the next time I get up to the plate.' I was pissed. I had let down my team. I had embarrassed my teammates."

In his last at-bat, Lamberg slammed an 0-1 fastball out of the park to tie the game, setting up an eventual tenth-inning victory.

"My teammates were all pumped up for me. That's one of the best feelings I've had since I've been here."

Psychic powers or mere coincidence? It all depends on whom you ask. But by the end of the game, all that really matters is the final score. But the mind games within the ballgame still continue.

Superstitions

Superstitions in baseball most likely go back as far as the mythical first game ever played in Cooperstown, New York. Although the fables concerning Abner Doubleday as the founder of the game and Cooperstown as its home have long since proven to be little more than a fairy tale and marketing scheme, it is quite possible that rabbits' feet, horseshoes, and other tokens of luck were on hand when the first inning ever was played.

There are the "normal" superstitions like wearing the same socks or underwear everyday during a hot streak. Unfortunately for some teammates, the individual partaking of this ritual sometimes believes that laundering the garments will wash away the magic touch. This superstition even affected one baseball wife.

Ned Pettigrew was managing the Cushing Refiners of the Oklahoma State League in 1923 when he got a chance to visit his wife at home in Oklahoma City while the team was passing through the town. As time grew short, Pettigrew had to leave to meet the team while his laundry was still being done, leaving him with only one set of underwear—the set he was wearing.

Following his short visit at home, the Refiners began a winning streak. Convinced that his streak of consecutive days in the same underwear was the cause of the team's success, he refused to change his fraying garments. It even came to the point where he returned a package of clean underwear his wife had sent him for fear it would jeopardize the team's winning ways.

All good things must come to an end, as did Cushing's string of victories. A three-game losing streak convinced Pettigrew that it was time for a change. The much put-upon Mrs. Pettigrew soon received a telegram from her husband that read, "Team losing; send me clean underwear."

Chris Bourjos had one teammate on the Phoenix Giants who did change his clothes regularly, but not his chewing gum. Mike Rex, with whom Bourjos shared a room on road trips, had been chewing the same piece of gum since he was eight years old.

"He made sure he put that gum somewhere at night so he could get it in the morning," Bourjos recalled.

And while some players are willing to loan someone their glove, their bats are another story. Even the act of someone else picking up the bat may cause a permanent curse. The ultimate defilement may be if a pitcher touches a bat. Outfielder Adam Hydzu recalled seeing one teammate throw away a perfectly good bat after a pitcher actually dared to pick up the sacred object.

In 1950, the McAlester Rockets of the Sooner State League had a pitcher, Roger Hanners, who was also a good hitter and was sometimes called upon to pinch hit. Since he didn't hit regularly, he would simply take any bat that was close by. After flying out in one game, he was greeted angrily in the dugout by Clint Weaver, a teammate whose bat Hanners had just used. Weaver, who would slug thirty-five homers that season was furious at the possibility that Hanners may have put a jinx on one of his bats.

This is not to say that all ballplayers go walking around wearing strands of four-leaf clovers and garlic cloves around their necks. There are many who studiously avoid any superstition, not wishing to have nonsensical things or random occurrences mess with their heads. The more common practices are simply habits that help them relax and focus before the game—things like putting one's uniform on in a certain order or tying the shoelaces a certain way.

Rick Asadoorian found that he was sometimes tying himself into mental knots with his habits. He eventually discovered that overall consistency was the best way to keep the baseball demons at bay.

"Personally, I'm superstitious," he explained. "I try to do everything the same when things are good. When things are bad, I think I did something wrong before the game and I change everything. Finally, I got to the point that I did the same thing if I was good or bad."

Despite his professed beliefs in witches and extraterrestrial beings, Bill Lee was not superstitious as a player. Said the man who became known during his major league career as "Spaceman," "I didn't even think that far ahead. I was really spontaneous. I kind of liked things to be . . . different."

But for every player who shuns superstitions, there is another one who seemingly collects them.

"I've got too many," sighed pitcher Woody Fullencamp. "Too many. I put my socks on the same way, my pants on the same way. When I'm on the mound, the rubber always has to be clean. Between each pitch, I'm always dusting it off."

If Phil Dauphin had a good game after drinking the night before, he would drink the same thing that night to help repeat the performance. However, this practice sometimes caused him to be a victim of his own success. "If you're on a really good streak of like fourteen or fifteen games, that starts to wear on you," he recounted.

In the Texas League, players used to drink two beers after the game in the belief that it would help get their strength back. Babe Martin didn't drink, but made a rare exception while he was playing for San Antonio in the 1940s.

"I was a good malt man," Martin said. "I ate ice cream like a fifteen-year-old kid."

Spending many innings in the bullpen gave Bryan Eversgerd time to refine his practice of lucky glove positions. Not only must his glove be in the same place on the bench, but also pointing in a certain position (presumably to protect his luck, he would not divulge the actual position). Before entering a game, the glove was then turned 180 degrees to point in the opposite direction.

Another denizen of the bullpen, Tommy Kramer, gave new definition to the term "leaving it on the field," which usually means that a player has given all of his effort out on the field. Not content to wait until he stepped out onto the grass, he would vomit up his pre-game meal in the bullpen before entering the game.

Despite being repeatedly fined for his practice during his minor league years in the 1940s, Billy Loes would fill up on hot dogs while sitting in the dugout prior to the game. Fortunately for his teammates, the future big league pitcher for Brooklyn, Baltimore, and San Francisco had a stomach that was apparently made of sterner stuff than Kramer's.

Pat Ahearne had a teammate in Tacoma who somehow got it into his head that a particular fan was bad luck. The fan, an ordinary woman who attended many of the home games, had done nothing to warrant this suspicion. Nevertheless, she unknowingly created an odd ritual.

The player, fearing that he would be jinxed if she spoke to him, would hide in the dugout, cautiously peering around the corner to observe her. As soon as her head was turned away from the dugout, he would sprint out and away before she could curse him with any diabolical phrases like "hi!" and "good luck, tonight!"

Pitcher Turk Wendell gained notoriety in the majors for his superstitions, but he already had a strange regimen established early on in the minors. On the days he was scheduled to be on the mound, he ate or drank nothing but two cans of Jolt Cola (a soft drink with a high caffeine and sugar content). On the days he would eat, the only utensils he would use were a baby-sized fork and spoon. During every inning, he would brush his teeth— a helpful habit since he was also prone to write in the dirt with his finger, then licking the dirt off. While on the mound, he never wore socks.

Many superstitions were carried well beyond the ballpark. Nate Minchey had been a teammate of Wendell's in 1989. A few years later in Pawtucket, Minchey had another teammate with a personality full of quirks. The player (whom Minchey charitably kept anonymous) had a phobia of germs, carrying a can of spray disinfectant with him at all times. Seats in taxis, buses, and airplanes got the Lysol treatment before he would sit in them. Even his girlfriend was not exempt before he would hug her (his girlfriends never lasted long). As an extra precaution, he even took his own pillow, sheets, and towels on the road with him.

Kelly Gruber had a teammate in Triple-A who, if someone touched him, had to touch that person back. He had to be the last person doing the touching. Naturally, this set him up as a target. While dozing during a plane trip, someone would attach a note saying something like: "You don't know who I am, but I touched you." The player would wind up walking through the plane, touching everyone to get rid of his jinx.

Like the game itself, baseball superstition has no national boundaries. Rex Hudler recalled a Japanese player who would tape a marble to his chest before putting on his uniform. Jim Pankovits ran across one memorable ritual while playing winter ball in Venezuela. One of his teammates, Vic Dabilillo, would give himself a full body massage with snake oil before every game.

The fans themselves sometimes get involved in the quest to bring their teams good luck. Lefty O'Doul was a very popular player with the San Francisco Seals before his eleven-year major league career. When he returned to manage the Seals in 1935, the fans were ecstatic. One booster, a rabbi from Fresno, sent O'Doul a mezuzah, a small case containing a portion of scripture meant to offer Divine protection, along with a letter wishing the new manager and his team the best of luck.

Though O'Doul was not of the Jewish faith, any edge was appreciated. Under O'Doul's leadership, the Seals won the Pacific Coast League title that same year and four consecutive championships from 1943 to 1946.

Practical Jokes

For players enduring the anonymity of the minors and independents, the long nights of travel and the unsure future of their careers, a little laughter can go a long way. Granted, the laughter comes at someone else's expense, but the victim will usually be on the giving end the next time that particular stunt is pulled on another unsuspecting teammate. As Woody Fullencamp, a veteran of professional baseball and all of its accompanying pratfalls pointed out, the jokes are good for keeping everyone loose.

There are those jokes that range among the classics. Rubbing heat-treatment ointment into a teammate's jockstrap, nailing someone's cleats to the floor, and splattering a player's face with a shaving cream pie are among the time-honored gags of the game. Also to be included in this category is the rubbing of eye black on the eyepieces of a pair of binoculars before someone looks through them. One such victim, Myrtle Beach outfielder Ryan Langerhans, played for a couple of innings with rings around his eyes before someone finally informed him of his raccoonlike appearance.

Cal Ripken was a notorious prankster long before there was any mention of him breaking Lou Gehrig's "Ironman" streak. Tom Chism was a veteran when Ripken came up to Triple-A and recalled the antics of the future big league star.

"He and his buddies were always having a good time, putting things in people's shorts, that sort of stuff."

Chewing gum has a myriad of uses in the practice of practical joking. The gum itself has "mysteriously" found its way onto players' uniforms, usually the cap. Sometimes the gum is artfully shaped into an object, or perhaps merely containing a partially blown bubble before gracing the top of some unsuspecting, walking art museum's head. One bullpen favorite is to use the gum as an adhesive to hold a burning twig on someone's hat.

Early in his professional coaching career, Marty Dunn fell victim to another dugout classic goof—the hot foot. To add to the experience, a local newspaper reporter caught the perpetrating players in the act and duly included the deed in his game coverage. For the next few weeks, Dunn got to listen to everyone's take on the matter when he was out in town. In the following years, he became a jaded observer of these shenanigans.

"There's always something," he noted, listing a few of his favorites. "There's constantly gum on the caps, tags on the backs . . . things of that nature."

Cal Hogue recalled a teammate who always fell asleep on the bench. "Guys would wait until he dozed off—then yell out loud to grab a bat and pinch hit. Always when we were on defense." More than one game was interrupted by the would-be pinch hitter stepping toward home plate while his team was in the field.

Then there is the "Three Man Lift," another tradition that has transcended (or crawled beneath) the borders between organized and independent baseball, as Ty Levy, a veteran of both, can attest to.

A bogus bet is made with a large teammate, challenging him to lift three players at once. A rookie, unaware of what is about to happen, is asked to participate by being the middle and bottom of the three "liftees." His other two teammates get on either side of him and grab hold of him, the object of the challenge supposedly being that the lifter will raise the other two players up by lifting the middle one up. With the middleman now pinned in place, the other conspirators then empty a bucket or cooler full of water or Gatorade ("or pretty much anything we can put in it," according to Levy) onto their helpless victim.

Matt Buirley, who has pitched in both independent and affiliated baseball, shared his favorite stunt. Minor leaguers certainly don't have the money to spend on Hollywood-caliber special effects, but improvisation is affordable and often in great quantity.

Before one game, a fallen branch was found that had a few unusual twists in it, vaguely resembling the form of a snake. After covering it in black tape and attaching some fishing line to it, Buirley and his teammates were ready to test their serpent on the visiting team.

Placing it on the ground next to a baseball just outside the locker room door, they hollered to exiting players to please get the ball. As the victims did so, the fishing line was tugged to make the "snake" move, getting a startled reaction followed by laughter by most cases . . . with an emphasis on *most*.

When the biggest player (whose name Buirley, possibly fearing retribution, did not provide) on the team obliged the request to retrieve the ball and suddenly found himself confronted by the snake, he revealed to one and all his long-standing phobia of snakes.

"He jumped three feet off the ground and let out a scream like a five-year-old girl," reported Buirley.

The player scrambled back into the clubhouse and barricaded the door before sitting down for a prolonged session of hyperventilation.

Teamwork is as paramount to a successful prank as it is to a successful ballgame. But plays on the field during the game do not require planning with the radio broadcaster.

While playing for Fargo-Moorhead, infielder Chad Akers did some pre-game practice with the Redhawks radio man Jack Michaels to set up the team's closer, Barry Nelson. The Minnesota state lottery jackpot had climbed to over ninety million dollars. Like many others in the state, Nelson stocked up on tickets prior to the next drawing. In order to keep up with the game as well as the lottery, he had a radio playing in the bullpen.

As the team was warming up on the field, Akers snuck into Nelson's locker, took his tickets, and copied the numbers. He had already arranged for Michaels to announce the "winning" numbers during the game.

Unaware as to when Michaels was going to make his bogus broadcast of the lottery numbers, the Redhawks were surprised to see Nelson walking through the dugout in the middle of the game while they were at bat. Nelson never said a word; he just quietly strode past his baffled teammates and into the locker room with an eerie calm about him.

Once inside the locker room, Nelson let loose, beating on anything he could reach. As players went into the locker room to see what was happening, Nelson yelled, "I think I just won the f—ing lottery!"

Nelson then ran back onto the field, roaring and pumping his fists as the coaches, umpires, and the other team stared at him in open amazement, and perhaps a bit of alarm.

His teammates, however, just sat calmly in the dugout smiling.

Once he was informed of the gag, though, Nelson really lost control. Running amok with the game still in progress, he doused the entire dugout and all of its inhabitants with water. Finally, he left the dugout, himself none the richer, and his teammates all the wetter.

The Court is Now in Session

Another time-honored tradition in pro ball is the kangaroo court. About once a week, or as circumstances dictate, a court is called to session in the team's locker room to judge those accused of various "crimes." The purpose of these courts is not to enforce arcane rules but to give everyone a chance to loosen up and have a few laughs in a forum where anyone may be on the giving or receiving end of a charge. No players are safe from being brought up on charges, and often coaches (although rarely the manager) are included in this due process of the law. However, if the accused player is found innocent, the accuser must pay a fine.

As paychecks are tight, the fines are equally modest—usually five or ten dollars at the most, often even less. The money collected during these courts may go to any number of uses—charity, beer, an end-of-the-season party, etc.

The offenses that can lead to an appearance in the court are myriad. Simply being promoted up to the team will merit an indictment. Talking to a girl during the game is a no-no. Bone-headed plays are a surefire way to get brought before the judge, but the laws of the kangaroo court extend well beyond the playing field. These crimes include wearing part of the uniform (such as a cap) out in town (with the exception of team functions), wearing the same clothes off the field for two days in a row, or antics during a night on the town.

Four months into his first pro season, Josh Lamberg found that he still couldn't avoid paying weekly fines.

"I'm still getting it every week," he said, slowly shaking his head but grinning nonetheless.

CHAPTER 17

Independence

*I was not drafted. I basically had to go and try out,
not knowing what to expect or really thinking
about my future. I just wanted to play.*

—David Dalton, infielder

Pat Ahearne knows about second chances. In 1995, he pitched in four major league games for the Detroit Tigers. Two years later, he was playing in the Dodgers farm system and spent the winter of 1997-98 pitching in the Australian Baseball League. In January of 1998, while he was still in Australia, he was informed by the Dodgers that they had released him. With only a month before Spring Training, he had to scramble to find a potential team. Finally, he received an invitation to attend camp with the Yankees.

However, once he got there, Ahearne found that he was feeling burned out from the whole experience. He left Spring Training and returned home, seemingly through with baseball.

"I wouldn't even watch it on TV," he said.

By mid-summer, he began to have second thoughts about retirement. Then a team from Taiwan called him with an offer, so he began to get himself back into pitching form. By the time his arm strength was once again at its peak, the deal with the Taiwanese team fizzled out.

A relative of Ahearne's was working in a hotel used by visiting teams in the Atlantic League, an organization made up of teams with no major league affiliations, and he had met several players who knew Ahearne. The relative then told Ahearne about this independent league.

Ahearne called the league's president, Joe Klein, who had also been the Tigers' general manager in 1995, to let him know he was interested in finding pitching work. Klein put Ahearne's name out on the wire, and five of the league's teams called Ahearne with offers.

Ahearne chose to sign with the Bridgeport Bluefish as he knew many of their players and knew of the manager, veteran big leaguer Willie Upshaw. He joined the team in August and stayed with them through the playoffs, until they lost to Atlantic City in the finals.

He returned to Australia the following winter and once again returned without a Spring Training job with a major league organization. In mid-April, he rejoined the Bluefish at the start of the Atlantic League's Spring Training. After getting off to a 6-0 start, he was signed by the Seattle Mariners and assigned to their Double-A team in New Haven, Connecticut, only twenty minutes from Bridgeport.

"I didn't even have to move my apartment," he said of his return to affliated ball.

Aside from a few cases where major league owners also owned a minor league team, all of the original minor league teams were independent of any major league affiliation. It wasn't until 1919 that baseball pioneer Branch Rickey proposed the idea of a structured system of minor league clubs who developed and provided players for solely the major league team to which they were affiliated. This was the beginning of today's minor league farm system.

By the late 1940s, relatively few independent teams existed, with most of them in the lowest levels of Class C and Class D. Many established leagues were a mixture affiliated and independent teams, with the affiliates gradually becoming the majority. Throughout the 1950s, as the number of minor leagues shrank, most of the teams to fall by the wayside were the independents. By the end of the decade, only a handful of minor league teams outside of the Mexican leagues were independent. The 1960s and the first half of the 1970s saw few independent teams, and in some years, none.

In 1976, a Class A league comprised solely of independent teams, the Gulf States League, was begun under the auspices of Minor League Baseball (then called the National Association). The league had a rocky start. In August, the East Division-leading Baton Rouge Cougars ceased operations due to financial problems.

The league, rechristened as the Lone Star League, returned in 1977, but so did its problems. The playoffs never got underway when the South Division champion Corpus Christi Seagulls, who had won the division in both halves of the season, refused to play after the regular season. That left the North Division winners Victoria Rosebud (first half) and Texas City Stars (second half), but those teams decided to cancel their playoff series. This lack of post-season play carried over to the entire league. By 1978, the league was no longer in existence.

Another independent league, the Triple-A Inter-American League, existed briefly in 1979 before folding in June. The league was an ambitious idea, with its six teams spread out in the United States, Caribbean, and South America. Unfortunately, poor transportation arrangements and even worse weather doomed the league. Although independent teams would continue to exist within affiliated leagues, this marked the end of independent leagues until 1993.

Beginning in 1902, the Northern League had existed in various forms before folding as a four-team Class-A league in 1971. Twenty-two years later, the league was resurrected with six independent teams in Minnesota, South Dakota, Iowa, and Canada. The players were a mix of undrafted college players, minor league veterans, and a few ex-major leaguers like Leon Durham.

During that same year, another independent circuit, the Frontier League, made its debut with eight teams in Ohio, Kentucky, and West Virginia. While the Northern League got off to a reasonably strong start, the Frontier League was soon beset by internal problems. With less than fifteen games into the season, two teams had already folded. The remaining franchise owners banded together that same season and fired the league president. Despite its rocky inaugural season, the league returned in 1994 with two new teams joining the surviving six from the previous season. ·

The 1994 season also saw three more independent leagues begin operation. In 1995, the total number of independent leagues shot up to eleven. Expansion, however, did not translate into stability. During the following years, franchises within leagues would change location or fold, sometimes in midseason. New leagues formed as others folded, many after only one or two seasons. A handful of franchises jumped ship to surviving leagues as their own collapsed. In 1999, the Northeast League merged with the Northern League to leave five leagues remaining from the fourteen overall leagues that had started during the decade. By 2003, there were the two leagues from the beginning of the new independent era, the Northern and Frontier (now grown to ten and twelve teams, respectively) leagues, along with six others, including the Northeast League which had ended its merger with the Northern League. While the Northern, Northeast, Frontier, Central, and Atlantic leagues have achieved stability and prosperity, only time will tell how the other current and future leagues will fare.

"It's amazing that we're still here, to tell you the truth," says Chillicothe general manager Bryan Wickline of the Frontier League's smallest market-sized, yet oldest, franchise. "It's the fans, the business community, and the season ticket holders that have kept us here."

This prosperity is no accident. The so-called stigma of non-affiliation doesn't seem to last for successful franchises. Chillicothe has drawn fans from as far away as Cincinnati who are willing to drive a few hours to see some small-town, grassroots baseball in favor of the nearby major league team. This is seen in even more dramatic fashion in St. Paul, where the Saints often outdrew the nearby Minnesota Twins in the late 1990s.

There has been friction generated between the independent and affiliated leagues with issues such as territorial rights at stake. Unlike their predecessors from earlier in the century, the independent leagues are not part of the association of Minor League Baseball. Some independent owners resent the attitude of the affiliates toward them. Conversely, some owners in affiliate ball are concerned that the instability of some independent teams has hurt the image of all minor league teams. However, there have been some efforts for cooperation that continue to this day.

From the major league perspective, the independent leagues offer an opportunity to scout players who have had a little more time to develop their skills. Major leaguers such as Kerry Ligtenberg (Braves), Jeff Zimmerman (Rangers), Brian Tollberg (Padres), and Morgan Burkhart (Red Sox) started out as unknowns in independent baseball.

Although reaching the major leagues remains a long shot for players, the independent leagues offer many opportunities to still strive for that goal or, at the very least, prolong their playing days. Some players find themselves cut from their major league organization due to simple economics. The player who is a good second baseman will get very limited playing time if the team's other second baseman is a first-round draft pick. Regardless of the statistics, the parent club will want the player they have invested a large signing bonus in to get the playing time. Other players are simply overlooked in the draft.

Consider the following: Mike Piazza was a sixty-first round draft pick for the Dodgers in 1988. With the draft now capped at fifty rounds, Piazza would not be drafted today. This is not to say that teams playing in Yuma, Schaumburg, and Evansville are brimming with Piazzas. But for many players, the independents are their last remaining hope to prove that they have what it takes to become major leaguers.

"I think it's a good thing," says Jack DiLauro, who saw players forced to leave the game as the minors were pared down in the 1960s, "for kids from smaller towns and smaller schools that didn't get the exposure that truly love the game. It might take them longer to develop, but they're still going to develop."

Like Leon Durham in 1994, other former major leaguers can be found on the playing fields of the independents. The Atlantic League in particular has seen several big names from the majors such as Jose Canseco and Ruben Sierra who have used the league as a springboard to return to The Show.

With the affiliated minor leagues offering a finite amount of managerial and coaching positions, former big league players have taken the opportunity of the independent leagues to stay in the game and gain some coaching experience. Al Gallagher, a former infielder with the San Francisco Giants and manager in the Atlanta Braves and Cleveland Indians farm systems, left the game for ten years to teach. After deciding to get back into the game ("My Major League pension kicked in—I could afford it," he explained), he took the reins of the Northern League's Madison Black Wolf in 1998.

Former big league slugger Jack Clark managed the Frontier League's River City Rascals before becoming hitting coach for the Dodgers. Other familiar names from the majors who went on to manage in the indy leagues include the Frontier League's Dick Schofield (Springfield), the Atlantic League's Butch Hobson (Nashua), and Sparky Lyle (Somerset), the Northern League's Ron Kittle (Schaumberg), and the Western League's Steve Yeager (Long Beach).

Players looking for teams will respond to open calls for

tryouts and even send resumes to specific teams as they would for any other job. The teams in turn do their own searching through various networks of contacts, scouts, and college coaches. Lists of players cut from affiliated team rosters quickly make their way around to the front offices of the independent leagues.

The tide has shifted somewhat since the early 1990s as independent teams have more players coming to them instead of seeking them out.

"They [college coaches] will call us now and say that, 'We have this outfielder, this catcher, this pitcher who didn't get drafted, but we think he should have,'" says Chillicothe's John Wend. "That happens a lot."

The players arriving to an independent team largely know they are fortunate to get this opportunity to play again.

"We're very up front with them," says Wend. "It's not big money. They'll be able to get by. But we tell them if they perform well, their chances of being picked up by a major league organization are pretty good."

Wend points out that overlooked talent is a part of the game. Scouts often have but a few innings to observe a player and make their best estimate and projection before moving on to the next potential prospect.

"I talk to scouts every time they come in. They don't hesitate to admit that they make mistakes all the time."

Heading for the Frontier

Unlike other independent leagues like the Northern and Atlantic, which attract players of all ages and experience, the Frontier League is more restrictive in the maximum age and professional experience of its players, opting for an overall younger player base. No player in the league can be twenty-seven years of age before May 30 of a given season. Additionally, the teams' twenty-four-man rosters are limited in terms of player experience as each team must have at least ten rookies and no more than seven 2nd-year players, along with maximums of two 3rd-year players and three players in their fourth or higher season.

In 1994, Brian Tollberg was out of college and out of baseball. Despite pitching well at the University of North Florida, he was passed over in the draft. Fortunately, his college coach knew Roger Hanners, the manager of the Chillicothe Paints, and arranged for Tollberg to audition for the team. He signed with the team the night of his tryout and was playing professionally a week later. Following his thirteenth start for the Paints, Tollberg, who had set a two-year goal to get into a major league farm system, was signed by the Milwaukee Brewers.

"I was elated, to say the least," recalled Tollberg, who remained aware that he still had a long road to travel. "I had planned on going back to Chillicothe if nothing panned out, though."

Tollberg steadily worked his way through the minors. In 1997, he was traded to the Padres. Upon reaching Triple-A with the Las Vegas Stars, he began to see the light at the end of the tunnel.

"I think once I reached Triple-A it could become a reality, but I needed a few breaks and needed to be pitching well at the time, too."

The pitches and the breaks finally came together on Father's Day, 2000. Las Vegas' pitching coach Darrel Akerfelds informed Tollberg that he was to pack his bags for San Diego.

"It gave me a good reason to call my dad back, along with others, to let him know the news."

After playing two seasons of baseball in Europe, Chris Dickerson wanted to try pro baseball in the United States before hanging up his glove for good. He checked out the Northern, Western, and Frontier Leagues on the Internet, sending resumes to every team. Finally landing in Chillicothe, he was content to give the game one more year, regardless of the outcome.

"Anything is possible right now," he said early in the 2000 season. "If nothing transpires this year [as far as being signed by a major league organization], then I'll probably hang it up. But at least I'm playing some quality ball here in America."

Ben Crowley had major league aspirations while playing for Catholic University in the Washington, D.C. area. During his senior year in 1999, he had spoken the Mets and Braves about his possibilities in the draft. That same season, he was named the Capital Athletic Conference's Co-Player of the Year. After graduation, he went to Florida to play in a summer amateur league while waiting for a phone call with draft news. The call never came.

A coach from college still felt that Crowley could play on a professional level and arranged a tryout for the outfielder with the Johnstown Johnnies. The rest was up to Crowley. He arrived in Johnstown for a weekend tryout along with two pitchers the team was interested in. Due to roster limitations, only one of the three would be signed. After watching him hit against the two pitchers, the Johnnies signed him and sent the two pitchers home.

After his success as a mid-season replacement, he spent the winter in Sydney, playing in the Australian Baseball League. In February, he received a call from Johnstown, asking him to return for a full season. While in his second season, he saw two former Frontier League players become the first players from the league to reach the majors.

"It's fantastic," said Crowley. "They may be late bloomers, but they're guys who worked their butts off."

As his college days came to an end in 1998, Mike Robertson found his baseball career to be at an apparent end after going unselected in the Major League draft. Like a growing number of other ex-collegiate players, he tried his luck with the Frontier League, which focused on these younger athletes with little or no professional experience. The effort seemed to pay off, as the Cook County Cheetahs signed him. After ten games, however, his season came to an end with an injury and subsequent release.

In 1999, he returned to the Frontier League, this time with the River City Rascals. His solid play earned him a return to the Rascals in 2000. Due to the age restrictions in the league, this was to be his final year in the league—and professional baseball. But baseball wasn't through with him yet. On August 1, he finally received what he was unable to get in college—a contract with a major league organization, the Red Sox.

"I had no idea, to tell you the truth," said Robertson when asked if he knew he was being scouted. "We were just having a team lunch when the manager came up to me and said, 'Would you like to sign with the Red Sox? They're interested in signing you.'"

Robertson understands that a contract in organized baseball does not guarantee a path to the majors. Despite the leap from the indies, there remains a long, grueling trail from the Ed White Stadium in Sarasota, Florida to Fenway Park. Regardless of where the journey will take him, he remains appreciative of what he has now.

"I'll continue playing for a year or two at the most . . . and then see what happens."

Like Robertson, pitcher Matt Buirley found himself outside of professional baseball until joining the Frontier League with the Chillicothe Paints. The Paints were an ideal choice for him as they were close to home as well as giving him the chance to play with former college teammates Woody Fullencamp and Andy Lee.

During the 2000 season, he was signed away from Chillicothe by the Cincinnati Reds and moved west to Dayton, a Class-A affiliate. To add to the excitement, the Dayton Dragons were playing in their inaugural season and consistently sold out their games, with over 8,500 fans packing the stands each night.

Having worked his way to several stops in the professional ranks, Buirley maintains his optimism.

"There's always the chance and dream that you'll make it to the top. Thoughts always cross your mind of finally stopping and getting on with your life. But not yet."

Woody Fullencamp was ready to call it a career after going undrafted at Ohio State University. He planned to spend the summer of 1999 taking the last few classes he needed for his degree. By chance, the classes were cancelled, leaving Fullencamp with a summer devoid of plans. Around the same time, he and fellow OSU pitcher Andy Lee received phone calls from Paints manager Roger Hanners, inviting them to try out for the team. Accepting Hanners' offer, they both proceeded to make the team.

"I kind of fell in love with it ever since," said Fullencamp. "It's been a pleasure to play here and play for Roger Hanners, having the opportunity to play as a professional—just going out there, having fun, doing the things you can do.

"As the season goes on, you realize there are scouts in the stands. The chance to sign as a free agent is no sure thing, but you can see if you can make it to the next level."

Fullencamp did manage to get an invitation to Spring Training 2000 with the Braves. However, after competing with younger players with more time in the Braves organization, he was once again on the outside. This time, though, he knew where his next step would be. Both he and Lee returned to the Paints for the 2000 season.

His tryout with the Braves did add something to Fullencamp's perspective on playing for a career and a promotion versus playing just for the sake of the game.

"You can be released anywhere, but here [in independent ball] you get a better chance. In affiliated ball, you're almost rooting against the guys you're playing with. Here, it's, 'Let's win. Let's try to get that championship.'"

After pitching in the Reds organization, Tye Levy was out of baseball, but still felt he could compete in pro ball, perhaps eventually with another organization. With the Frontier League, he had that opportunity. After discussing some options with his agent, the pitcher tried out for and signed with the Johnstown Johnnies in 2000.

"I decided to come here, get in some good innings, prove to myself that I still have confidence to pitch at this level, and hopefully get picked up by an organized team. I live an hour away, so Johnstown is a good place to play for me."

Joining Levy that season on the Johnnies' pitching staff was Takuro Seki, from Japan.

Like many of his teammates, he looked to pitching in the Frontier League as a means to prove that he belonged in pro ball. Obviously, language was a barrier, but he was soon able to communicate with his coaches and teammates through a mixture of words and hand motions.

What was not as easy to overcome was a visa problem. He originally came over to North America with a visa to play ball in Canada. After being cut by the Montreal Expos in Spring Training, he tried out for and was signed by Johnstown. Unbeknownst to anyone on the team, Saeki's visa expired during this season.

The expired visa was eventually discovered while the Johnnies were on the road, returning from a series in London, Ontario against the league's only Canadian franchise. Seki was not allowed to cross the border back into the United States. With no other recourse, Seki and pitching coach Bill Masching remained behind on the Canadian side of the border for three days until the Japanese consulate in Toronto processed the paperwork Seki needed to continue playing in the United States.

In 1998, David Dalton played for Chillicothe, having gone undrafted after playing college ball at Liberty University. Dalton points out that he was a late bloomer and had only one good season—his senior year—which may have been enough to keep teams from drafting him. After hearing about the Paints from a college teammate, he contacted Chillicothe's manager, Roger Hanners, who invited him to try out for the team.

After putting together a strong season for the Paints, Dalton went back to Liberty University early in 1999 to work out with his old college team in preparation of what he figured to be another season in the Frontier League. Unknown to him, Roger Hanners had been in contact with the Atlanta Braves' director of scouting, Paul Snyder. Snyder then contacted Dalton to offer him a contract to play in the Braves farm system.

After playing in Jamestown and Macon in 1999, he spent

the 2000 season with the Myrtle Beach Pelicans of the Carolina League. During that season, Brian Tollberg and Morgan Burkhart became the first two Frontier League alumni to make it to the major leagues. While Tollberg was long gone from the Paints when Dalton played in Chillicothe, Burkhart, who starred for the Richmond Roosters, left a lasting impression—and gave Dalton some perspective.

"Obviously, seeing guys I've played with make it gives me hope, but then I think how good they were. At this point in my career, I'm not half the hitter Morgan is, but I can do some things he can't.

"The love of the game is my motivation. The love of the game for me can be defined as the feelings I get when I make a great play or hit the ball hard. Those feelings and hearing the crowd—I love to thrill the crowd."

Alejandro Bracho may have been the most traveled player in the history of the Frontier League. The pitcher from Caracas, Venezuela first came to the United States while playing in the Yankees farm system. Following his release, he went to Taiwan for a year in 1999. Desiring to play once more in the United States, he returned to earn a spot with the Richmond Roosters. Every winter, he returned to his native Venezuela to play winter ball.

Following his junior year of college, pitcher Jason Baker was drafted by the Dodgers in 1995. After spending three years in the Dodgers organization, he was traded to the Expos, for whom he played in the minors for another two seasons. During his stint in the Expos farm system, he was converted from a starter to a closer. While he was willing to make the change, his arm was not, so he retired.

A year later, he found that he still wanted to play. Having been both a pitcher and outfielder in college, he decided to make his comeback primarily as a hitter. After contacting his former college teammate, David Dalton, he tried out for and signed with Chillicothe. Having played five seasons in affiliated ball,

Baker knew how much of a long shot he was, but he still wanted the opportunity to hit. He got his opportunity, but it was short-lived as a leg injury stopped his comeback and forced him to reconsider his baseball future once again.

"I've always had a burning desire to play in the big leagues. I'm left-handed and I throw hard. If I want to get to the major leagues, it's probably going to have to be as a pitcher."

During Spring Training of his third year in the Atlanta Braves system, catcher Chris Poulsen was released. During the eight-hour drive from the Braves training site to his home on the Florida panhandle, he resolved to stay in baseball. After arriving home, he researched independent leagues on the Internet and tried out for the Northern League. After failing to make a roster, there, he returned home once more to work out in preparation for the Atlantic League's spring tryouts.

While at home this time, he received an invitation from Roger Hanners to try out for the Paints. Hanners, using his network of contacts, had heard of Poulsen's release from the Braves and thought a catcher with a couple of years of professional experience would be an excellent fit for his young pitching staff. Although appreciative of Hanners' offer, Poulsen had already committed to a tryout with the Atlantic League.

The initial workouts went well, and Poulsen was able to get a roster spot with an Atlantic League team. However, he was released again on the last day of Spring Training.

Fortunately, Hanners had kept his offer open, and Poulsen became the Paints catcher following an open workout session.

Even part of his catching equipment made the transition to the Frontier League. He arrived in Chillicothe with a catcher's helmet sporting the Atlanta logo. Since the color scheme already matched that of the Paints (blue cap with a red bill), it was simply a matter of replacing Atlanta's stylized "A" with Chillicothe's "C" and leaping pony logo.

Like Poulsen, Matt Sheets found himself out of a job at the

end of Spring Training. After being released by the Twins, he tried out for and was signed by Johnstown. The Frontier League described itself as being at a level comparable to Class-A ball, with which Sheets agrees—except for the accommodations.

"The talent level is better than what I played in last year [which was Advanced Rookie]. The hotels we stay at here, though, are much better that what we had in affiliated ball."

It was a typical Midwestern afternoon in early August of 2000. The sun blazed down on the field in Chillicothe, keeping the temperatures well in the nineties, with the humidity levels to match it. As players were loosening up with some infield drills, Paints manager Marty Dunn focused his attention on the tall, lanky pitcher firing pitches to one of the catcher Chris Poulsen in the bullpen along the outfield line. Pitch after pitch, the ball hit the catcher's mitt with a sharp snap that turned peoples' heads that way.

The pitcher had no uniform—just a T-shirt and shorts. A tryout near the end of the season may sound futile, but both the manager and the player had much riding on this. For Dunn, thrust into the manager's job unexpectedly, the season is winding down too quickly. His team had turned its play around following a midseason slump largely caused by injuries and key players moving on to the affiliated ranks. But there may not be enough games in the season left to catch a playoff spot. Desperate for any edge, he closely watched the mechanics and delivery of the pitcher, breaking to occasionally glance down at the radar gun display.

An August audition in Chillicothe, Ohio would never have surfaced as a possibility for the future when Dennis Bair was drafted by the Chicago Cubs in 1995. His plans were more direct and simple: to ride his pitching arm to the major leagues. For two years, his plan seemed to be coming to life from the drawing board. In Spring Training of 1997, he was pitching for the Cubs' Double-A team and, given the turnover in pitching on the Chicago staff, had a shot to make the majors that year. But a shoulder injury that year and more shoulder surgeries in the 1998 and 1999 seasons put an end to his ride to Wrigley Field. Now, five years later, Chillicothe is the gateway for his possible return to the sport.

A week earlier, Bair pitched for the Padres in Fort Wayne, Indiana in hopes of being signed. While the Padres saw some potential, they did not have any open roster spots on any of their affiliates. The team's scout, who knew Paints coach Jamie Keefe from Keefe's playing days in the Padres farm system, suggested that Bair try out for the Frontier League team.

Despite his setbacks, Bair looks at his comeback as not just a resuming of his game, but a resuming of his journey to the major leagues.

"My arm is still alive and I'm still young," he explained. "I want to pitch my way to the big leagues and I hope this will give me an opportunity."

As Bair was pitching, a player on the infield was drawing looks and appreciative comments from a handful of stadium workers and booster club members as he took part in practice drills. Wearing a plain gray T-shirt and uniform pants of some unknown team, Josh Turner easily stood out from the Paints players in their dark blue practice shirts and white pants. But it was his throws from all points of the shortstop's range that caught people's attention. Thrown with seemingly little effort, they repeatedly and squarely struck the first baseman's mitt with loud pops that almost matched the sound of Bair's pitches.

"I'm hoping this will work out," said Turner, an undrafted collegiate player from Lander University in South Carolina. Like Bair, he came to Chillicothe on the recommendation of a Padres official, hoping this would lead to an eventual spot in a major league team's farm system.

But the eyes of a seasoned baseball professional catch things that escape those of the casual observer and rabid fan. There are still concerns with Bair's delivery, and he returns home. For Turner, the tryout illustrates how a professional baseball career can take an unexpected turn. Passed up by the Paints, he was signed to play by the Dubois County Dragons, the visiting team in town during his audition with the Paints.

Having established himself in the majors, Brian Tollberg still looks back fondly on his time in the Frontier League. When asked if he had any advice for those still playing there, he had this to say.

"Keep your priorities straight and remember why you're there in the first place. Anything is possible. I was always told I'd have to prove myself at every level. I did—and was rewarded for it."

Going on to the Farm System

For the independent teams whose players go on to farm systems, the success is a double-edged sword. When a team or league gets a reputation for being scouted by major league organizations and sending players on to affiliated leagues, they attract better talent.

"It starts making Chillicothe look like a farm team," said Bryan Wickline.

However, replacing these players is not as easy, particularly during the season. In the middle of the 2000 season, Wickline saw three of his top players leave the Paints for the Reds' and Yankees' farm systems. Despite a late-season surge, the team never quite recovered from the loss of those three, and finished one game away from making the Frontier League playoffs.

"We've become a victim of our own success," said Wickline, with no regret in his voice.

For the players making the transition from independent ball to the minors, the differences both on and off the field become apparent. For Mike Robertson, the most noticeable difference between the Frontier and the Florida State leagues was the pitching. In the Sunshine State, there were fewer mistakes being offered from the mound. The fastballs were quicker, and the curves broke harder. David Dalton found it to be the same in the New York-Penn, South Atlantic, and Carolina Leagues.

"As far as the game," he explained, "it's the pitching that makes the difference. I don't get many good pitches to hit, and it's a lot more of a mind game."

Having gone from affiliated to independent baseball, Dalton's former Jamestown teammate Chris Poulsen also saw differences in the pitching. Young pitchers are often drafted based on the speed of their fastball and don't expand their repertoire until they move to higher levels of play.

"Out here [in the Frontier League], you see a lot more breaking balls than you do in the low levels of affiliated ball," said the veteran catcher.

As the pitches become quicker, the off-field aspects of organized baseball become larger. The opportunity for promotion becomes a tangible thing as teammates are sent up to a higher league. Looming just as large is the specter of demotion or release. These are no longer the decision of the team manager and the local owner, but of an organization of largely unseen (by the player) people whose purpose is to develop and provide talent for the major league team.

After Spring Training in 1996 in which he was assigned to return to Double-A ball as a utility man, Chad Akers decided he was done with baseball. Feeling that he had nowhere else to go in the Reds organization, he returned to his home in West Virginia. But the decision did not bring him much in the way of peace of mind.

"About a month into it," said Akers of his retirement, "I decided I needed this game more than I thought I did."

Akers got in touch with a coach from Charleston, West Virginia who was with a new team in the Northern League, the Fargo-Moorehead RedHawks. For the next three seasons, he played in Fargo, including the team's championship year in 1998. Having proven himself in the Northern League, yet still unsigned by a major league organization, he tried his luck in the Atlantic League with the hope that more scouts would see him. Partway through the season, his plan came through as he was signed by the Seattle Mariners. He spent the rest of the season with their Double-A and Triple-A clubs in New Haven and Tacoma.

As the new breed of independent leagues nears their start of their second decade, they have established themselves as a legitimate proving ground for overlooked young players and even for former big leaguers. But regardless if the sweat poured out on the fields in Sioux Falls and Dubois County leads to major league glory, these leagues do give many players at least a few more cherished seasons in the game.

CHAPTER 18

The Foreign Experience: Summer Ball

I'm getting paid to do the same thing I was doing
when I was six years old. That amazes me.

—*Nate Minchey, pitcher*

For decades, baseball in Mexico and Japan presented an option for veteran minor league ballplayers unable to get past the ceiling of Triple-A or ex-majors unwilling to return to the minors. In other circumstances, non-free agents have had their contracts sold to a foreign club, usually in Japan. Over the last decade, other countries such as South Korea, Taiwan, Italy, and the Netherlands have also become destinations for those with a few years left in their arms or bats.

Playing overseas is not necessarily the last stop in a player's career. For those who were given little chance to play at the big league level due to competition at their position, a year or more in the top level overseas may show their worth to other ball clubs in the United States. Additionally, the money to be made playing in the majors in another country is usually better than a Triple-A contract will provide in the United States or Canada. For a player in his late twenties who can see little major league playing time in his future in North America, the opportunity to make enough money to provide lifetime financial security is very tempting.

Once overseas, they experience many of the same things that foreign players coming to the United States do. They must adapt to a new language and a new culture both on and off the field. Once they do adjust to their new surroundings, some decide to remain playing there for years, even after they are presented with offers to return to the majors in North America.

Don August saw much of the world during his pitching career. He got his first taste of international competition as a member of the 1984 United States Olympic baseball team. August, who compiled a 34-30 with the Milwaukee Brewers from 1988 to 1991, also played in the minors for the Astros, Giants, Tigers, Indians, Padres, and Pirates.

Outside of the United States and Canada, August spent parts of 1993 and 1994 playing in Mexico. After starting the 1995 season with the Pirates' Triple-A club in Calgary, he left for Taiwan where he would play through the 1999 season. During one year there, he spent a month of Spring Training with this team in Australia. He also played winter ball for two years in Puerto Rico and the Dominican Republic. In 2000, he played in Italy for the final season of his career.

August started playing in Mexico for Puebla Pericos. The pay was better, tax free, and he had a special arrangement with club. Usually, a player could be released from his Mexican contract if he was offered a major league deal. He worked it out so that he could be released if he had a Triple-A deal. All that remained was his indoctrination into playing in a foreign land. That he played abroad for years attests to the fact that he was a quick learner.

"If you're going to play in Mexico, you have to be tough," August explained. "I saw the same thing in Taiwan. Guys going to Mexico and going to Taiwan—they're in a different culture and a different situation. You can watch them ruin themselves. Everything was aggravating and frustrating. If they had a bad game, they took it off the field. They'd order something and screw that up and get pissed about it. Then in the hotel room, the maids were knocking on the door and they couldn't understand them. So I watched these guys disintegrate.

"I learned that that instead of getting mad and getting upset about these things, you had to laugh at it. You just had to joke and expect that these things were going to happen.

"I started learning that that's how baseball works altogether. Baseball is not really fair or unfair to anybody. You learn to make sense out of a lot of stuff."

The Netherlands

Out of college and undrafted in 1998, Chris Dickerson still had the desire to play baseball. Unsure of what avenue to take, he received help from a former coach who had contacts in Holland. After several transatlantic discussions, Dickerson found himself on an airliner going to a country he had never been to, much less thought much about.

"I was there on the plane, thinking, 'Oh my God, what have I gotten myself into?'" recalled Dickerson, one year later. "I had no idea. It was a different country, a different language. But once I got over there, I adapted. It was a great, great experience."

His major obstacle was the language barrier. Also, he quickly understood that, while growing in popularity, baseball ranked well below soccer as the country's sport of choice.

Professional baseball in Holland is divided into four levels. The Head Class is their equivalent of a major league, with three tiers below it comprising their version of the minor leagues. As in many other countries, the teams practice a couple of times during the week and play their games on the weekends for a fifty-plus game schedule. The crowds remain small throughout the season, but increase as the playoffs begin.

Expectations of American ballplayers are high, considering that they have come from a much deeper baseball background. Dutch players and coaches have had mostly instructors with a few years of baseball experience. Ballplayers from the States have been coached by people who are passing on knowledge from generations of baseball.

"They think we're going to be superstars," said Dickerson. "But that's not the case. As it turns out, they have some pretty good ball players over there."

While Dutch players aren't nearly as prevalent in the United States as Latin players or even those from the Far East, they have begun to trickle over. Pitcher Win Remmerswaal, outfielder Rikkert Faneyte, and infielder Robert Eenhoorn are three Dutch-born-and-raised players who have climbed all the way to the majors. When their U.S. careers were over, both Faanyete and Eenhoorn returned to play in the Netherlands, with Eenhoorn managing the National Team in world competition following his retirement as a player in 2000.

After two seasons in which he compiled a .383 batting average, Dickerson decided to return to the United States and hang up his glove. However, after a few months with no baseball in sight, he decided that he wasn't done with the game yet—as long as the game wasn't done with him. In 2000, he was signed to play for the Frontier League's Chillicothe Paints.

The Highlands

When thinking of baseball beyond the borders of North America, Scotland is not a location that quickly comes to mind. Although the game lags far behind soccer in popularity there, it has taken root and is gaining a loyal following.

Baseball was played in Great Britain as long ago as the 1890s. A major push was made in the 1930s to increase the awareness of the sport. Today, the game is played in a club system similar to that of other European countries, where players play on the weekends while working regular jobs through the week. Under the governance of the British Baseball Federation, Britain is divided into two conferences, the Northern and Southern Conferences, with Scottish teams placed in the Northern Conference.

The Federation has also been instrumental in bringing coaches with professional experience into the country to work with the players and clubs. This has given American players at the end of their careers an opportunity to gain some coaching experience to use back in the States.

Nick Clark has seen the game progress in his native Scotland, not only in club play but with the growing popularity of baseball in youth sports. Clark manages the Edinburgh Diamond Devils as well as playing first base and outfield for the team. As a country, Scotland's major claim to baseball fame thus far has been as the birthplace of Bobby Thomson, who hit the famous home run to wrap up the National League pennant for the New York Giants in 1951.

But Thomson was only two years old when his family moved to the United States, giving him an American upbringing with the game. Although the Atlanta Braves have a scout, Ronan Dunne, who routinely patrols the Federation games, Clark is pragmatic about a player moving on from the club circuit to the major leagues.

"The majors would be great," said Clark. "But in reality, the first Scottish MLB player is about thirty years away."

Still, the competition in the Northern Conference remains fierce. The Diamond Devils won the conference championship title in 2001 with a roster largely composed of Scots but with also a handful of other nationalities—English, Irish, South African, Canadian, and American. Former Oakland Athletics farmhand Joe Gagliardo was the first ex-professional to play for Edinburgh.

"He was a major asset to our club both on and off the field," said Clark.

Toward the end of the 2001 season, the team added another American, Tim Garren, to its roster. Garren grew up watching his hometown Cubs at Wrigley Field. After graduating college, which he attended on a baseball scholarship, he was signed to a pro contract by the Detroit Tigers. However, he was released after one season, bringing an end to his professional career.

Over ten years later, he moved to Scotland to work for a manufacturer of sausage skins. During his first three years in the country, he was unaware that baseball was being played there. After discovering the team in Edinburgh, he returned to the game. In three games and twelve at-bats for the Diamond Devils, he hit .667 with two home runs and ten RBIs.

At age thirty-eight, however, Garren harbors no hopes about a possible run to the major leagues—nor is that the important thing to him.

"I just play for the love of the game," he told a local reporter. " . . . I'm happy to play anywhere."

Scottish baseball has also made inroads in international play. Until recently Team Scotland only played England (think of Scotland versus England like the Red Sox versus the Yankees) and Ireland in international play. These contests within the United Kingdom began with college players on June 2, 1934, when the Scots routed the English by a score of 24-3.

For larger international events, Scottish players participated as part of the British team. But in the summer of 2001, Team Scotland won a berth to play in the Confederation of European Baseball (C.E.B.) Cup of Cups tournament held in Prague, its first European experience.

Clark does have broader goals in mind for Scottish baseball. Having played a key role in setting up Scotland's National Team and establishing a Little League, he hopes that some day baseball will be recognized in his country as a major sport.

The Land of the Rising Sun

Baseball has been a popular sport in Japan since Professor Horace Wilson and others introduced the game there in the 1870s. In the following decades, visiting collegiate and professional teams from the United States would tour the country to play local teams. In 1936, the first professional league began. For over fifty years, the country has had two major leagues—the Central and Pacific Leagues—that have seen many players come from the Americas to continue their careers. Some have returned to the

States to play, others have stayed for years and flourished in the Far East.

"I was surprised at how popular baseball is here," said Nate Minchey, a pitcher who came to Japan after parts of four major league seasons with the Red Sox and Rockies. "It is definitely the national sport. If you are good, you are treated like a god."

After the 1997 season, Minchey was tired of bouncing back and forth between Triple-A and the majors. When an offer to pitch in Japan for more money than he had made during the previous seven seasons combined, he jumped at the chance. After winning fifteen games his first year, he made the decision to stay longer.

For players who have spent their careers learning and playing in North America, the biggest change for most of them in Japan is the work ethic and expectations to follow it. It begins in Spring Training, where players typically take over one hundred ground balls each day. Likewise for pitchers, who throw at least one hundred pitches daily in the pre-season.

"American players try to work less and have more fun, so this naturally causes conflict," explained Minchey. "Sometimes an American player will draw the line and say, 'No, I am not taking a hundred ground balls' or 'No, I am not throwing a hundred and fifty pitches in the bullpen today' because we know it will only hurt us in the long run later on in the season."

As long as a player is successful, he is left to do things his way. However, if he struggles and does not conform to the practice regimen, he may quickly find himself on a one-way flight back to the United States.

The other major adjustment is adapting to a new culture and language. Minchey and his wife quickly found that the best way to learn the language was to immerse themselves in the culture. Each team has an interpreter to help players during the game, but that was of little help to Minchey and his American teammates during the 2000 season.

The interpreter for the Hiroshima Carp, for whom Minchey

played, quit the day before the season began. His hastily hired replacement was a nice enough guy, but barely spoke English. When asked by the foreign players why he took the job, he replied that he did it to *learn* English.

"It was like having a conversation with Scooby Doo," recalled Minchey.

George Culver, a nine-year major league veteran, went to Japan in the middle of the 1975 season after spending the first few months in Triple-A. The biggest difference he noticed in the game there was that the crowd was more reserved. If a foul ball went in to the stands, nobody moved. An usher would retrieve the ball and toss it back onto the field.

In Japan, the teams provide their players with apartments. With the exorbitant cost of housing on the island nation, size is scaled down. During their first two years in Hiroshima, the Mincheys and their children lived in a nine hundred square foot, three-bedroom apartment which the Japanese referred to as a mansion.

"We later found out that anything with more than one bedroom in Japan is called a mansion," explained Minchey. "I then found out that our apartment cost the Carp five hundred thousand dollars to purchase. Prices are even higher in Tokyo."

Taiwan

"You knew you are definitely somewhere else," said Don August about his first impression of the Far East. August was joined on the team by a couple of American teammates, Les Straker and Cecil Espy. Although August was a veteran of playing outside the United States, it still helped that Straker, who had been there for six years, was able to show him the ropes. August thrived during his five years in Taiwan and was named the league's Most Valuable Player in 1998.

When the Yankees released Alejandro Bracho, the ex-minor league pitcher was not ready to hang up his glove. In 1999, he went to Taiwan where he was one of five foreign players—one American, one Japanese, and three Latin—on the Brother Elephants of the Chinese Professional Baseball League. The manager was well versed in three languages—Chinese, English, and Japanese—which left him well equipped to speak with two of his foreigners but not with the Spanish-speaking South Americans. Fortunately, Bracho and the other two Latin players spoke enough English to communicate with him.

The teams practiced as much as they played, if not more. The weekly schedule included four games (with pre-game practice) and three all-day practice sessions.

Despite the large crowds, good pay, and having fun, Bracho left after one season to pursue a playing career back in the United States with an independent team.

Sadly, another factor that led many foreign players to leave Taiwan after 1999 was the involvement of organized crime in the game and its attempts to rig games. While the league has cleaned house, it faces a long road to regain the fans it lost because of the scandal. With the corresponding loss of revenue, the incentive of higher pay for foreign players disappeared, and many chose other locations in which to continue their careers.

Italy

By the end of the 1999 season, Don August knew his playing career was nearing the end. Having joined the exodus for foreign players from Taiwan, he weighed his options. Outside of his career, he had a wife and son and had to consider doing something else where he wouldn't be away from home for so long.

Finally, he decided to play in Italy as a fun place to be in his last year. The schedule of the professional game in Italy was the same every week—practice from Tuesday through Thursday, a single game on Friday, a doubleheader on Saturday, and Sunday and Monday were off days.

Although the pay wasn't nearly as much as he was used to, the benefits were incredible. The team, Rimini, flew his family from the United States, provided a car and an apartment in a resort area on the Adriatic Sea. Rimini won the league title that season, allowing August to retire as a champion.

CHAPTER 19

The Foreign Experience: Winter Ball

You go through two hundred and fifty rides a game.
With every pitch, you're riding a roller coaster.

—*Chris Nichting, pitcher*

For those players not going to school or working elsewhere, winter baseball presents a means for both extra money and extra playing time to improve their skills. Some off-season leagues like the Arizona Fall League are comprised of co-op teams in which several major league organizations provide players and coaches to a given team. The players, often top prospects, find themselves in a more competitive environment as the overall talent level is higher than what they were used to in the regular season. The primary purpose of these leagues is to provide additional instruction for these players as well as to evaluate how they play against other similar talent.

During the 1990s, other co-op winter leagues existed in Hawaii, Maryland, and California. In the Hawaiian Winter Baseball League, players on each team were also joined by prospects from Japanese teams. Most teams in the Australian Baseball league also had working agreements with one or more major league organizations, with the Americans and Canadians providing some players and coaches to the Australian clubs.

Other leagues thrive in Mexico, the Caribbean, and South America. The competition can be fierce, with Latin American players—some of them established major league stars—playing alongside or against the minor leaguers. It is always the player's option to go play in these leagues, although sometimes their parent clubs suggest that they do so. Regardless of the country, the winter league experience is never quickly forgotten by the ballplayers who journey there.

Pat Ahearne, a veteran of multiple seasons in both Australia and Venezuela, summed up the opportunities that playing winter ball provides:

"It's a chance to see different parts of the world. It's a chance to play more baseball. And it's a chance to make a little extra money in your occupation instead of going to work for UPS back home."

Winter baseball also presents opportunities to up-and-coming managers. Jim Pankovits played in Venezuela for a season, Columbia for another one, Puerto Rico for two, and later returned to Venezuela as a manager. Having managed up to the Double-A level in the United States, the opportunity in Venezuela gave him a chance to manage a higher caliber of talent, including some major leaguers.

You're Not in Kansas Anymore

Regardless of the lack of a "major league" classification, the fans in South America and the Caribbean are extremely passionate about their teams. The crowds are unlike any attending a North American minor league game, where the diehard rooters are sprinkled among the more casual masses that are just there to relax with friends and enjoy nine innings. These fans bring an enthusiasm to each game that rivals any seen at the premier level of any other sport in the world.

"The people there sort of have a funny way of doing things," said John Romonosky, a veteran of several winter leagues during the 1950s. "These people would take something like a bunch of rags stuffed into a sock, kerosene soaked. They would light it, twirl it around over their heads, and throw it through the stands. Then somebody would get it, do the same thing, then throw it someplace."

If things have toned down at all over the years, they haven't done so by much. Players who have gone there more recently tell of firecrackers being thrown around as a common occurrence. When crowds do "the wave," it is done at full force—any beer in someone's hand will go flying.

Pat Ahearne pitched for Magallanes during the 1999-2000 season. The team's archrival was Caracas and the rivalry was on a scale of that of the Yankees and Red Sox. Every game between the two teams took on a life of its own.

"They'd have dancing girls in center field. You'd walk out onto the field an hour before game time and people were blowing horns, waving flags, and chasing around the stadium," Ahearne recalled. "It was a big party atmosphere."

To keep the party in check during the game, guards armed with sabers and attack dogs stood on the foul lines, spaced every twenty to thirty feet, from the dugouts to the bullpens. Although it was an effective means for keeping fans off the field, any visiting player who had to chase a ball near a foul line or warning track was prime target for thrown ice, firecrackers, and whatever else might be at hand.

"It's blood and guts over there," said Trey Hillman, who managed a Venezuelan team in 1997. "It's their major league season."

While playing in South America is an unforgettable experience, the trip to simply get there can also create some vivid memories, as Mike Smithson learned when he played in Venezuela in 1979. Smithson and his wife were greeted by the driver who took them to the town where he was to play. After loading their belongings into a 1957 Chevrolet, he took them on an unforgettable three-hour ride, careening through the mountains at wild speeds while the Smithsons sat in the back, clutching each other for dear life.

"We knew we were into something special, it was just trying to get there—crazy," Smithson recalled.

Afoul of the Law

George Culver became familiar with the police during his years of winter ball in Venezuela. During the 1964-65 season, he was playing for Valencia and living in nearby Maracay. His North American teammates included Adrian Garrett, Tom Kelly (a pitcher, not the future Twins manager), and future Cy Young Award winner Jim Lonborg.

The first incident came about when Garrett was driving a rental car and struck a drunken woman who had suddenly staggered in front of the automobile. Fortunately, the woman was not seriously injured, but the police showed up and wanted to know who was driving. The players were reluctant to name Garrett, since the car wasn't registered to him, so they identified Kelly as the driver. Kelly wound up spending a week in jail, but was allowed out during the day. (Every morning, he would help the officers push the police car so it would start and then get dropped off at the hotel.)

The next winter, Culver was back in Venezuela and got a closer, more personal look at their prison system. After a night of drinking, he wound up in jail over a trumped-up assault charge.

"There was these wild characters in there," Culver recalled of the jail. "The guy next door to me was in there 'cause he cut a guy's head off and was bowling down the street with it."

Culver was soon released (with his head still attached to the rest of his body) and rejoined the team, but the legal problem wasn't over. The team owner called him during a game in Caracas in which he held a 1-0 lead. The owner informed him he had to leave the country because civil charges had been filed against him. With nowhere else to go, he hid in the owner's house while lawyers worked out a deal. When everything was hashed out, he wound up serving another three days in jail before the case was put to rest.

Culver was ready to head back to the United States when he got out, but the Valencia owner persuaded him to stay for the playoffs. Culver owed him three thousand dollars for legal fees, but the owner was willing to forget the debt if Culver stayed. Culver chose to remain so he would have some money with him when he finally departed. When he received his final pay envelope, the three thousand dollars was not there.

Whether it was a miscommunication or a deception is not known, but the owner, when confronted by Culver, claimed that he said he would waive the debt for the legal work only if the team won the playoffs. Not willing to risk any more trouble, Culver left the country while he still had the chance. He returned in 1981 as a coach, but fortunately, no one remembered him.

Revolution

Following the 1954 season, John Romonosky went to play in Guadalajara, Mexico. His fiancée, whom he had met that summer, flew out to join him there. Shortly after her arrival, they were married. This would be the first of several winters spent in warmer climates while the baseball games continued.

If the 1954-55 winter season was memorable for Romonosky for personal reasons, the 1958-59 even more so for a historical one. Having been called up to pitch for the Washington Senators in 1958, he took the mound against the Indians for a game late in the season at Cleveland Stadium. By the end of the fifth inning, he had amassed ten strikeouts, generating a buzz in the crowd and among the press as to whether he would break the current single-game record of eighteen held by Indians great Bob Feller.

Although he did not break Feller's record (in fact, he struck out no more hitters that game), he did impress the owner of the Cuban League's Almendares team, who was attending that game and who promptly signed the pitcher to play that winter.

"We thought we had a team that could beat a lot of the major league teams," said Romonosky of his Almendares club.

The team was stocked with past, present, and future major league talent as well as some of the cream of the Triple-A ranks. Its roster included the following position players:

- Rocky Nelson, first base; won the International League triple crown with Montreal in 1955, had already played for the Cardinals, Pirates, White Sox, Dodgers, and Indians and would return to Pittsburgh and play on their World Series championship team in 1960.
- Tony Taylor, second base; broke into the majors in 1958 with the Cubs—the first of nineteen big league seasons, made the National League All-Star team with Philadelphia in 1960.
- Jim Baxes, third base; previously played for the Kansas City Athletics.
- Willie Miranda, shortstop; played nine years in the majors for the Senators, White Sox, Browns, Yankees, and Orioles.
- Dick Brown, catcher; spent nine seasons playing for the Indians, White Sox, Tigers, and Orioles.
- Carlos Paula, outfield; had completed a three-year, big league stint with Senators.
- Bobby Allison, outfield; made his major league debut with the Senators the previous summer and would remain with the team after they moved to Minnesota until his retirement in 1970, played on three American League All-Star teams.
- Sandy Amoros, outfield; spent seven years in the major leagues with the Dodgers and Tigers.

To complement the batting order, the pitching staff boasted

its share of talent. Along with Romonosky, who had pitched for the Cardinals and Senators, the staff included the following:

- Tommy Lasorda; had brilliant success in the minors, but was winless on the mound in three seasons with the Dodgers and the Athletics by the time he played that winter. As a major league manager, he would win over 1,500 games during his Hall of Fame career.
- Orlando Pena; began his big league career the previous summer and pitched in the majors until 1975, throwing for the Reds, Athletics, Tigers, Indians, Pirates, Orioles, Cardinals, and Angels.
- Art Fowler; a four-year big league veteran with the Reds by the winter of 1958-59, would pitch another five seasons for the Angels. After retiring, he became the Angels pitching coach for a season, then returned to the majors to coach under Billy Martin throughout nearly all of Martin's managerial career with the Twins, Tigers, Rangers, Yankees, and Athletics.
- Mike Cuellar; would make his major league debut with the Reds the following summer and pitch fifteen seasons for the Cardinals, Astros, Orioles, and Angels, during which time he had four twenty-win seasons and was a member of four All-Star teams and a World Series champion (Baltimore, 1970).

Although baseball was a popular passion in Cuba, it was not at the forefront of current events in late 1958. The country was in great political turmoil as the regime of Fulgencio Batista was fighting a losing war against rebels led by Fidel Castro. The underlying tension was felt in the country's capital, Havana, which had been famous for its boisterous nightlife.

"Everything was real quiet at night," said Romonosky, describing the tension. "All because they knew something was up. Something would happen any time. It finally did."

On January 1, 1959, Castro arrived in Havana to assume

power of the island nation after Batista fled the country. For their own protection, the players and their families were confined to their motel for one week. Fortunately for Romonosky and his wife, who now had three small children, they had just done their weekly shopping prior to the New Year's celebrations.

While the city remained quiet during the day, the chatter of automatic rifle fire would start shortly after the sun went down as Castro's troops battled Batista loyalists. Although the U.S. embassy did what it possibly could for the players and their families, there still were scary moments. After an anonymous threat was made to burn down the hotel where the players were staying, Castro sent his own troops in to guard the building.

When the residual fighting was largely over, baseball resumed and Castro himself attended several of Almendares' games in the company of around one hundred soldiers. Despite the previous violence and the political cold war that was to come, the American ballplayers were loved and respected by the Cuban fans.

"Every time one of our American players hit a home run, there would be six or eight of the soldiers running out to carry the man back to the dugout," said Romonosky.

The Almendares club dominated the other teams in Cuba, sweeping the championship series and earning a berth in the Little World Series, the tournament made up of the eight champions from the other winter leagues. With the revolution still fresh and viable threats to his new regime existing, Castro sent a squad of soldiers with the team to the tournament in Caracas, Venezuela to prevent anyone from threatening "his" players.

Allowed to take two extra players with them, they filled out their ranks with Indians all-star outfielder Minnie Minoso, who, at the time was in the prime of his major league career and Senators hurler Camilo Pascual, another future all-star. In the opening game of the Series, they defeated future Hall of Famer Juan Marichal in a 1-0 contest.

The tournament progressed, with the games played in a constantly packed stadium that held about 40,000 spectators. As they did in the Cuban championships, Almendares swept through their competitors in the Little World Series, reaching the final game against the "home" team of Caracas. Despite the overwhelming numbers rooting for the Venezuelan squad, Camilo Pascual threw a shutout to seal the championship title for Cuba.

After the game, the team got into limousines waiting outside the stadium to take them to the airport. However, the cars were soon surrounded by angry fans who were in no hurry to let the players go. A thrown brick shattered the rear window of the car that Romonosky was riding in, covering him with broken glass. Fortunately, the police were able to clear a path for the cars to exit without further incident.

Down Under

The obvious benefit of playing "winter" ball in Australia is the geography. November, December, and January are prime summer months well south of the equator.

Jim Saul already had decades of minor league managerial time under his belt when he arrived in Australia in late 1995 to manage Adelaide. The biggest difference he saw was in how the sport was treated as a profession. He had a handful of minor leaguers from the United States who were used to playing full time during a season. But like its European counterparts, the league's native players fit practice in around their regular jobs during the week and play on the weekends.

"You might have a plumber. You might have a service station attendant or something else. It's more like semi-pro than professional," said Saul.

Still, there is an abundance of talent in the league, both with foreign players looking to hone their skills between seasons in North America and with Australians looking for a shot at a contract to play ball in the other hemisphere. Regardless of their professional status to the north, American players quickly blend in with their Australian teammates.

"You go over and you think you're going to be treated

differently and as special," explained Frontier League outfielder Ben Crowley. "At first they want to see what you can do. After that, it's up to you. You're just another guy and there's not a whole lot of difference."

Pat Ahearne dealt with a little mistaken identity while playing in Perth, a port city frequently visited by Navy ships.

"I'd walk into any place, talking with an American accent, and the first thing they'd ask me was if I was in the navy. I don't know what reputation the navy boys have—I can only imagine—but their faces seemed to brighten up a bit when they found out I was just there to play baseball."

There are very few baseball-only venues in Australia. The typical baseball park is often a soccer or Australian-rules football field with a pitcher's mound built up and a backstop erected nearest the closest set of bleachers.

Despite their limited playing time at home, more Australians are making their way to play in North America. The major leagues have already had Australians on their rosters such as pitchers Graeme Lloyd and Damian Moss, infielder Craig Shipley, and former catcher/outfielder Dave Nilsson, who now owns International Baseball League Australia.

CHAPTER 20

Strange Innings, Part 4

Baseball's a crazy game. Maybe that's why it's so interesting.

—*Dennis "Oil Can" Boyd, pitcher*

Playing Long Ball

The home run: a baseball classic. The dramatic hit that wins the game. The "frozen rope" line drive that seemingly rips through the sound barrier on the way to the fence. The majestic skyrocket shot that soars out of site above the outfield before gracefully arcing its way from the heavens to the stands. These are the stuff of baseball poetry. But some have resulted in some rather strange verse.

Determining how far a ball flew may not always be an exact science, but any decent legendary smash should have at least an extra fifty feet added during the retelling of the tale. The one that has them all beaten, according to several former players from the early and mid-twentieth century, is one hit in Lynchburg (or Pulaski, depending on the storyteller), Virginia. According to the legend, the ball sailed over the fence and landed in the coal car of a passing train whose tracks ran just outside of the park. In keeping with legendary distances, this train was bound for California. Thus, some unknown baseball journeyman slugger may have very well hit the longest ball ever in the history of the game.

One similar occurrence has been documented. Early in the 1982 season, the Toledo Mud Hens' Randy Bush knocked a ball over the fence in Charleston, South Carolina that did indeed land on the coal car of a passing train. The final destination of the train was not reported at the time.

Seventy years earlier, on June 17, 1912, another ball caught the train. A foul ball hit during an American Association game in Louisville, Kentucky careened out of the park and toward a passing train that was rolling along at forty-five miles per hour. The train's engineer, William Madden, spotted the ball in flight and, while leaning out of his cab, snared the sphere.

Are We Done Yet?

By the end of April 1960, the players for the San Antonio Missions and the Rio Grande Valley Giants could be excused if they felt like they had already played half of a season. On April 29, the two Texas League teams squared off for a Texas-sized game that lasted twenty-four innings with the Giants emerging as the victors.

San Antonio catcher Gordon Massa, who caught all twenty-four innings, had a front row seat for plenty of good pitching as the final score was a mere 4-2. The biggest casualty of the game for the Missions was not a player, but their scoreboard. The unfortunate piece of the park caught fire. The common belief was that the conflagration started because the lights had been on for so long.

Bats in the Belfry

Things weren't going well for the Alexandria Aces during the 1999 Texas-Louisiana League playoffs. Their offense, in particular, had come up short. Robert Hewes, who played for the Aces for several seasons, recalled a teammate who decided that the bats, rather than the players, were to blame for this untimely slump.

The player (who remained unnamed) called a bat meeting to correct this problem. After setting all the bats side by side on a couch, he removed all of his clothes and sat down in front of the small assembly and began to lecture them. He explained to each of the bats what they were doing wrong and admonished them to get their wooden heads out of their wooden butts.

Unfortunately, even this inspirational monologue was not enough to make the Aces' bats come to life. The team was swept in three games by Amarillo in the finals.

Thanks for the Encouragement

Hiroshima Carp pitcher Nate Minchey was rocked for four runs in the first two innings of a Central League game in August 2000. After the second inning, he shut down the opposition's hitters while his teammates began to chip away at the lead. With one out in the sixth inning, the Carp were only down by one run with runners on first and third and had Minchey coming to the plate. As he approached the batter's box, the team's interpreter yelled for him to come back to the dugout.

Minchey figured that there was some special strategy afoot; a pinch hitter or perhaps a chance for him to initiate a squeeze play. Manager Mitsuo Tatsukawa did not want to take one of his better pitchers out of the game yet, but he also had no illusions about how well pitchers did with a bat in their hands. Fearing that Minchey would ground into a double play, he gave the pitcher his assignment via the interpreter.

"The manager says," instructed the interpreter. "Strike out, please."

It Wasn't Pretty, But the Run Still Counts

The Bluefield Orioles had Pulaski outfielder Manny Baez dead in the basepath during an Appalachian League game in the late 1990s. Caught in a rundown between third and home, he was trying to avoid being tagged when he was struck in the head by the ball as it was thrown to the catcher. As the ball rolled toward first base, Baez was able to safely scramble to home plate and score before retreating to the dugout for some high fives and a couple of aspirin.

Fielding Practice, Anyone?

By mid-season, players are usually in top form. With the winter well behind them, they have meshed together as a team, and their skills have been fine-tuned. On July 14, 1946, the Zanesville Dodgers must have thought it was still January.

The Dodgers were hosting the Lima Terriers in an Ohio State League contest when their manager, Clay Bryant, probably aged twenty years over the course of one inning. In the top of the second, the first two Lima hitters, Wayne Reside and Van Hoff, were walked. Ray McLeod followed them to the plate and soon thereafter hit a routine ground ball to Zanesville first baseman Red Hughs. Then all hell broke loose.

Hughs bobbled the ball and let it slip behind him, allowing Reside to score from second. Right fielder Lou Ott backed Hughs on the play, nabbing the ball cleanly but throwing off the mark in an attempt to nail Hoff at third. Hoff then scored as left fielder Bob Sloss scrambled after the ball.

Sloss recovered the ball and threw it to third baseman Joe Stefano, who apparently forgot what his glove was for as the throw went sailing past him. Stefano chased the ball down and threw back to third, where McLeod was trying to reach while shortstop Jim Masser covered the base. As Fate would have it, Masser proved to be as slick with the glove as Hughs and Stefano. McLeod proceeded on to home plate unchallenged as the ball bounced away from the shortstop's mitt.

The Dodgers' ineptitude was matched during a Southern League game on May 20, 1982 when the Charlotte O's embarrassed themselves against the Knoxville Blue Jays. Knoxville's Toby Hernandez was on second with two out and Carlos Rios coming to bat. All the O's needed was one out to end the inning, but they couldn't get it in four tries on the same batted ball.

Rios grounded to second baseman Jeff Shaeffer, who scooped it up before dropping it. After recovering the ball, Shaeffer fired it to first. The first baseman, for reasons unknown, was not covering, and the ball sailed harmlessly over the bag. Catcher Tim Derryberry, who had been scrambling down to first to back-up the first baseman (who wasn't there to be backed up), snatched up the ball and threw to second in an attempt to get Rios. Instead, the ball flew into centerfield where John Tutt continued the travesty by throwing wildly to third base, allowing Rios to continue safely to home.

Triple Jeopardy

Unlike Zanesville and Charlotte, the Albuquerque Dukes had their defense with them when they turned a triple play against the Hawaii Islanders during a 1981 Pacific Coast League contest. What made the rare accomplishment all the more unique was that it all began with a perfectly good, run-scoring base hit.

The Islanders had the bases loaded with Rick Lancellotti on third, Jim Beswick on second, and Curtis Reed on first when John Alvarez came to bat. Alvarez singled to center field, allowing Lancellotti to score before everything else went wrong.

Beswick was thrown out at home plate while trying to score for out number one. Reed had stopped at second to see if he should try for third when the speeding Alvarez accidentally ran past him. According to baseball rules, a base runner is not allowed to pass another one, so Alvarez was promptly called out. Reed, watching what was going to be a close play at home, decided to advance, but was tagged out following a sharp throw by the catcher to the third baseman.

Nothing Lasts Forever

All hot streaks eventually come to end. All athletes are aware of this and accept it as part of their sport. But Erik Schullstrom probably wished that he had stayed in bed on the day his streak came to a crashing halt in 1991.

Schullstrom, a pitcher for the Frederick Keys, had put Carolina League scoreboards into a deep freeze by holding opponents scoreless for thirty-six consecutive innings. To top it off, he had thrown a no-hitter in his last start. Then he faced the Salem Buccaneers.

In the bottom of the first inning, Salem batter Roman Rodriguez snapped the scoreless streak with a home run. The next hitter, Paul List, followed suit. So did Alberto de los Santos after him, and then Ken Trusky.

It was only the second time in league history that four consecutive batters had hit home runs. By the game's end, Schullstrum's ERA had risen by nearly a full run, from 1.96 to 2.86.

CHAPTER 21

Promotions

*Sometimes, you just have to spend an afternoon in
the asylum to come up with a couple of ideas.*

—Mike Veeck, on creating promotions

Promotions have been around minor league baseball for about
as long as grass has been in the outfield. Tales of these extra
attractions to entice fans to attend games reach far back into the
nineteenth century. "Ladies Day," band performances, and
fireworks displays are but some of examples that have over a
century of history in the game.

During the 1950s, promotions evolved from a business
option to a necessary tool for survival. The migration of the
population to suburban areas left cities and their teams with smaller
fan bases. Also, baseball attendance was adversely affected by
improvements in technology available to the average family.
Television offered the option of baseball and other entertainment
within the home. Air conditioning meant that the living room
would provide more comfort on a hot summer night than a
breeze in the ballpark bleachers. The promotions became bigger,
with pre—and post-game auto races and beauty pageants taking
place on the field.

In some instances, promotions were born out of a different necessity. Shortly before the start of the 1920 season, Columbus Senators club secretary Charley Thomas and his wife attended a movie in downtown Columbus. After they left the show, they discovered that his Ford sedan had been stolen. The team offered a season pass in reward for the person who would reunite Mr. Thomas with his "gas buggy."

Pre-game promotions in all levels include celebrities of all kinds throwing out the first pitch—former ballplayers, musicians, movie stars, and politicians. In the minors, though, part of the fun is getting the ball onto the field. Dogs, horses, pigs, and goats tend to be the popular four-legged choices of delivery.

Another mode of transportation calls for little use of the legs at all as skydivers aim to bring the ball to the pitcher's mound. As with most promotions, however, this is also done at the mercy of the elements. Forceful winds have kept more than one would-be arrival from reaching the park, let alone the pitcher's mound. On one occasion, the skydiver and ceremonial ball landed in a wheat field over five miles from the stadium.

A quartet of skydivers with the ceremonial ball for the Little Falls Mets' season opener did manage to land on the diamond—it was just the wrong one. The pilot of the plane carrying the crew was already off-course when one of the parachutists mistaken thought he saw a flare on the ground to mark the jump point. The group jumped out and landed safely on a softball field about ten miles from the Mets' park. Nearly an hour later, the skydivers and the ball arrived at the correct venue.

Fireworks are another popular attraction—one that also has its share of technical difficulties. At the Chillicothe Paints' 2000 season's Fan Appreciation Night, the second-to-last game of the season, general manager Bryan Wickline had to take the field before the game to apologize for the lack of fireworks. The show was scheduled for after the game, but he received word two hours prior to the game that the pyrotechnics company would not be able to be there. With a packed audience and high expectations, he was able to provide some unexpected entertainment by proposing marriage to his girlfriend, who promptly accepted.

Johnstown, Pennsylvania wasn't as fortunate on July 4 of that same year. The team's and city's plans called for an afternoon ballgame followed by an orchestra concert and fireworks. They might have been better off planning for checkers and TV.

The previous day's game was postponed due to rain, with the make-up scheduled as a doubleheader to start at 1 p.m. on the Fourth. The rain continued into the holiday, delaying the start of the first game by over an hour. The crowd of ten thousand got to see even more extra baseball as the first game went into extra innings and wasn't finished until the late evening.

The second game, the one originally scheduled for 1 p.m. on the holiday, didn't get underway until 9 p.m. At 10:30, just as a pitcher was winding up to throw, Johnstown's mayor announced over the public address system that due to time constraints of the orchestra and the fireworks, the game would be stopped immediately. This didn't sit well with his pastime-loving electorate, who promptly—and loudly—booed him away from the microphone.

The home plate umpire was no less thrilled with the mayor's decision.

"This is my game," he said, chastising the mayor. "I'm the only one who can stop it."

The game continued, finishing at 12:30 a.m. An hour later, the *Fifth* of July holiday fireworks show proceeded. Unfortunately, they were fired from the wrong location and exploded above and behind the grandstand so that only the fans in the left field bleachers could see them.

One promotional event that has been gaining popularity, particularly in the Western United States, is the Grateful Dead Night or Jerry Garcia night. The event is usually held on the anniversary of the death of the psychedelic rock band's front man,

Garcia. The promotion is not just limited to the stands, where fans come dressed in their 1960's finest. The players take the field in tie-dyed jerseys as the Dead's music plays from the public address system.

In Sonoma County, even the mascot participated with a size XXXXXL tie-dyed uniform shirt. The team had band member Phil Lesh throw out the first pitch one year. Other optional events during this promotion include a Jerry Garcia look-alike contest, with fans of all ages and both genders lining up in bushy wigs and beards.

For Kevin Wolski, the Crushers' Director of Sales and Promotions, the creativity involved in these promotions was the favorite part of his job.

"This is a job where you can make something up and do it," he explained. "In the minor leagues, you can be stupid and be rewarded for it."

Another popular promotion is the guest appearance of an on-field character to provide entertainment between innings. This began primarily in the 1930s with the likes of Al Schacht and, later, Max Patkin. Today, the choices include BirdZerk!, ZOOperstars!, Myron Noodleman, and Elvis Himselvis.

One often-repeated promotion involves fans bringing their pets, usually dogs, to the park. One night in the Pacific Coast League in 2000, R.A. Dickey was on the mound for a "Bring Your Dog to the Game" promotion. Although he had pitched in front of hecklers in other games, it was his first time pitching before 150 barking dogs.

"I'm trying to strike out an ex-big leaguer and I have a bunch of dogs yelping in my ear," Dickey remarked.

Pre-game cow-milking contests are another time-honored promotion. One such contest may have cost the Paducah Chiefs a game against the Centralia Sterlings in a Mississippi-Ohio Valley League game on August 29, 1950. Paducah player-manager Walter DeFreitas was facing off against Centralia skipper Lou Bezeka beneath the udders when DeFreitas' cow kicked him in the shins.

DeFreitas was unable to play due to his hoof-induced injuries and the Chiefs lost to the Sterlings.

On occasion, a horse will get into the act. In the early 1980s San Jose outfielder Don Carter, noted for his speed, was pitted against a horse in a forty-yard dash and won.

August 2001 saw the ninety-race losing streak of glue factory candidate Zippy Chippy come to an end. The horse, who was 0-89 versus fellow horses and 0-1 against the species *homo sapiens*, pulled his record with humans up to the .500 mark by out-legging Rochester Red Wings outfielder Darnell McDonald.

Another horse was involved in a 2000 Bowie Bay Sox promotion, not as a contestant but as the prize. The Bay Sox got into a promotional partnership with the nearby Rosecroft Racetrack, whose new ownership was looking to attract a more family-oriented crowd. The attendees at the ballpark made for a perfect target audience, so the racetrack owner approached the team with the idea of giving away a racehorse.

During the promotion, the horse made weekly appearances at the ballpark, which in turn drew more people through the turnstiles. On August 13, the winner was drawn from a pool of thousands of entrants. The winning couple was split on how to take the prize; the wife wanted the horse, but the husband preferred the five thousand-dollar cash option. In the end, cash won out over hoof.

"We didn't have any protests," said Gary Groll, who worked in the Bowie front office. "In fact, a lot of people thought it was cool. We did have a few logistical activities—making sure the horse was here when it was supposed to be and having someone running behind the horse with a shovel when it was on the field. It only let loose once."

To draw more fans to a May 14 game, the 1982 Clinton Giants of the Midwest League held a drawing in which the luck fan won the team's manager, Wendell Kim. During the week, fans in attendance received a raffle ticket and had to be at the game on the fourteenth to win. What the winner actually received was a lunch with Kim, although the initial press release stated that women could to go out dancing with the manager instead.

"If it came up to that, my wife trusts me," Kim commented.

Fans attending the Tacoma Rainiers game on Easter Sunday stood no chance of winning a manager, but there was plenty of ham on the menu. The Rainiers had Ryan Anderson, who was leading the Pacific Coast League in strikeouts, on the mound for the game and gave away a ham for every strikeout Anderson recorded in the game. Seven fans left the park that day with dinner tucked under their arms.

The undisputed, if not officially titled, king of baseball promotions is Mike Veeck. Veeck's father, Bill, owned three major league teams at different times, the St. Louis Browns, the Cleveland Indians and the Chicago White Sox.

The elder Veeck was also once the president of the Milwaukee Brewers in the 1940s when the team was part of the minor league American Association. During World War II, Veeck's Brewers played several morning games every season so that night shift workers at war production plants could attend. Throughout these games, ushers wearing brightly colored nightshirts served the workers free coffee and doughnuts.

During his ownership of the Browns, Bill Veeck made baseball history by using a midget, three-foot, seven-inch tall Eddie Gaedel as a pinch hitter. Gaedel had instructions not to swing, but to let his small stature shrink the strike zone to the point where he would be able to draw a walk.

When his father later owned the Sox, Mike Veeck made a name for himself in the annals of baseball promotions by staging Disco Demolition Night at Comisky Park. The event involving the burning of disco records and got so out of control that the White Sox had to forfeit the game.

After leaving the White Sox years later, Veeck was out of baseball and started an advertising agency. In 1989, Marv Goldklang called Veeck about returning to baseball. Goldklang, comedian Bill Murray, and singer Jimmy Buffett had just purchased the Miami Miracle, an independent team operating in the Florida State League. Roland Hemond, who had known Veeck in Chicago, told the new owners, "If you're dumb enough to buy the Miracle, you're dumb enough to hire Veeck."

Veeck sold his agency and went to work for the Miracle. Over the next ten years, the Goldklang Group acquired four additional teams.

"Now I have a hand in lousing up the operations for five teams," Veeck proclaimed in 2000. The five were the Northern League's Saint Paul Saints and Sioux Falls Canaries, the Hudson Valley Renegades (New York-Penn League), Charleston Riverdogs (South Atlantic League), and the relocated Fort Myers Miracle. (The Sioux Falls Canaries were later sold by the Goldklang Group.)

Veeck took a couple of years off from the minor leagues in the late 1990s to work with the Tampa Bay Devil Rays, but returned to the minors. Working the majors at the time, Veeck admitted, "wasn't a good fit. It's become a little corporate for my taste."

While not ruling out an eventual return to the major leagues, he still felt drawn to the minors. "I missed the minor leagues. I missed the game itself. I missed not being close to the players and the fans."

Veeck was also involved in the original planning of the Northern League with Miles Wolff, to whom Veeck gives a majority of the credit for the league's success.

"We wanted to start a league with baseball guys and people who love the game," Veeck explained. "It was designed by fans for fans."

Promotions are a creative outlet for Veeck. "The importance of promotions is to appeal to many different segments of the audience. On any given night, we might bring in three different groups by doing something that attracts them."

One of the seemingly more mundane sights at a ballgame is that of the grounds crew dragging rakes or other implements over the infield dirt between innings to smooth out the playing surface. Charleston took a different angle on this chore and brought in drag queens to drag the diamond's dirt. Another game in Charleston was dubbed "Lawyers' Night," to which lawyers were admitted for free—only to be billed by the inning for their attendance.

On July 7, 2002, the River Dogs staged another promotion that set a new attendance record for a professional baseball game. For "Nobody Night," the gates were locked to keep the fans out and attendance at zero, thereby breaking the 121-year-old record for the lowest attendance, which had been twelve. Once the game was official after five innings had been played, the gates were thrown open and the fans, who had been gathering outside and listening to the radio broadcast, entered the park to find candy and souvenirs waiting for them in the empty seats.

Veeck's personal favorite was with the Miami Miracle when the club held a tribute to the unsung hero of night baseball, Thomas Edison (in recognition of the lightbulb). A medium was brought out onto the field to attempt to communicate with Edison's spirit. The crowd was in hysterics, although the medium didn't find the reaction very amusing.

Veeck is quick to praise his front office staffs for their efforts in creating and implementing many successful promotions. "They come up with the majority and I just try to steal the credit," he joked.

In 2000, Jim Lucas, part of the Riverdogs' broadcast team, originally came up with the idea of having a contest for a free funeral, in which participants submitted their own eulogies. Team officials stated that they hoped the winner would not have to cash in the prize any time soon.

Not all of Veeck's promotions have gone smoothly. The Tonya Harding mini-bat night raised some controversy with some of the fans and media. An idea for a drawing for a free vasectomy during a River Dogs game on Father's Day caused too much uproar and Veeck cancelled the promotion.

"You have to be willing to make mistakes. But what I find is that people are very forgiving and if you admit you made a mistake."

Another misfire was St. Paul's "Mime-o-Vision" Veeck used mimes to recreate close plays on top of the dugout. The fans responded by throwing everything they could find at the luckless performers. By the seventh inning, the mines refused to come out, but Veeck was unfazed. The following year, Veeck responded with another promotion entitled "A Mime is a Terrible Thing to Waste."

"Other minor league teams don't have the nerve to do a third of what he does," said Chillicothe media relations director John Wend, with a hint of admiration in his voice.

Like Veeck's ill-fated Disco Demolition Night, the minor leagues have had plenty of promotions backfire. As described earlier, wayward skydivers and missing fireworks happen on occasion, but there are those promotional stunts that rise (or perhaps sink) from the others as they go awry.

During the 2000 season, the Cape Fear Crocs of the South Atlantic League staged a contest for second half season tickets. The contestants would stand up at the start of the game and have to remain standing until only one remained upright to claim the prize.

The contest was doomed to failure largely by fan apathy. The team was slated to move to Lakewood, New Jersey to become a Phillies affiliate after the season, so fan interest—and attendance—was abysmal. The team averaged a mere 550 fans per game and only two of those attending that night were willing to give the season tickets a try.

To their credit, both fans were still on their feet when the ninth inning came to a close three hours later. This caused a momentary dilemma for Cape Fear's general manager, Buck Rodgers, who quickly decided he had little to lose and gave both fans their tickets to the second half.

Two years later, the South Atlantic League saw another promotion come to fruition, at a cost to the team's management.

To be more precise, it was accomplished at a cost to the team management's hair.

Lexington Legends president Alan Stein had publicly vowed to shave his head if the Legends lost their home opener of the season. For nine innings the battle between Lexington and the Greensboro Bats raged; pitcher against hitter, runner against fielder, follicles against scissors. Then came the extra innings—the tenth, then eleventh—when the Legends finally fell to the Bats and Stein's hair fell to the floor.

As baseball has a way of adding unexpected twists to the drama of life, so went this saga. Following Stein's scalping, Debra Hensley, a Lexington-area insurance agent, rented advertising space on the team president's freshly mowed head for the team's next homestand. Thus, the team gained extra revenue despite the loss on the field.

There was one promotional mishap with baseball that never occurred at a park. During the 1939 World's Fair in San Francisco, an exhibition was planned that involved one of the city's baseball players and a dirigible blimp. San Francisco Seals catcher Joe Sprinz was to be on the receiving end of a ball dropped from a height of 1,200 feet.

The ball left the airship and was tracked all of the way down by Sprinz, who managed to catch the ball—with his mouth. (It was unintentional; he had planned to use his glove.) After being revived, he found himself minus five teeth while sustaining multiple fractures to his jaw. Sprinz would recover and later go on to play in the majors for the Cleveland Indians.

Leave it to one of Veeck's teams, though, to stage the promotion to end all promotions—literally. In 2001, the River Dogs introduced "Traditionalist Tuesday," on which Tuesday home games would feature no promotions at all before, during, or following the game.

CHAPTER 22

Mascots

Everything was an experience is baseball.
It was a fun time for all of us.

—*Tom Chism, first baseman*

As with promotions, team mascots are part of the draw beyond the game itself that brings fans to the ballgames. From a business perspective, the existence of a successful mascot means even more profit from the sale of dolls, T-shirts, and other memorabilia bearing the likeness of the mascot.

Other performers, such as "Birdzerk!" and the "Zooperstars!" are not affiliated with any team, but travel from stadium to stadium to provide more between-innings entertainment. They could be considered as a cross between promotions and mascots.

One of the most famous was the late Max Patkin. Patkin, who was billed as "The Clown Prince of Baseball" simply appeared as himself wearing a uniform with a question mark on the back and a cap perpetually turned in odd positions. He even made it to the silver screen, appearing, once again, as himself in *Bull Durham*.

Behind the stunts and zany antics, though, was a man who knew the sport well. Growing up in Philadelphia, he excelled in baseball when he wasn't cutting up. Marty Good, who knew Patkin during their school years, described him as "a great pitcher and a real comedian."

Patkin was well liked by the players, who often regarded him as one of their own. Like them, he spent long seasons on the road, performing on the same fields in small towns across the country.

"He brought a lot of smiles and added some entertainment to the game," said pitcher Steve Grilli. "He had a lot of passion for the game. I respected him in that manner."

Before Patkin, Al Schacht held the "Clown Prince" title, appearing on diamonds from coast to coast in a baseball uniform over which he wore a long tuxedo coat with tails and a top hat. Before his clowning days, Schacht was a pitcher and spent time in the major leagues, compiling a 14-10 record with the Washington Senators from 1919 to 1921. When ballplayers joined the armed forces by the hundreds in World War II, Schacht followed them, providing entertainment to the troops in far-flung corners of the world.

Like the characters they represent, the roles of the mascots vary from team to team. Some are limited to on-the-field promotional events and walking through the stands. Others take their act to the players, coaches and, on occasion, even umpires. These stunts are limited to between innings, never to interfere with the game itself. Well, almost never.

So what brings an otherwise average person to the point in life where they don a costume and transform themselves into giant birds, frogs, horses, and nearly anything else that can be found on the planet—or on the front page of a supermarket tabloid?

Free Agent Fowl

When the Louisville Redbirds made an offer to their top choice to play their mascot, Billy Bird, he turned it down. Turning to their second choice, Dominic Latkovski, they made the offer again and were rewarded with an acceptance. In April of 1990, Latkovski donned the feathers for the first time, making $35 per game. It was the start of an entertainment success story.

Latkovski had previously done some mascot work in high school and college and for a radio station. He also spent some time on a local television show.

"I was always a goofball, trying to be the class clown," he said.

After gaining a reputation for his costumed antics, he began performing around the United States and Mexico with his brother Brennan and a friend. The act billed themselves as "Billy Bird and Friends." As the pair became more successful, the Redbirds informed Latkovski that they wanted a larger percentage for the use of the name and costume. Latkovski weighed his options and made a decision.

In December of 1994, Latkovski left the Redbirds and formed BirdZerk!, Inc. Although BirdZerk! is now a promotion like Max Patkin was, his roots remain as a mascot—just one for rent.

BirdZerk! (the capital letters and punctuation are part of the correct spelling) is a man-sized avian with green and purple plumage and is one of the few mascot characters that do speak. As Latkovski described this, his voice instantly morphed into a high-pitched, cartoonlike one.

"When I talk to the kids after the game like this," he joked in his normal voice. "It's not very funny."

As the trio took their show on the road, they did encounter some inevitable problems. In the early days, when the BirdZerk! costume was still being carried in duffel bags, a suspicious customs agent in Mexico didn't know what to make of the large bird head in a bag he had just opened, despite not finding any contraband. A few dollars under the table later (to bypass hours worth of forms and endless questions), he let the group through so they could arrive in time for the game.

The act eventually expanded to include two other BirdZerk! characters, Air BirdZerk! and BirdZerk!, Jr. The new BirdZerks!

are inflatable and also require batteries and motor-powered fans. The entire inventory has grown too large for duffel bags and is now packed down into three traveling crates. In a full-size rental car, two crates can fit in the trunk and the third in the back seat.

In Canada, the BirdZerk! team was stopped for speeding. The police officer was naturally curious about the trunks in the car. They explained what they were doing and by the time the conversation was done, the traffic ticket was no more, and the officer had game tickets for him and his family.

On a typical game day, they usually arrive two hours before the game to set up. This includes talking to the host team's front office personnel, managers, players, and umpires to determine what will and what will not take place during the game. Before they were well known, it was more difficult to get cooperation from managers and players. Over the years, their reputation has made it much easier to get volunteers.

As a rule, most ballparks don't have a bird changing room, although some of the newer parks do have auxiliary changing rooms for extra needs or events. Otherwise, they use a corner of the locker room, weight room, laundry room, hallway, office, or any other available space to bring BirdZerk! to life.

BirdZerk!, Inc. was not content to remain a one-bird show that performed seventy to seventy-five games each summer in the United States, Canada, and Mexico. Dominic Latkovski and Aaron Flaker created the ZOOperstars!, which feature performers inside of inflatable, mascotlike characters in 1998.

During their first year, the ZOOperstars! appeared in twenty-eight parks. By 2001, the number of appearances had grown to over 150, including places as far away as Japan. The ZOOperstars have also branched into other sports.

What's at, er, on the plate in San Antonio?

At least his face is memorable. When asked for this book

which mascots stood out from others, many players mentioned the one in San Antonio, if not necessarily by the right name. "Puffy the Taco," "Puffy the Giant Taco," "Super Taco," "The Puffball Taco" and "that hopping burrito guy or something" were some of the identifications given. For the record (courtesy of the San Antonio Missions' media and public relations director Jim White), his name is Henry the Puffy Taco.

One of the Missions' longtime sponsors is a local restaurant, Henry's Puffy Tacos. The mascot was the advertising brainchild of San Antonio General Manager Dave Oldham in 1989 and has been a fixture at the park ever since. However, it wasn't until 2000 that the team had their own official mascot, Ballapeno. Ballapeno, a giant jalapeno pepper who wears a Missions jersey and cap, is Henry's cousin, according to White. There's no word as to whether a team of nachos will be hired as the grounds crew.

The Flying Bear

One day, Jimmy Kowalski happened to be going into a store next to the Schaumburg Flyers' temporary office. The team was still preparing for its inaugural season in 1999. On a whim, Kowalski, who had been a mascot at his high school and happened to know the team's merchandising director, Michelle Arrigo, went into the Flyers' office and asked if they had anyone lined up for the mascot's job.

Soon, the job was his and "Bearon" was born. The mascot is a bear dressed as an old-fashioned aviator.

For Kowalski, putting on the costume is like changing personalities. "When I talk to someone about the sketches, it's not what I'm going to do on the field, it's what Bearon is going to do," he explained. "Bearon and Jimmy aren't the same person."

Away from the ballpark, Kowalski works as a bartender. His customers know what he does, which is good for business as they'll come in and talk to him about the game.

The Abominable Sonoman

During the existence of the Western League, Sonoma County's Rehnert Park was inhabited by a creature known as Crusher the Abominable Sonoman. Crusher was a purple creature with huge (size 32) feet—a homage to the old practice of stomping grapes for wine making.

The mascot was first played by Tim Cox. During Cox's stint, Crusher became the first mascot to be thrown out of Western League game after patting an umpire on the back and leaving a sign that read "Blind Man Working" on his shirt.

In 1995, Justin Davis began working for the Sonoma County Crushers as an usher. The following year, Davis moved to the front office as the team's director of group sales. On one fateful day, Davis was asked to fill in as Crusher at an off-field event. The gig went so well that Davis became the new full-time Crusher. Between working the games and appearing at other events in the community, Davis eventually dropped the sales job.

Later, Davis accepted a position as general manager at a local manufacturing company, a job that demanded less time than the team's sales job and allowed him to keep his part-time job in the giant purple suit. Still, a season spent in the eighty-pound costume took its toll.

"By the middle of September, I'm a complete mess, but I just can't give it up," said Davis.

Davis always refers to Crusher in the third person, not as himself. For him, Crusher is an alter ego. "You can do things you couldn't do in a regular setting," he explained.

Although Davis' employees were aware of what their boss did, they still couldn't believe the antics they saw Crusher perform were the work of the man they knew.

"When I'm in the suit, they're doing double-takes, saying, 'That's not Justin!'"

Wild Horses

Mark Jackson was working in the stadium operations

department at Lawrence-Dumont Stadium in Wichita, Kansas in 1992 when the person who portrayed the Wranglers horse mascot, Wilbur T. Wrangler, hung up his hooves. With their costumed star having put himself out to pasture, the team asked Jackson to fill in. Jackson wound up enjoying the gig so much that he still remains in the role.

Although he works full time as a supervisor for a truck parts dealer, Jackson is also a year-round mascot. In the winter, he plays a mascot for a local hockey team, which keeps in shape and well practiced for his summer character.

Portraying Wilbur has led to plenty of time well outside the norm. Jackson spent a day in costume atop a billboard along Kellogg Drive, a major thoroughfare in Wichita, in order to sell game tickets. Amid all of the strangeness, the best part of his job, according to Jackson, is the interaction with the fans.

"Young and old like to play with Wilbur. I really enjoy signing autographs [no easy task with a hoof] during the fifth inning. You do have some that will give you a hard time, but over all, I am treated very well. The players treat me real well."

Rodney Fender had been a clown with the Ringling Brothers Circus before moving on to other work. When the opportunity to be Chief Crazy Horse, the equine mascot for the Chillicothe Paints arose, he didn't hesitate to take on a second job. His circus experience was an excellent background for doing performance work that relied on exaggerated movements instead of words.

Several of Fender's stunts involve the Paints players and occasionally someone from the visiting team. Umpires (by mutual agreement before the game) sometimes are included for an act between innings, but only when the circumstances of the game permit this. Fender is appreciative of any support he gets, understanding that the game itself is the top priority. The positive response he gets from the fans is at times overwhelming.

"Sometimes you don't hear a lot from the team, and that's fine because they're supposed to be concentrating on the game.

But when fans come up to you, send you Christmas cards, send you e-mail from California just because they used to be here and enjoyed the game, that's really neat."

Mixed Results

While mascots are supposed to provide some friendly entertainment, the design of their costumes can sometimes create an unintentionally scary-looking character. While it is understandable that some small children may be afraid of someone dressed up in a costume, it is unusual to find an adult, particularly a player, who is hesitant to come near the creature. Unusual, but not impossible.

The mascot for the Frontier League's Springfield Capitals is a character with a giant baseball for a head. He reminded Chillicothe's Chris Poulsen of the Jack Skellington character from the movie *The Nightmare Before Christmas*.

"He had big eyes, a big, evil-looking smile. Scary," explained Poulsen of his strange phobia. "Everytime he came over to the dugout, I kind of slid over into the corner. I was afraid of him."

When asked if kids were also scared of the mascot, Poulsen laughed.

"Oh, I don't know about the little kids, but I was frightened. He was scary enough to me."

Just a few weeks into his managerial debut, Dubois County skipper Fran Riordan nearly lost a game because of the team mascot. After a questionable call at the plate, the mascot, a dragon named "Slammer" began kicking dirt onto the home plate umpire. Unaware that the game resumed, he was still behind home plate, kicking away, when the next pitch was thrown. The umpire ordered him off the field, but the man inside the costume did not speak or understand English and kept kicking dirt. Finally, Riordan came onto the field and guided the mascot away.

Later that game, the Dragons' pitcher was ejected after arguing a questionable call during extra innings. The second base umpire approached the mound in an attempt to calm things down. However, the unfortunate arbiter was waylaid by the dirt-kicking Slammer. The umpires ordered the mascot off the field again, this time warning Riordan that he would have to forfeit the game if Slammer came on the field again. Fortunately for the Dragons, Riordan was able to communicate well enough with the man inside Slammer to let him know that the field was now off-limits.

Being on the inside of the costume is no picnic, either. The entire outfit often weighs a hundred pounds or more. And ventilation, a must during the hot and humid baseball season, is scarce.

Both Jackson and Fender have had their horse outfits redesigned to make them more comfortable and to allow for better movement. Fender was performing one stunt during which he was "clotheslined" by a player. One of the straps that held the head on broke and slammed a metal support into Fender's face.

Jimmy Kowalski, on the other hand, raved about his "Bearon" costume, which was easy to work in right from the start as it was designed with stunts in mind. There is extra material from the head that gets tucked down into the suit. Between that and the scarf that Bearon wears, the head remains very secure. Allows him to do cartwheels and flips without becoming headless.

The costume is also very comfortable and very light. This is handy for some sketches that involve Bearon wearing rollerblades. "I think it's one of the best costumes in the league," Kowalski said.

The biggest problem that he has had with the costume was when he has been at a gathering away from the game with small children for too long. One hour around children is the limit. After that, they get bored and decide to make their own entertainment by pulling on his scarf and seeing if they can get their hands inside the costume.

One of the biggest hazards a mascot faces is when playacting goes too far. While wearing an oversized head fixed with a huge, permanent smile, it becomes quite difficult to convince anyone else in the act that you're serious.

A common event at games is a foot race around the bases between a mascot and a young fan. If the mascot pulls ahead, he is inevitably foiled by someone who "distracts" him from the race, trips him up, or otherwise keeps him from finishing first.

Henderson Stadium, Lethbridge, Alberta, 1996: The base race was on. As the host Black Diamonds' mascot rounded third, Great Falls Dodgers skipper Mickey Hatcher, deciding to get in on the act, stuck his arm out to "clothesline" the mascot. However, the mascot never saw Hatcher's arm and ran full force into it, knocking his costume head off and bloodying his nose (the real one). It made for quite a scene as the mascot performer left the field with a goofy-grinned moose head in one hand and a bloody nose dripping behind the other, shouting curses at the stunned Hatcher.

Lightning struck again—right on the nose—during a routine with Midland manager Don Long. Long was supposed to smack BirdZerk! across the beak. But the manager, not realizing the difference a direct hit would make, punched BirdZerk! straight into the beak and gave Dominic Latkovski a bloody nose.

Other unrehearsed stunts have actually turned out quite well. Before one game in Schaumburg, Sioux City manager Ed Nottle came up to the Flyers' Bearon to compliment him on his performance and shook his hand. While their hands were clasped, Nottle told Bearon that he was going to flip him. Bearon nodded in agreement and soon went airborne, then landed safely. The stunt drew a roar of approval from the crowd.

Sometimes, when a stunt goes awry, it turns out for the better. Before one game, Rodney Fender, as Chief Crazy Horse, was involved in an act with Paints pitcher Stephen Byrd. Byrd, who had previous experience in roping cattle, was attempting to do the same with the team's mascot. Fender, while trying to "escape," began to climb a chain link fence when part of his costume became caught on the top. With the weight of the costume's horse head dragging him down, Fender was left hanging upside down on the fence, much to the amusement of the fans.

Despite the discomfort and the occasional mishaps, the people behind the masks have a deep appreciation for their craft and rewards that it brings.

"I have met come wonderful players coming through here on their way up to the big leagues," said Wichita's Mark Jackson. "It is nice to be able to say that I knew these players when they were just starting out."

CHAPTER 23

The Pitchers

It's a lot better than pitching to aluminum bats.
You don't have to hear that 'Ping' anymore.

—Jeff Heaverlo, pitcher, comparing professional
baseball to the college game

While accounts of pitching performances by Walter Johnson, Bob Gibson, and Pedro Martinez in the major leagues have always been well detailed nationwide, from the early pages of *The Sporting News* to multiple broadcasts of *Sports Center,* a single game pitched somewhere in Kinston, Peoria, or Ogden will barely make a showing beyond the local papers and radio broadcasts. But for the pitchers, their teammates, and the opposing hitters, some performances from the depths the minors make a lasting impression. Be it an inning, a season, or a career in the minors, these are some of those feats from the mound that stand above so many others.

Wins and Losses

Cy Young holds the major league records for both career wins and career losses with a lifetime record of 511-316. Like the major leagues, the minors also have both career records held by the same pitcher. Over a twenty-seven-year career in the minors, Bill Thomas pitched in 1,105 games (itself a record). During that span, he won 383 games while losing 347. He retired in 1952 without ever having played in the major leagues.

Ending on a High Note

When Pawtucket's Tomokazu Ohka threw a perfect game against the Charlotte Knights in 2000, it was the first such game in the International League in nearly fifty years. As memorable as the game may have been for Ohka, it had an even bigger impact on his battery mate, Joe Siddall. Siddall, a journeyman catcher who had made several appearances in the majors for Montreal, Florida, and Detroit, had been thinking about retiring from the game. After catching Ohka's perfect performance, he decided that this was an opportunity to go out on top, and he retired the following day.

No-Hit Déjà vu

The Greensboro Yankees were the home team for a Carolina League doubleheader on May 15, 1966, but their bats must have been on a road trip. In the first game (both games were limited to seven innings as was common for minor league twin bills), Rocky Mount pitcher Dick Drago held the Yankees hitless as the visiting Leafs beat the Yankees 5-0. Drago's roommate, Darrell Clark, helped the Leafs overstay their welcome in the second game with another no-hitter. The final out of the 2-0 win marked the first time that two no-hitters had been thrown in a pro ball doubleheader.

"Most of the things in the minors are just a blur, people coming and going so fast," said Fred Scherman, another pitcher on the Rocky Mount staff. "That's the one thing from the minors that stands out."

Missed it by That Much

A countless number of pitchers have lost perfect games and

no-hitters with one out left in the ninth, but John McFarland found a unique way of losing perfection in that situation. On July 29, 1908, McFarland, pitching for Helena in the Arkansas State League, went eight and two thirds innings against Pine Bluff without allowing a runner to safely get on base. However, Pine Bluff's twenty-seventh batter, presumably not wanting to be on the wrong side of a perfect game, refused to go to the plate. His refusal resulted in a forfeit, giving Helena an automatic 9-0 victory, with no credit of a perfect game being given to McFarland.

Although lacking the glamour of a perfect game or no-hitter, the one-hitter is quite an accomplishment unto itself. Hitters in the New York-Penn League had to be checking their bats for holes after facing the pitching staff of the Lowell Spinners in June of 2000.

The Pittsfield Mets left the field with only one hit to show for their efforts against Lowell pitchers Mauricio Lara, Mark Martinez, and Ian Perio. Four days later, the New Jersey Cardinals had similar luck against another trio of Spinners—Felix Villegas, Brian Bentley, and Daniel Glese.

Cal Hogue did not get off to a good start while pitching a South Atlantic League game for the Jacksonville Tars against the Columbus (Georgia) Cardinals during the 1950 season. The first batter he faced, Frank Dean, smacked Hogue's first pitch for a home run. Hogue followed up by retiring the next twenty-seven hitters. Despite his perfect finish, he lost the game, 1-0. To add insult to injury, Dean's home run would be the only one he would hit that year.

Who Needs a Pitch Count?

The number of pitches thrown in a game has become an obsession for pitching coaches and player development personnel. As the count climbs over ninety or a hundred, the nerves and trigger fingers in the dugout begin jumping. However, this did not develop as a wide-ranging phenomenon until around the late 1970s.

In simpler times, for better or worse—or both, a pitcher remained on the mound until his manager decided that he was "out of gas." This method was illustrated in grand fashion on August 31, 1942 during a Middle Atlantic League contest between the Zanesville Cubs and the Canton Terriers. Bob Snider was pitching for the visiting Cubs while Mel Parnell was on the mound for the Terriers.

The Cubs quickly jumped on Parnell for three runs in the top of the first inning. Canton manager Floyd Patterson wanted to take Parnell out, but relented when Parnell asked to stay in the game. The scoreboard was then filled with zeroes until the bottom of the sixth, when Canton scored three times to even the score. As the game went into extra innings with the teams knotted three to three, Snider and Parnell kept firing to the plate. Both teams struck for one run apiece in the eleventh before being blanked for another six innings. Parnell had a chance to end the game by scoring the winning run in the seventeenth, but was thrown out at home plate.

Parnell shut out Zanesville for the seventh consecutive inning in the top of the eighteenth inning, but the innings finally caught up to Snider, who walked the winning run home with bases loaded and one out in the bottom half. All told, Snider pitched seventeen and a third innings, allowing eighteen hits, four walks, and five runs in a losing effort. In his eighteen innings of work, Parnell allowed seventeen hits and four runs while walking eight and striking out ten for the win. And though pitch counts were not in existence then, it is estimated that each pitcher threw over three hundred pitches in the game.

Parnell would pitch in the major leagues for ten years and was selected as the starting pitcher for the American League All-Star Team in 1949. He still believes that pitchers should be allowed to pitch more.

"I think they baby pitchers too much in the big leagues," he commented in 2000. "It's a ridiculous thing."

Trailblazing

The box score of the Northern League game between St. Paul and Sioux Falls on May 31, 1997 gives no inkling that history had been made. Listed under the St. Paul pitchers' line was simply the name "Borders." What the box score line could not tell was that men's professional baseball had another barrier broken when Ila Borders took the mound.

While the All-American Girls Professional Baseball League, made famous in the movie *A League of Their Own*, was supposed to be for women, the Northern League was a "men-only" club on the field. Some questioned the signing of Borders by the Saints, claiming that team president Mike Veeck was looking for another publicity stunt. But Borders was no fluke.

At age five, she began playing in a girl's softball league. At age ten, she attended a Dodgers game and traded softball for baseball. After pitching on her high school team in California, she received a scholarship to play baseball for Southern California College. Earlier, Julie Croteau had become the first woman to play NCAA baseball, but Borders was the first to be awarded a scholarship for playing.

During her senior year in college, she was scouted by the St. Paul Saints, who invited her to Spring Training. At the end of the pre-season, she made the final cut, signing a contract on May 29, two days before her professional debut.

After appearing in seven games for the Saints as a reliever, she was dealt to the Duluth-Superior for infielder Keith English. While she took the trade in stride, English was rather unhappy with his place in baseball history.

"I got traded for a girl," he moaned. "It can't get any worse for that."

Whether or not things got worse for English, they definitely improved for Borders. The Dukes soon went on a tear through the league and eventually won the championship that year.

She returned to the Dukes in 1998 and appeared in three games for them in 1999 before being picked up by the Madison Black Wolf. Under manager Al Gallagher, a former major league infielder, she prospered. Gallagher felt that although she could match up well against professional hitters in the Northern League, she was best when her innings per game were limited to three. Pitching under this limit, she went 1-0 with a miniscule ERA of 1.67 in thirty-two innings. That success rubbed off on the team, which was 9-3 in the games that she pitched.

"She was a great worker, a hard thrower," said Gallagher. "She was five-foot-seven and a hundred and thirty-seven pounds. Had she been six foot and a hundred and eighty pounds, she could have pitched in the big leagues. Unfortunately, with the limited rosters in baseball, it hurt her. If there was a twenty-five-man roster, we definitely could have used her because they couldn't hit her for three innings."

During the 2000 season, she was placed on the Black Wolf's inactive list and later traded to the Zion Poineerzz of the Western League. Later that season she retired, but not before leaving a legacy in professional sports for other female athletes to build upon.

Maybe that's what they mean by giving "110%"

The math seems like it's fairly simple. Three outs in an inning means that a pitcher can strike out a maximum of three hitters in an inning, right? No, this *is* baseball, after all. According to the rules of the game, if the catcher drops the third strike, the hitter has the opportunity to run to first base since the ball was mishandled on a play that should have resulted in an out. In most situations, the catcher has plenty of time to retrieve the ball and to throw the batter out. However, if the batter safely reaches the base, he is credited with getting on base with an error while the pitcher, who threw the third strike, is still credited with the strikeout.

If the 2000 season quickly witnessed single-game strikeout

history with Brett Gray's gem, it also saw more than its share of single-inning miracles. In the second inning of a Texas-Louisiana League game against the Lafayette Bayou Bullfrogs, catcher Ricky Van Asselberg lost control of the third-strike pitch from Jim Wollschied. Although he was able to recover the ball, his throw did not get to first base in time. Wollschied was unfazed by this misfortune and went on to strike out the rest of the hitters he faced that inning for a total of four K's. He wasn't much easier for the rest of the game, keeping the rest of the batters from the bases for a no-hitter and a 7-0 win for the Ozark Mountain Ducks. The one error, which had allowed him to strike out four batters in one inning, had also cost him a perfect game.

Daytona Cubs manager Richie Zisk had planned to give Chris Booker one quick inning of work in order help his confidence after battling control problems. Booker wound up throwing thirty-five pitches in that "quick" inning on May 26, 2000 with some help from a split-fingered fastball.

Booker took the mound against the Charlotte Rangers and promptly gave up a double to the first batter for the only hit he would allow that inning. Booker recovered to strike out the next two hitters. He followed that by striking out the next Ranger, but was done in by his split-fingered pitch. The third strike (the batter swung at the pitch) bounced off the plate and over the catcher. The catcher recovered the ball and threw to the first baseman, who dropped the ball. The hitter was safe at first while the runner who had been on second advanced to third on the bounced pitch and then scored on the bobble at first.

Booker got two strikes on the next batter, but the splitter went wild again, hitting the dirt behind home plate and rolling under the catcher. By the time the ball was in control, the hitter was on first and his predecessor on second. The next batter safely reached first by more conventional means, a walk.

Having already struck out four batters and still seeking the third out, Booker tried another tactic—a pick-off throw to first. Unfortunately the throw was wild, allowing the runners on second and third to score. With little else left, Booker resumed throwing to home and struck out the batter with the ball landing firmly in the catcher's mitt on the third strike.

Booker's tally for the inning was one hit, one walk, one error, one wild pitch (on the third strikeout), one passed ball (on the fourth strikeout), three runs scored, and five strikeouts. He was also tagged with the loss after becoming only the fourth pitcher in minor league history to fan five in one inning. Booker was less than impressed with his place in the annals of the game.

"It kind of sucked, having five strikeouts in one inning, because I got flustered," he said of his bittersweet achievement.

The K Factor

The strikeout is a favorite of statisticians and storytellers. Much has been made of the pitcher's act eluding the bat. The numbers are manipulated to compare a bush leaguer to the likes of Cy Young, Bob Feller, and Roger Clemens. As years pass and the tale is repeated, the fastball gains twenty miles per hour and the break of the slider is given another thirty degrees in angle. But the fact that some magic was spun from the mound remains undeniable.

On August 10, 1962, Columbus Jets pitcher Bob Veale struck out twenty-two Buffalo Bisons batters in nine innings pitched. Unfortunately for Veale, he did not get the win as the game went twelve frames, with the Jets winning 6-5. Buffalo outfielder John Herrnstein remembered facing Veale in their International League days.

"He was a big, tall, left-handed pitcher who could throw the ball through a wall," recalled Herrnstein. "But he didn't necessarily know where it was going to go. When he was on, he was untouchable."

If any Frontier League fan was waiting for a new league record to be set in 2000, they didn't have to wait long. In the Opening Day game in London, Ontario, Werewolves pitcher Brett Gray shut down the Chillicothe Paints batters with twenty-five strikeouts en route to a 9-1 victory. Gray was no stranger to the art of the whiff, having set the league's single-season (which was three months long) record of 129 K's the previous year.

For minor (and major) league strikeout artists, the standard set in 1952 by Ron Neccai may never be surpassed. The high point came on May 13, 1952 while Neccai was pitching for the Bristol Twins in the Appalachian League. That Neccai, a Pittsburgh Pirates farmhand, threw a no-hitter that day was noteworthy in and of itself. But by the end of the game, he had become the first pitcher in pro ball to ever strike out twenty-seven batters in a regulation nine-inning game.

Eleven days prior, Neccai had fanned twenty in a game against the Kingsport Cherokees. His total in that game was one less than the league record. On May 13, he cruised past the record, allowing one walk, one error and hit one batter. Another hitter reached base on a dropped third strike. Consequently, the extra out in the game came on an infield grounder.

While aware of the no-hitter in progress, Neccai didn't give any thought to his mounting strikeout total. He didn't realize he had struck out twenty-seven until he was in the locker room after the game. As he was getting dressed, Manager George Detore and catcher Harry Dunlop told him what he had done.

"Being a smart-ass kid as I was in those days, I said, 'So what? They've been playing this game for a hundred years. Somebody's done it, so what's the big deal?'"

It wasn't until the next day that the team learned that no one had accomplished this feat before.

Although he never equaled his twenty-seven-strikeout total in another game, Neccai was in no way charitable to the hitters he faced. His next start came on May 17 against the Johnson City Cardinals. Like Chris Booker would do forty-eight years later, Neccai struck out five hitters in one inning due to a pair of dropped third strikes.

On May 21, he struck out twenty-four Kingsport Cherokees. That turned out to be his last start in the league as Pittsburgh promoted him to the Carolina League. In his forty-three Appalachian League innings, he had struck out 109 batters. With the Durham Bulls, he continued to make life miserable for Carolina League hitters, fanning 172 in 126 innings before being called up to the majors.

"I threw hard, had a decent curveball," said Neccai, explaining his strikeout success. "But I was a little on the wild side, so it wasn't unusual for them not to dig in too much."

In throwing the no-hitter, the feat usually doesn't sink in with the pitcher until the later innings, when the end of the game is in sight. By about the seventh inning, the dugout atmosphere begins to change. Neccai recalled this vividly.

"Nobody wants to sit by you. They don't want to talk to you or do anything. They're all superstitious and they don't want to be the one to jinx you. It gets awful quiet in there and all of the sudden, you find that you're alone."

Two of Neccai's Bristol teammates experienced this during the same season. One day after Neccai's twenty-four strikeouts against Kingsport, eighteen-year-old Bill Bell threw a no-hitter against the unfortunate Cherokees. Bell repeated the feat in his very next start, on May 26, against the Bluefield Blue-Grays. Bell's back-to-back no-hitters by one pitcher were the first in professional baseball since Johnny Vander Meer's pair in 1938 for the Cincinnati Reds and the first in minor league baseball since Dayton's Clarence Wright did it in the Western Association in 1901.

Bell wasn't finished with Bluefield, as the Blue-Grays discovered later that season. On August 25, he again silenced the Bluefield bats for his third no-hitter of the season. But Bluefield's trouble against Bristol's pitchers wasn't quite done. On August 26, yet another Twins hurler, Frank Ramsey, held the Blue-Grays hitless again.

The Wild One

In the movie *Bull Durham*, viewers are introduced to the

character of Nuke LaLoosh, a young pitcher who was wildly talented, but cursed with wild control. His statistics, laden with an extraordinary number of strikeouts and walks, seem purely like a Hollywood invention. But the truth was indeed stranger than fiction.

In 1960, Stockton pitcher Steve Dalkowski achieved a mark of 262 K's and 262 walks in only 170 innings of terror for California League batters. Although he would never pitch in a major league venue, Dalkowski did things on the mound that professional baseball may never see the like of again—to the relief of hitters everywhere. Years later, Ron Shelton, a teammate of Dalkowski's, used him as the basis for Nuke LaLoosh when he wrote the screenplay.

"Steve could really throw smoke," said Tom Parsons, who had pitched against him. "But he couldn't throw it anyplace. He threw it all over."

"He was off the wall," remembered Brooks Robinson. "A typical left-hander."

Even in the days before relief pitchers were used to limit the starter's pitch count, Dalkowski rarely lasted past the fifth or sixth inning. With all of the strikeouts and walks in the first half of the game, he was usually well past the number of pitches thrown by anyone else over the course of a complete game. In a 1957 game, he struck out twenty-four, walked eighteen, hit four batsmen, and threw six wild pitches for Kingsport.

His primary pitch was, naturally, the fastball. People who hit (or attempted to hit) against him swore his pitches were in excess of 110 miles per hour. His fastball was supposedly clocked at 108 miles per hour in 1962, but this was in an age where portable radar guns were a thing of science fiction.

In an attempt, to find out just how fast he was, the Orioles sent their puzzling pitching prospect to the Army's proving grounds in Aberdeen, South Dakota. There, his fastball was clocked at 98.6 miles per hour but the test was quintessentially Dalkowski-esque. Already having thrown 150 pitches in a game the night before, Dalkowski spent an hour throwing more pitches at Aberdeen before he could finally locate the ball in an area where the detectors could pick up the ball.

In a more unscientific test of his speed, teammate Herm Starrette bet Dalkowski five dollars that he couldn't put a baseball through a wall. On his first pitch from fifteen feet way, he drilled the ball though boards of a wooden outfield fence. (Fortunately for Dalkowski, he had a large target to aim for.)

Like the tales of his strikeouts, the stories of his wildness are myriad. Teammates hated it when he threw during their batting practice. They would have to wear catcher's gear—shin guards and masks before stepping to the plate.

Before game time, Orioles manager Paul Richards would have him warm up for forty-five minutes in the bullpen in order to tire him out so that he wouldn't be so wild. In an often futile attempt to get him to throw the ball over home plate during practice, a fifty-dollar bill would be placed on the plate—his reward if he could nail the strike zone. More times than not, the bill did not leave the field in his pocket.

As Herm Starrette had learned for the price of five dollars, Steve Dalkowski was no friend to the walls of a baseball park. In 1958, he drilled an outside pitch through the backstop at Fleming Stadium in Wilson, North Carolina. The team officials in Wilson must have been impressed, for fifteen years later, the hole still remained, untouched.

In one unfortunate incident while pitching for Kingsport in 1957, one of Dalkowski's pitches tore off part of the hitter's ear. Some believe that this accident, so early in his career, affected Dalkowski to the point where he feared that he might kill a hitter, which only served to hurt his fragile control.

Three years later, it was an umpire who fell victim to a Dalkowski pitch. During a California League game, the umpire behind home plate was hit by a fastball that sent him flying backward nearly twenty feet, broke his mask in three places, and put him in the hospital for three days with a concussion.

The end began in Spring Training of 1963. While fielding a bunt, Dalkowski felt something let go in his arm as he threw to first base. After returning from the disabled list late in the season, he found that much of the speed had vanished from his fastball. In 1965, he was released by the Orioles. Over the course of the 995 minor league innings he pitched, he amassed 1,396 strikeouts while walking 1,354 batters.

Sadly, he never enjoyed success in life after baseball. A heavy drinker whose exploits in the bar were as notorious as his exploits on the mound, he drifted from job to job and home to home as his drinking increased. After the death of his wife in 1994, he returned home to Connecticut with the assistance of his family and a former teammate. There, he lived in a convalescent home where he was treated for alcohol-related dementia.

So indelible were the impressions he made that the mere mention of his name brings back memories of encounters with him with startling abruptness and clarity.

"Steve Dalkowski, 1958," recited John Romonosky. "I was with Charlotte, North Carolina and he was over in Knoxville with the Baltimore Orioles farm team. They say that he was one of the very few people who could throw a baseball through a car wash and have it come out dry—that's how hard he was throwing."

Brooks Robinson was in Spring Training with Steve Dalkowski and had to bat against him in practice. "Scary," was how he described the experience, "I never liked to hit against guys who had no idea where the ball was going. And he was one of them."

CHAPTER 24

The Hitters

It seems like a dream when you get drafted. Then, all of the sudden, you find out that it's either produce or be gone.

—*Phil Dauphin, outfielder*

The "success" of a ballplayer's career is often measured by whether or not that career included any time in the major leagues. Many talented players have seen their careers unexpectedly stall in double or Triple-A. Regardless of how far they went, some players have made their mark in professional baseball when everything came together, if only briefly, to become pure magic.

Although he was a talented hitter, Rocky Nelson spent many seasons in the Dodgers minor league system. Nelson, a first baseman, was stuck behind the great Gil Hodges on Brooklyn's depth chart for much of his career, although he did play in parts of nine seasons from 1949 through 1961 with the Dodgers, Pirates, Cardinals, and Indians. Nelson made the most of his time in the minors, which included two remarkable single-day feats. During a doubleheader while playing for the Western Association's St. Joseph Cardinals in 1946, he collected hits in nine consecutive at-bats. In 1955, he drove in eleven runs in one game for the Montreal Royals. He won the Triple Crown in the International League in 1955 (leading the league with a .364 batting average, 37 home runs and 118 RBIs) and again in 1958 (.326, 43, 120).

Uncommon Averages

Skeeter Barnes raised some eyebrows in the Cincinnati Reds organization in 1978 as he batted at a .368 clip for the Billings Mustangs of the Pioneer League. However, Barnes' effort fell short of the league—and team—title by ninety-four points. Fellow Mustang Gary Redus tore up the league, finishing with a .462 batting average. Redus' single season mark was the highest in minor league history (based on a minimum of two hundred at-bats in a season) eclipsing the eighty-two-year-old record of .452 set by Bill Krieg of the Western Association's Rockford team in 1896.

Both Redus and Barnes would play in the major leagues following their dream seasons. Redus' best average in the big leagues was .288 for the Rangers in 1993 while Barnes topped out at .286 with Detroit in 1994. Krieg's banner season in the minors came nine years after his last year in the majors. During his four-year big league career, his best season was 1886, during which he managed a .255 average for the Washington Senators.

The Streak

During four years in the majors with the Braves, Pirates, and Giants, outfielder Joe Wilhoit never made much of an impression, compiling a .255 batting average before moving on to the Pacific Coast League in 1919. After the first few weeks of the season, Wilhoit was hitting an anemic .165 for the Seattle Rainiers. He was then traded to the Wichita Jobbers of the Western League. With Wichita, he fared marginally better but still was no threat at the plate with a .198 batting average. Then, in mid-June, everything changed.

Over the next sixty-nine games, Wilhoit hit safely in every contest. During the streak, he batted .505 and finished the season with a .422 batting average. After the Western League's season was over, he moved east to Boston and hit .333 in eighteen at-bats for the Red Sox. After 1919, he spent another four years in the minors before retiring.

His sixty-nine-game hitting streak was a new record for all of professional baseball. In the years that followed, his record remained intact. The biggest threat came in 1933 when San Francisco Seals outfielder Joe DiMaggio hit safely in sixty-one straight games, five better than the major league record he would establish eight years later with the Yankees.

Home Run Derby

In his nine-year career in the major leagues, Justin Clarke hit a total of six home runs. This was nothing unusual for a player during baseball's "Dead Ball Era," the period of baseball in the early twentieth century when balls had an all-rubber core as opposed to the later cork-and-rubber core that made the balls livelier. (During the Dead Ball Era, it was also legal for pitcher to doctor the balls in order to make their pitches harder to hit.) What does stand out in Clarke's statistics is that his big league home run total is two short of the number he hit in one minor league game.

On June 15, 1902, Clarke's Corsicana Oil Citys (this was the team's spelling) were playing hosting the Texarkana Casketmakers in nearby Ennis, Texas because Sunday games were banned in Corsicana. The Texas League match was a blowout, with the Oil Citys burying the Casketmakers 51-3. In twelve at-bats, Clarke slugged eight homers, driving in sixteen runs. Clarke's teammates Bill Alexander and Ike Pendleton also contributed eight hits each in the offensive effort.

This game offered a glimpse into the future of that season. Less than a month after the game, the Texarkana team was disbanded. Corsicana would cruise to the Texas League title, finishing 28 ½ games ahead of second-place Dallas.

Long Distance

John Romonosky remembers the stadium in Guadalajara, Mexico, where he played winter ball, as "a pitcher's paradise." The distance to the outfield fence was 370 feet down the lines and 450 feet in center field. This did not hinder Luke Easter in one game, as he crushed one of Romonosky's pitches well past the 450-foot mark and deep into the centerfield stands.

Before becoming a big league manager, Don Baylor was well known for his hitting exploits in the majors, where he slugged 338 home runs. Jack DiLauro faced Baylor in the minors and will never forget one home run in Spokane. DiLauro threw a pitch low and inside ("shin high," according to DiLauro) that Baylor took downtown.

"He hit me over the friggin' light towers," recalled DiLauro. "Ain't nobody hit a ball that far! I mean *over* the light tower in left center! In those days, the ball wasn't juiced. With the height and everything, that ball had to have gone four hundred and eighty feet. "I was in awe. I just turned around and watched it."

Roy Campanella made a habit of terrorizing pitchers during his major league career with the Dodgers. But the three-time National League MVP and Hall of Famer accomplished something in the minors that he was never able to duplicate over the stretch of 242 big league home runs. During an American Association game in St. Paul, he slugged five home runs in consecutive at-bats.

Another future Dodger great, Duke Snider, also had his share of success in St. Paul. The stadium had a hill in right field with a scoreboard sitting above the outfield fence. To hit a ball far and high enough to clear the fence was a tremendous accomplishment, but Snider drove one ball well over the scoreboard.

"That was a hell of a drive in a jeep," said outfielder Babe Martin, who witnessed the flight.

The longest officially estimated distance of a home run in

professional baseball came during a 1929 Fourth of July game in Oakland, California. The Pacific Coast League contest pitted the visiting Mission Reds against the hosting. On the mound for the Reds was Ernie Nevers, who rose to fame as an All-American football player at Stanford University. The hero-to-be was outfielder Roy Carlyle.

Both participants were ex-major leaguers. Nevers pitched for the St. Louis Browns from 1926 until 1928, compiling a meager 6-12 win-loss record. Carlyle played for the Senators, Red Sox, and Yankees in 1925 and 1926, hitting only nine home runs but batting a very respectable .318.

Carlyle's home run off of Nevers flew into the deepest part of Emeryville Park's cavernous centerfield. Just beyond the outfield fence was the clubhouse, which the ball completely cleared before finally reaching earth beyond it. Using the mark established by eyewitnesses of the landing, the total length from home plate to the spot was measured to be 618 feet.

It Took Long Enough

In the major league box scores that appeared in newspapers on August 2, 1950, Indianapolis Indians first baseman Dale Coogan was credited with a home run in Brooklyn's 21 to 12 thrashing of the Pittsburgh Pirates. Coogan was playing for the Pirates when the game began on June 24 and had homered. Due to approaching darkness, the game was halted in the eight inning with the Dodgers ahead, 19 to 12.

The game was completed when the teams met again on August 1, but by this time, Coogan had been sent down to the American Association. Once the game was finished, all of the statistics became official, finally giving a minor league player his major league home run. It would be the only home run of Coogan's major league career.

A Hint of Things to Come

In 1950, a young Mickey Mantle was playing shortstop for

the McAlester Rockets in the Class-D Sooner State League. Because of his hitting prowess, many of his teammates knew he would be a big leaguer some day, but never as a shortstop. Mantle's defensive skills in the infield were erratic at best.

During one game that season, Mantle committed five errors. He compensated for his fielding at the plate, though, hitting a home run from each side of the plate and driving in eight runs.

Seasons of the Sluggers

While Babe Ruth was setting and resetting major league records in regard to most home runs in a season, he was often coming in second as far as the professional record was concerned. His fifty-four home runs in 1920 broke the twenty-five-year-old record of forty-five set by Minneapolis' Perry Werden in 1895.

Ruth's major league single-season record had grown by fifty-nine before being nudged out by his future teammate Tony Lazzeri. In 1925, Lazzeri led the Pacific Coast League with sixty homers for Salt Lake City. Ruth tied him in 1927, but by that time a new pro record had already been set again the previous year when the Tyler Trojans' Moose Clabaugh lit up the East Texas League with sixty-two round-trippers.

While Clabaugh's mark of sixty-two eluded major leaguers, including Roger Maris, for over sixty years, it did not last long as a minor league record. In 1930, Joe Hauser knocked in sixty-three while playing for the Baltimore Orioles in the International League. Three years later, he eclipsed his own record as a member of the Minneapolis Millers (Perry Werden's old team) when sixty-nine of his hits cleared the fences in parks throughout the American Association.

A share of that record moved south to the lands of the West Texas-New Mexico League in 1948 when Bob Crues also hit sixty-nine home runs while playing for the Amarillo Gold Sox. The new record would last for only six years.

In 1947, an unidentified object crashed down into the desert outside of Roswell, New Mexico. The debate as to whether it was a weather balloon (according to the air force) or an alien spacecraft (according to witnesses) has given birth to countless conspiracy theories, books, and movies.

In 1954, Roswell experienced more phenomena of flying objects, but this time they were headed in an opposite trajectory—away from earth. To find proof of these, however, there is no need to delve into shadows of Area 51 or the realm of science fiction. The proof lies in the six-foot-five-inch form of Joe Bauman, who launched seventy-two homers that season while playing for the Roswell Rockets in the Class C Longhorn League.

Up to that season, Bauman had reached as high as Triple-A in 1948, playing for the Milwaukee Brewers, a franchise of the Boston Braves at the time. Also during that season, he played in Amarillo and got a firsthand look at Bob Crues' home run record. After playing semi-pro ball for three years while running his gas station, he arrived in the Longhorn League in 1952, playing for the Artesia Drillers.

During his two seasons with the Drillers, he hit a total of 103 home runs. During one game against Roswell in 1952, Bauman was held to a single in his first two at-bats by Rockets pitcher Rudie Malone, who had employed a unique strategy against the slugger. Malone, normally a right-hander, pitched left-handed against Bauman, but only lasted a little over three innings as the other Artesia batters pummeled his right-handed pitches. In 1954, Bauman took his potent bat to Roswell and made history.

Hitting in Roswell was a mixed bag for home run hitters. The ballpark was over 3,500 feet above sea level, positioned so that the usual prevailing winds would help carry the ball even further through the thin air. However, a problem for all hitters was the typical minor league lighting of the day. The poor field lights in the minors gave pitchers a huge advantage over their adversaries at the plate.

Along with his seventy-two round-trippers, Bauman also posted a league-leading .400 batting average, 224 RBIs, and a

.916 slugging percentage in only 138 games, which was the length of the Longhorn League's season. Bauman credited his season with the fact that, while he didn't have any specific hot streaks, he didn't suffer through any slumps, either.

"Usually you have three or four slumps a year; short ones, long ones, whatever," he explained. "For some reason, I didn't have any that year. I can't explain it."

Bauman's former Amarillo teammate, Bob Crues, heard about Bauman's assault on his record and wished the Rockets' slugger well. The two players, in fact, remained lifelong friends. Bauman played two more years before retiring from baseball in 1956. With a business to run and a family to support, remaining in baseball on a miniscule salary simply didn't make sense.

Bauman's professional home run mark was eventually passed by Barry Bonds in 2001. The record had almost been broken two years earlier when Mark McGwire topped out at seventy. Bauman was interviewed for this book shortly before the 2001 season began. When asked if he was rooting for any of the game's premier sluggers to break his record, he replied, "Yeah! Hell, these damn records were made to be broken. Whoever can do it, more power to 'em."

While the major leagues twice boasted of two sixty-plus home run hitters in the same season (McGwire and Sosa in 1998 and 1999), the minors can still claim the title for having the most sixty-plus home run sluggers in a season.

In 1956, Dick Stuart led all of professional baseball with sixty-six home runs while playing first base for the Western League's Lincoln Chiefs. (Stuart, a future major league all-star, hit 228 home runs in his big league career, with a personal single season high of forty-two in 1963.) At the same time, Shreveport's Ken Guettler was busy terrorizing Texas League pitchers with sixty-two homers. Finally, Frosty Kennedy of the Plainview Ponies gave pitchers a case of whiplash as they turned to watch their pitches disappear into the heavens above Southwestern League stadiums at a rate of sixty for the season.

Major League Preview

In earlier years, it was common for major league team to occasionally play their minor league affiliates. Not only was this of benefit to the host minor league team as far as attendance was concerned, but it gave the minor league players a chance to show the big league team what that could do.

In 1955, the Baltimore Orioles came to York, Pennsylvania to play their Class-B team in the Piedmont League. Although four levels below the major league, the York White Roses routed their parent club, 13-1.

Although the Orioles players were glad to see no more of York, it would not be the last they would see of some of the York players that year. Impressed by his four-hit performance in the game, the Orioles brought up first baseman Bob Hale the following day. Another York infielder, third baseman Brooks Robinson, who had homered in his first at-bat of the game against the Orioles, would join the team in September of that year.

Fans in attendance at another major-minor league game in 1937 got to see a glimpse of current major league talent and class, courtesy of the Yankees star first baseman, Lou Gehrig. The New York Yankees had come to Butler, Pennsylvania to play their affiliate in the Pennsylvania State Association. In Gehrig's first at-bat, Butler's pitcher struck him in the head with a fastball and knocked him down.

Gehrig refused to take first base and asked the umpire to simply count the pitch as a ball. Hank Sauer, who was playing first base, still vividly recalled Gehrig's reaction more than sixty years later.

"He said, 'People came here to watch us play ball, not walk to first base. I'm going to hit.'"

Gehrig followed through on his promise and promptly followed his beaning with a home run.

All in a Game's Work

August 19, 1958 was not a happy day for the pitching staff of the Chihuahua Dorados in the Class-C Arizona-Mexico League. In their game against the Douglas Copper Kings, they gave up a home run against all nine hitters in the Douglas lineup. This is the first (and to date, only) time in professional baseball history that every member of a team's lineup homered in the same game. Leading the way at the plate, on the mound, and in the dugout was manager and pitcher Bob Clear.

CHAPTER 25

Strange Innings, Part 5

Every single day, you see something you've never seen before—that's the beautiful thing about this game. It never gets boring. I can tell you that much.

—*Eric Wedge, manager*

The Foggiest of Ideas

In the fifth inning of an Appalachian League game during the 1958 season, players and spectators began to notice a bank of fog slowly descending from the surrounding mountaintops. As the game progressed, the fog crept closer, finally enveloping the outfield by the bottom of the ninth inning. The visiting Johnson City Phillies held a slim lead over the Pulaski Cubs, but had to contend with the potential havoc of the fog as well as the Cubs batters.

The Phillies held fast for two outs, and seemed to be on the verge of victory when the next Pulaski hitter turned a pitch into a skyrocketing shot that disappeared into the murk of the outfield air. As the hitter began to run the bases, the Phillies held their breath. However, the centerfielder soon jogged in nonchalantly, cradling the ball in his glove. Upon seeing this, the umpired called the batter out and the win was sealed for the Phillies.

After the team boarded the bus to leave the park, pitcher Joe Short asked the outfielder how he had managed to catch the ball with all of the fog in the field. As it turned out, the fielder never saw the ball. Before the bottom half of the inning, Johnson City manager Eddie Lyons, anticipating problems with the fog, sent each of his outfielders out with a ball tucked in their glove for just such an event as the one that had occurred.

You're Out!

Howard Cosell made a name for himself in broadcasting major sporting events, so it may have come as a surprise that he was ejected from a Texas League game in 1981. During the season, the Tulsa Drillers would play a tape of Cosell saying "It is purely and simply a disgrace." after any questionable call that went against the Drillers.

This occurred repeatedly without incident until the umpiring crew of Larry Dagate and Pam Postema came back into town. Dagate told the Drillers he did not want the tape played while he and Postema were on the field. Team officials, not willing to risk a forfeit, complied.

A Short Loss

Nate Minchey was pitching in a Midwest League game for the Rockford Expos in 1989 when the team found out that he had been traded to the Braves for big league closer Jeff Reardon. Manager Mike Quade immediately pulled Minchey out of the game during the top of the second inning with the Expos behind, 1-0. Never given the chance to help keep his team in the game, Minchey wound up taking the loss for a team to which he no longer belonged.

Long-Distance Scoring

During the 2001 season, Columbus first baseman Nick

Johnson belted two home runs during the Clippers' 15-10 win over the Charlotte Knights. What made Johnson's feat remarkable was that Johnson's homers landed over four hundred miles apart from each other.

Johnson's first bomb came in the first inning at Knights Stadium in Charlotte, South Carolina. The game was suspended in the bottom of the first due to heavy rain and was scheduled for completion a week and a half later when the Knights were in Columbus, Ohio. When the game was resumed in Columbus, Johnson struck again, more than four hundred miles north of where the game had begun.

In another odd twist, Portland Beavers pitcher Brett Jodie was charged with two of the Knights' runs, despite the fact that he was playing in the Pacific Coast League and the Knights and Clippers belonged to the International League.

Jodie had been the Clippers' starting pitcher when the game began in Charlotte and had two Knights on base when the game was suspended. Before the game was resumed, the Yankees (Columbus' parent club) traded Jodie to the San Diego Padres, who placed him with their Triple-A club in Portland. When the game continued in Columbus, both of the Charlotte base runners scored, adding two earned runs to Jodie's statistics.

Too Much Celebration

Joe Nossek was playing for the Charlotte Hornets in the South Atlantic League in 1961 when a win got a little too wild. A teammate of Nossek's had just driven in the winning run when an overly enthusiastic fan ran on to the field to congratulate him. However, the fan tripped and stumbled into the player and both men fell to the ground. Charlotte manager Ellis Clary, believing that one of his players was being attacked, charged out of the dugout and pounced on the fan with both fists flying. As a stunned Nossek observed the scene, the other players managed to pull Clary off of the unfortunate and unwise spectator before much damage was done.

"This was my second or third game and I was thinking, 'What have I gotten myself into?'" recalled Nossek.

We Have Ignition

Dave Dennis, catcher for the Miami Indians of the Kansas-Oklahoma-Missouri League, was watching a nearby argument between his pitcher, Steve Jordan, and umpire George Carney. The words between the two quickly became heated, but it was Dennis who was soon the hottest.

Feeling an odd, prickling sensation on his torso, Dennis shifted his chest protector in discomfort and was amazed to see sparks fall from beneath it. He took the protector completely off, only to have flames begin growing from the cloth cover. Jordan and Carney's debate froze in midstream as the two turned to see Dennis throw his now blazing chest protector to the ground.

The best guess that anyone could offer was that a cigarette might have been accidentally tossed onto the protector as it was lying on the ground while the Indians were at bat the previous half inning.

Off to See the Wizard

Don August spent time with the big league club while in Spring Training with the Houston Astros in 1986. On a trip to Vero Beach to play the Dodgers, he wound up in the locker next to Yogi Berra, the colorful Hall of Famer who was an Astros coach at the time.

While they were changing, Berra began merrily whistling the tune, "If I Only Had a Brain" from *The Wizard of Oz*. As the song went on, Berra put more and more effort and verve into the song. August looked around, unsure if this was some kind of joke to see how he would react, but his teammates went about their business like this was the norm for Berra.

"I thought to myself, 'Wow, I guess this guy does have his goofy angle," August recalled.

Trading Catfish for Perfection

A trade made in 1998 between two teams in two different independent leagues may have been one of the most unusual ones in baseball history, competing with the "Lefty Grove for a fence" swap mentioned in Chapter 2. The Western League's Oxnard Pacific Suns sent pitcher Kenny Krahenbuhl to the Greenville Bluesmen of the Texas-Louisiana League for two players to be named later—and ten pounds of catfish.

The Suns may have enjoyed their catfish dinner, but the Bluesman must have enjoyed Krahenbuhl's Greenville debut even more. In his first start for the Bluesmen, Krahenbuhl faced the Amarillo Dillas, who were feasting on pitchers with a team batting average of .337. Unfazed by their hitting prowess, Krahenbuhl pitched a perfect game against the Dillas.

Atonement

After making an error, many a player desperately seeks the opportunity to redeem himself. Asheville Tourists shortstop Erv Palica was in dire need of such a chance during a Tri-State League game on May 8, 1946. Palica botched eight of his eighteen chances in the field, giving the Anderson A's the opportunity to take the game to extra innings.

The first part of Palica's redemption came when he drove in the winning run in the tenth inning. Shortly thereafter, Tourists manager William Sayles, with the approval of the parent club, shifted Palica from shortstop to pitcher. The move was a wise one, as Palica won fifteen games for the team that season. The following year, Palica was on the mound for the Brooklyn Dodgers for what would be the first of his nine big league seasons.

Great Hit, Lousy Running

Steve Turigliatto, a catcher for the Dallas-Ft. Worth Spurs, hit his first home run of the 1971 Texas League season on August

15. With the blast coming so late in the season, Turigliatto was obviously out of practice in jogging around the bases. During his home run trot, he stumbled and fell on his left arm, breaking his elbow.

CHAPTER 26

The Longest Game

I was thankful I was a baseball player and on the field that night. As time went by, I appreciated it more.

—Dallas Williams, outfielder

This is a game that has its own life now.

—Mike Tamburro, president, Pawtucket Red Sox

It was not exactly what anyone would have called perfect baseball weather on April 18, 1981. Instead, it was a cold, blustery Saturday evening before Easter in Rhode Island when the Rochester Red Wings, the Triple-A affiliate of the Baltimore Orioles, were to take on the hometown Pawtucket Red Sox, Boston's Triple-A team. While the weather was not terribly unusual for that time of year, all other traces of normality soon vanished from McCoy Stadium.

When the game finally emerged from the Twilight Zone, thirty-three innings, sixty-six calendar days, eight hours and twenty-five minutes of game time, and two hundred and nineteen total at-bats—all of these new records—had come and gone in the contest. A total of five runs were scored on thirty-nine hits. Thirteen dozen baseballs saw action, compared to the three dozen balls that are usually used in a game. The losing pitcher was in another team's farm system when the game began. Both third basemen would go on to have Hall of Fame careers in the American League and the winning manager was a part-time pitching coach.

Prior to the 1981 season, the longest game in professional history was a twenty-nine-inning marathon between the Miami Marlins and the St. Petersburg Cardinals. On June 14, 1966, the Florida State League affiliates of the Orioles and Cardinals completed the first nine innings with a 2-2 tie score. Both teams scored one run each in the eleventh inning, but would put no more runners across home plate until the twenty-ninth inning. With the bases loaded and one out in the top of the inning, Fred Rico hit a sacrifice fly to score Mike Hebert from third. Hebert, the current Marlins pitcher, returned in the bottom of the inning to retire the three batters in a row to end the game at 2:29 a.m., after six hours and fifty-nine minutes of play.

Back to 1981: The game was initially delayed when the lights in the left field tower went out, the only time any Pawtucket team personnel can remember that occurring. When the lights were restored an hour later, the game began with the Red Wings' Larry Jones and Pawtucket's Danny Parks starting on the mound for their respective teams.

The two hurlers remained locked in a scoreless duel until the top of the seventh when outfielder Chris Bourjos singled to left field with Mark Corey on second and Dan Logan on first. As Corey hustled around third base, leftfielder Chico Walker fired the ball to catcher Rich Gedman. As both the ball and the runner simultaneously arrived at home plate, Corey narrowly avoided Gedman's tag to give Rochester a 1-0 lead. With two men on and no outs, Red Sox manager Joe Morgan (not the Hall of Fame second baseman) brought in Luis Aponte to relieve Parks. Aponte promptly retired the next three Red Wing batters to begin his four-inning stint in which he allowed no hits while striking out nine batters.

In the ninth inning, Chico Walker got his revenge by hitting a double, then advancing to third base on a wild pitch by Jones. Designated hitter Russ Laribee hit a sacrifice fly ball to the outfield, allowing Walker to score. Pawtucket loaded the bases following Laribee's out, but could not capitalize on their opportunity when Rochester reliever Jeff Schneider came to the mound with two outs and slammed the door on the Sox.

As the game progressed into extra innings, the weather began to play its part. An incredibly strong wind blowing in remained steady, turning several line drives heading for the fence into long outs. Red Wing outfielder Dallas Williams had an inkling that the game would not end quickly after watching what happened to one of Pawtucket's big sluggers.

"When I saw Sam Bowen, a prolific home run hitter in the minor leagues, hit his best bolt out of the stadium and watched the ball come back to the infield, I knew it was going to be a long night."

The temperature continued to drop. The Red Sox attempted to stay warm by burning broken bats in a barrel placed in their dugout. (Although, as the night wore on and the broken wood ran out, it is suspected that more than a few perfectly good bats found their way into the flames—after all, it was still very early in the season to have very many broken bats.) Other fires were started in the bullpens. Players on both teams were running into the clubhouses between innings to soak up some heat. Inside the press box, a betting pool was begun to determine when the inning count would exceed the degrees in temperature. One thing that was not apparently affected by the cold was the fielding; both teams in the game committed a total of only four errors.

"By the seventeenth or eighteenth inning I was pretty much at a crawl coming out onto the field," recalled Pawtucket outfielder Chico Walker. "But tired or not, we were going to be there. Guys gave it their all."

The scoring opportunities remained scarce. In the fifteenth inning, Rochester had runners on first and third with one out before Mike Smithson, the fourth Pawtucket pitcher of the game, shut the Wings down.

Finally, in the twenty-first inning, lightning struck when Red Wings catcher Dave Huppert hit a double off of Win Remmerswaal to drive in Mike Hart and once again gave Rochester the lead. The Sox and the wind came right back in the bottom half, though. Pawtucket first baseman Dave Koza, who was robbed of a home run in the eleventh inning when the wind blew against his line drive to keep it in the park, was aided by the elements this time. Facing veteran hurler Steve Luebber, he hit a pop fly that was caught by the wind and driven just beyond the reach of Red Wings second baseman Tom Eaton for a double. Third baseman Wade Boggs followed Koza to the plate and doubled him in to knot the score at 2-2. The initial jubilation quickly wore off as realization set in.

"A lot of people were saying, 'Yeah, yeah, we tied it, we tied it!'" recalled Boggs. "And then they said, 'Oh no, what did you do? We could have gone home!'"

Luebber, who was usually used in short stints as a closer, pitched eight innings in that game. He described players joking about the length of the game in the fifteenth and sixteenth innings then getting quieter as the inning count grew and a sense of disbelief set in.

"By the twenty-third or twenty-fourth inning, it got to be kind of surreal," Luebber remembered.

"The guys who were out of the game started getting kind of goofy," said Red Wings left fielder Chris Bourjos, who left the game in the tenth inning when Doc Edwards sent a pinch hitter in for him.

Along with the cold, hunger began to take its toll. Pitcher Mike Boddicker had been charting the pitches for the Red Wings, but after the twenty-first inning, there was no room left on the chart to write. He went into the visitors' clubhouse and noticed the post-game meal that had been set up in the ninth inning.

Spying a bowl of potato salad, he immediately dove in—head first.

"He didn't even use his hand or a fork," said Bourjos, who witnessed Boddicker's feast. "He just put his mouth in and started eating it."

In the twenty-second inning, Red Sox skipper Joe Morgan was ejected from the game following an argument with the home plate umpire. Rochester's leadoff hitter was hit by a pitch and awarded first base. Morgan felt that the batter had been leaning over into the strike zone and was struck where his body was in the zone—nullifying the automatic base. Both the skipper and the umpire loudly held to their decisions, which inevitably led to the manager getting the thumb. Morgan's ouster left the managing duties to pitching coach Mike Roarke. Prior to the start of the season, Roarke had been hired as a part-time pitching coach in that he only worked with the team's hurlers when they were at home.

Roarke recalled his impression of his part-time job that had suddenly included a huge amount of unpaid overtime. Before Morgan's forced departure, he turned to the manager and said, "If we have more like this, you can forget it."

Roarke was not the only part-timer getting in some unexpected hours. Rochester's general manager, Bob Drew, had also taken on radio play-by-play duties for the Red Wings away games. In only his second game as a broadcaster, Drew was describing history in the making.

After his ejection, Joe Morgan remained at the park, alternating between the warmth of the team office, which at the time was located behind home plate, and a view of the game by peeking through the backstop. As the night grew late, the office phone rang and Morgan answered it. The caller was his concerned wife, Dottie, who was wondering why he hadn't returned home yet. When he explained that the game was still going on, Dottie Morgan, by now very confused, asked why he was answering the office phone instead of being in the dugout if the game was still in progress.

As the clock rolled past midnight, Pawtucket general manager Mike Tamburro asked the umpiring crew chief, Jack Leitz, when he would suspend the game. Lietz had checked his International League rulebook but had found no rule or guidance as to how late a game was allowed to last. Tamburro brought out a copy of the league charter, which stated that no inning should begin after 12:50 a.m. Unfortunately, that rule had been printed near the bottom of the page. When the rulebooks for that season were printed, a misalignment of that page cut off the last few lines, omitting the 12:50 rule. Without that in his rulebook, Leitz was not about to call the game, regardless of what was printed in the charter. His responsibility was to follow the rulebook only.

And so the game continued. Team officials tried to reach league president Harold Cooper at home to get a decision on suspending the game, but Cooper was out late at a social function. The original crowd of 1,740 fans was steadily decreasing, with cold, fatigue, and perhaps a little sanity getting the better of enthusiasm. Pawtucket owner Ben Mondor made an offer of a free season pass to those fans that remained until the end of the game. About 11:30 that night, the concession stands began giving out free coffee and hot food—whatever anybody wanted to help stay warm.

Mike Smithson's wife stayed at the park throughout the game. In the very late innings, she began picking up some discarded ticket stubs to keep as souvenirs. "We still have them," Smithson said, nearly twenty years later.

Stellar pitching marked the last ten innings in the April portion of the game as both teams were shut out. Joel Finch and Bruce Hurst went five innings apiece for Pawtucket, allowing a combined five hits and four walks while striking out another ten Red Wing batters. From the Rochester bullpen came Jim Umbarger, who pitched the last ten frames with four hits, no walks, and nine strikeouts. Umbarger had no intention of allowing Pawtucket to manufacture a run and warned third baseman Cal

Ripken, Jr. to be prepared for a Red Sox bunt. Ripken stared at his teammate for moment, the fatigue beginning to show.

"I've been watching for the bunt for twenty-three innings now," he sighed to his pitcher.

Like Ripken would later do in the major leagues, Rochester catchers proved themselves to be iron men as well. Dave Huppert had just returned to the lineup after suffering a knee injury and caught the first thirty-one innings before being pinch-hit for in the thirty-second. His replacement behind the plate, Floyd Rayford, had initially entered the game as a pinch-runner and was still in the lineup as the designated hitter. Despite the temperature, Rayford wore nothing heavier than a t-shirt along with his uniform jersey to the amazement of his teammate Dallas Williams.

"At around three in the morning I realized how much of an animal Floyd Rayford was," said Williams. "It must have been thirty degrees."

Finally, in the thirty-second inning, Harold Cooper was reached by phone and he gave the directive to suspend the game when the current inning was finished. At 4:07 a.m., the last out was made and it was time to go home. The teams would play their regularly scheduled game later that day and complete the suspended contest the next time the Red Wings were in town, which wouldn't be until June.

The twenty diehard fans remaining at the park received their season passes, and players headed to the showers. The excitement didn't end for some as the sun was rising that Easter morning. When Luis Aponte returned home, he found that his wife had locked him out of their home. She refused to let him in, not believing that his night-long absence was actually due to a baseball game. It took a phone call from team officials to convince her that her husband was indeed telling the truth.

"I don't think he got into that house until after seven o'clock that morning," said Mike Tamburro.

Aponte wasn't the only one having trouble getting some sleep.

The weary Red Wings players, unaware that of the record they had broken, began getting phone calls from reporters almost as soon as they got back to their hotel rooms. Mike Tamburro wasn't able to leave McCoy Stadium until after six in the morning. He went home, showered, attended Easter Mass, then returned to the ballpark to prepare for the afternoon game.

The string of extra innings nearly carried over into the game played that afternoon. The Red Sox came into the bottom of the ninth with the score tied at three apiece. Visions of another 4 a.m. finish were swept away, though, when Sam Bowen swatted a three-run homer in the home half of the inning to give Pawtucket the win after a mere nine innings.

(Pawtucket would have one more marathon contest in 1981. On July 26, the Sox dropped a 4-2 decision to the Richmond Braves in a game that lasted twenty innings.)

By the time the Red Wings returned to Pawtucket on June 23, the baseball world had radically changed. The major leagues were currently out of business due to the player's strike. Among those players on the picket lines was Steve Luebber, who had been called up to Baltimore before the strike. With no big league games to cover, and with a historical game to be completed, the media turned up in droves from all over the country as well as from overseas. The crowd of newspeople was too large for the facilities at McCoy Stadium. Pawtucket team owner Ben Mondor spent five thousand dollars on temporary media facilities behind home plate and on catering.

"It was the first time that most of us had been around that kind of media exposure," recalled Mike Smithson.

Joining the media was Bob Drew again, this time in a different capacity. During the season following the events in April, Drew was fired as Red Wings general manager. With the loss of his job also came the loss of his radio assignment. However, WFBR, the radio flagship station for the Baltimore Orioles, had been broadcasting Red Wings games during the strike. The station brought Drew back to Pawtucket, this time as a color analyst.

Although he would still have to sit out the remainder of the game, Joe Morgan was looking forward to becoming a part of history. "We wanted to play a forty-inning game—a record never to be challenged," said the former manager. "It was a World Series atmosphere with hundreds of media and TV people—a great attraction."

When the game finally resumed in the top of the thirty-third, Rochester managed one hit, but had nothing to show for it as Red Sox pitcher Bob Ojeda kept the scoreless streak alive. Taking the mound for the Red Wings in the bottom half of the inning was Steve Grilli, a major league veteran who had been with the Syracuse Chiefs, Toronto's Triple-A affiliate, when the first thirty-two innings were played. In May, the Blue Jays released Grilli, who was then signed by the Orioles and assigned to Rochester. Grilli was chosen by Doc Edwards to resume the game because he felt that Grilli's major league experience would be beneficial in handling all of the hype surrounding the game.

Grilli quickly ran into trouble when he hit lead-off batter Marty Barrett with a pitch. Barrett moved to third on a hit-and-run play off the bat of Chico Walker. Russ Laribee, whose sacrifice fly way back in the ninth sent the game into extra innings, followed Walker. Red Wings manager Doc Edwards had Grilli intentionally walk Laribee to load the bases and set up a possible force out at home. Edwards then replaced Grilli with Cliff Speck, another recent addition to the Red Wings.

The Red Sox had Dave Koza and Wade Boggs, the duo who had combined for the tying run in the twenty-first inning, coming to bat. Boggs never had a chance for heroics. With the count knotted at two balls and two strikes, Koza swung at a curveball that he admitted was probably a little outside and lined the pitch for a single to left field to safely bring Barrett home. As the years have passed since then, the strength and distance of Koza's hit have grown when spoken about by fans, much to the amusement of the hitter.

"It was a soft line drive to left," he stated emphatically. "It still is a soft line drive to left, but people come up to me and say, 'Jeez, you hit that home run!' No, it was a soft line drive."

At 6:20 p.m., the game was finally over. By coincidence, when Koza was at bat, the local newscast teams were doing live shots at the stadium and brought the game-winning hit directly into households throughout baseball-starved New England.

Koza's hit wasn't the only thing that grew in size after the game. If all of the claims from people who said they were at the game are true, McCoy Stadium must have been filled to over one hundred times its seating capacity.

"Everybody in Rhode Island was here for the longest game," Mike Tamburro said, laughing.

Among the oddities in the game were certain numbers and how they pertained to Koza. The game began on April 18 and years later, one of his daughters was born on the same date. The game's closing date, June 23, matched the uniform number, twenty-three, that he wore for Pawtucket.

While still in Triple-A, the participants from both teams did get their feet in the door at Cooperstown. Later that summer, the Hall of Fame created a display on the game, which included the official scorecard and Bob Drew's thirty-two inning broadcast among other items. Among the other professional records set in the game were most strikeouts by a team, thirty-four (Rochester); total strikeouts by both teams, sixty; most individual at-bats, fourteen (Pawtucket's Lee Graham, Chico Walker, and Dave Koza); and most individual plate appearances, fifteen (Rochester's Tom Eaton, Dallas Williams, and Cal Ripken, Jr.).

Koza had the most hits of any player in the game, getting five. Teammate Wade Boggs and Rochester first baseman Dan Logan each had four hits in twelve at-bats. Years later, looking back at Boggs' "mere" .333 average in the contest, Chico Walker quipped, "he had an off game."

Players in Triple-A, being on the cusp of the major leagues, are very much aware of their statistics, as they know the big league team is also constantly looking at those same numbers. In accordance with baseball rules, none of the statistics from the game had been entered into the players' records until the game was concluded. Once the numbers were factored in, they provided mixed results. Pitchers wanted their innings added to lower their earned run averages, but hitters were not looking forward to 1-for-11 additions to their batting averages.

Chico Walker, who was 2-for-14 at the plate, saw his batting average drop significantly after the game was finished. "After they added the stats on, I went from something like .315 [or] .318 to .292," he remembered.

When Rochester left fielder Chris Bourjos was replaced by a pinch hitter in the tenth inning, it was the first time in his career he had been pinch-hit for. "I was upset about it at the time," Bourjos remembered. "But by the twentieth inning, I wasn't too upset about because I was two-for-four and a lot of guys were having a pretty bad night."

The fortunes of the players in the game took many different paths in the passing years. Cal Ripken and Wade Boggs punched their return tickets to Cooperstown during their major league careers. Losing pitcher Steve Grilli, who had pitched for Detroit and Toronto in the 1970s, never returned to the major leagues. His son, Jason, made his major league pitching debut for the Florida Marlins on May 11, 2000 with a win over the Atlanta Braves. Other players, such has Luis Aponte, Bruce Hurst, Bob Ojeda, Mike Smithson, Marty Barrett, Chico Walker, Rich Gedman, and Floyd Rayford would see significant playing time in the majors. Dallas Williams played briefly in the majors with the Orioles and Reds and coached first base for the Colorado Rockies and currently for the Boston Red Sox. Dave Huppert played for the Orioles and Brewers before becoming a minor league manager. With over a thousand wins in his managerial career, he is currently the skipper of the Edmonton Trappers in the Pacific Coast League.

The managers in the game, all of them former big league players, returned to the majors as coaches and managers. Doc

Edwards served the Indians as both coach and manager and later coached the Mets. Joe Morgan coached and managed the Boston Red Sox, leading the team to two division titles in 1988 and 1990. Mike Roarke, the winning manager of record in the longest game, added St. Louis, San Diego, and Boston to his major league coaching resume.

Dave Koza, the game's final hero, never saw action in the majors. He still lives in Pawtucket and is recognized by many of the locals. While not actively involved in baseball on a full-time basis, he does participate in some area youth clinics for the sport. Despite the lack of major league time in his baseball career, he has many fond memories, and is proud to have been a professional ballplayer.

"People like the fans at McCoy make the game. I'm grateful to have been a part of it. Being able to do it all over again, I would. I would do some things differently, but all in all, I love baseball."

CHAPTER 27

This Is the Life: Welcome to the Show

Everything is bigger and better [in the majors]—
the crowds, paychecks, etc.

—Brian Tollberg, pitcher

There's no exact certainty as to when, or if, the call will come. When it does, the player has arrived. He is informed that he is now part of a select group of baseball players wearing the uniform of the major leagues. From convenience store cuisine and fast food to steak and lobster; from all-night bus rides to first-class charters; from the small-town fields in Pocatello and Bowie to the diamond palaces of New York and Chicago; the long, dusty roads of the minors have finally led to The Show.

When Steve Fireovid was brought up to San Diego for the first time in 1981, he found that the Padres clubhouse was slightly smaller than the one for their Triple-A team in Hawaii. But it was the atmosphere that made the physical size irrelevant.

"The thing that's different between the minor leagues and the major leagues is the electricity," Fireovid explained. "It's the adrenaline."

The call comes with no guarantee of fame, or even longevity. The majors are the final, grand stage where the athlete must prove once again that he belongs there. Whether it is by virtue of talent, the result of a trade, or an injury on the big league roster, the challenge and opportunity is given. Many players are sent back to the minors after their first big league appearance, but there is always the hope of the return.

"I had thirty-eight days in the big leagues," said Chris Bourjos, who played for the San Francisco Giants in 1980. "They were the quickest thirty-eight days of my life."

All of Brooks Robinson's minor league managers had stressed the importance of maintaining an emotional even keel. "Don't get too high, don't get too low. You could be a hero in one game and a goat in the next," was the oft-repeated mantra.

In his first game during his first call-up in September of 1955, he had two hits and drove in a key run. He then discovered how steep the slopes were after being on top of the mountain, going hitless in his next eighteen at-bats, including ten strikeouts.

"I knew that I had a lot to learn," said Robinson of his managers' advice. "That was a pretty good lesson."

Although the Orioles had called him up to the majors at the end of several seasons, Robinson was aware that his future was still in doubt. "There was a question as to whether I would ever be a big league player. No one offered me a lot of money when I signed. I was a very average—at best—runner, average arm, good fielder, good hitter in Legion Ball, but hitting is one thing. You could take the greatest hitters out of high school or college and maybe they won't make it. 'Will he ever hit big league pitching?' That was the question in the eyes of all the managers I played for."

In 1958, he spent his first full season in Baltimore and struggled at the plate with a .238 batting average. After the season, he spent six months on active duty in the Arkansas National Guard as part of his military obligation. He managed to still play ball and was looking forward to 1959 as his breakout year. He was platooned early in the season, but was still confident that he would eventually be made the everyday third baseman. On May

18, his twenty-second birthday, manager Paul Richards told him he was being sent down to Vancouver for a month to play every day and get himself back in to peak playing form.

"That was more of a blow to my ego than anything else. All these thoughts are running through my mind—'Do they want send me out because they don't think I'm going to be able to do it here? What are all my friends in Arkansas going to think? Here I was, playing in the major leagues and now I'm back in the minors.'

"What I thought was the worst thing that could have happened to me was actually the best thing that could have happened to me. It was like night and day. I was a different player when I got back. I had matured, had gotten stronger physically."

Robinson was called back to Baltimore shortly before the All-Star break and remained with the Orioles until his retirement in 1977. During his career in Baltimore, he set a new standard for excellence at third base, winning sixteen Gold Gloves and making fifteen All-Star appearances. He was voted the American League Most Valuable Player in 1964 and was elected to the Hall of Fame in 1983.

Rex Hudler was seventeen when he signed with the Yankees. At the time, he figured that he would be playing in New York in three years. During his eighth minor league season, he finally got his call to The Show when his manager called him in his hotel room to tell him that his flight was leaving in two hours.

If the years of toiling toward the majors can take their toll, those last few days can really push one to the edge. John Herrnstein spent his final six days in Triple-A playing a double header each day in Rochester, Syracuse, and Buffalo at the end of season to make up for previous rain-outs. Immediately following that twelve-game avalanche in 1962, he was called up to Philadelphia.

In 1984, Jim Pankovits was back playing for the Tucson Toros in the Astros organization after a stint in the Padres farm system. The Toros had just completed a series in Las Vegas. As was the practice, the players received wakeup calls at four in the morning to catch their six o'clock flight to their next stop in Hawaii. He had been up all night since it was usually fruitless to try to sleep between a night game and an early wakeup, "especially in Las Vegas." The team arrived in Honolulu at three in the afternoon, whereupon he was informed that had been called up to the big leagues. He had a six o'clock flight going back to the mainland and finally arrived in Houston at ten the following morning. "That was the longest travel day I ever had."

With the amount of time spent in the Astros organization and having played with the big league team in Spring Training, he knew many of the players on the Astros. Pankovits credits those teammates for his easy transition to the major leagues and as "the biggest reason I got off to a fairly good start." After his prolonged travel day, he did not play in the first game he was on the roster for. The following day, he was put in as a pinch hitter against the Pirates' Rod Scurry and got a base hit.

Unlike Pankovits, Jon Zuber knew virtually no one on the Phillies major league roster when he was first called to the big leagues just two and a half weeks into the 1996 season. In fact, his call-up was so unexpected that he had no way of getting from Scranton to Philadelphia, so he wound up riding there with a coach. Upon arriving in the Phillies clubhouse, he did his best to keep a low profile.

"I didn't want to make any waves. I just wanted to hide in the background until I got my bearings and figured out what was going on," recalled Zuber.

The call can come within a series of downs and ups. Bryan Eversgerd was feeling very upset with himself and the world one day in New Orleans. The Louisville Redbirds pitcher had given up four earned runs in one third of an inning. As he was walking through the hotel lobby, his manager, who was on the phone, motioned him over and handed him a note that read: "Go pack. You're going to St. Louis tomorrow!"

In his first game, he fired his first big league pitch to Steve

Finley, who stroked it for a single. Eversgerd then came back to retire the next three hitters, including one with a strikeout.

Dallas Williams' initial plans for making the majors in four years had come and gone by the end of the 1979. Despite that, he stayed in the game and got his reward two years later. The season of 1981 was already a memorable one for him, as he had played in the thirty-three-inning marathon for Rochester. After the Red Wings clinched a playoff spot in late August, manager Doc Edwards summoned Williams and teammate John Shelby to tell them the news that they were on their way to Baltimore.

Cal Hogue had already experienced plenty of trials in the minors. Signed by the St. Louis Browns out of high school as a pitcher and outfielder in 1945, he was released by the team after tearing up his knee in 1947. He got a second chance in the Pirates farm system the following year, this time as strictly a pitcher. He progressed through the organization and was told during Spring Training of 1952 that he would make the major league roster.

Instead, he was sent to Charleston, South Carolina, where he had a 10-3 record by mid-season. After giving up a game-winning home run with two outs in the ninth inning of a game in July, he found out that the Pirates had purchased his contract and that he was on his way the The Show.

In his first big league game, he pitched two innings of relief. Two days later, he pitched a complete game against the Phillies, winning 2-1.

As the 1961 Pacific Coast League season was coming to a close, twenty-one-year-old outfielder Mike Hershberger was looking forward to his team's road trip to Hawaii. However, his trip to paradise was rerouted to Minneapolis when the White Sox tabbed him to replace Jim Landis, who had just been injured. Although he missed some time among the beaches and palm trees, he got his first crack at the major leagues.

In his first game, he went one-for-three against the Twins' pitching ace, Camilo Pascual. In that same game, he had a bit of an adventure when Minnesota slugger Harmon Killebrew crushed a towering fly ball that disappeared into the fog above the outfield. After losing track of the ball, Hershberger attempted to guess the trajectory and was able to get close enough to catch the ball once it became visible again.

Hall of Fame second baseman Bobby Doerr was still a teenager when he reported to the Red Sox Spring Training camp in 1937. What stood out the most from his experience was meeting players whose careers he had followed as a schoolboy. He was practically speechless as he was introduced to stars Joe Cronin and Jimmie Foxx, two other future members of the Hall of Fame.

"I had these guys' pictures pasted on my wall at home," he recalled.

For Tom Parsons, the major leagues came so tantalizing close, only to fall hopelessly out of reach. While pitching for Columbus in 1961, Parsons was called up to Pittsburgh, but the team needed him to pitch one more game in Triple-A. During that game, he injured his arm and could not pitch again for the rest of the year.

He spent all of the 1962 season trying to get his arm back in shape. With the science of sports medicine still in its infancy, Parsons was forced to throw repeatedly to tear the scar tissue loose in his arm. The year 1963 was another repeated season in Triple-A, but his struggles paid off with a September summons to the Pirates.

His first game was against the Braves in Milwaukee. Before the game, a sportswriter asked him how it felt to be going up against big leaguers. Parsons responded, "It doesn't bother me. They put their pants on one leg at a time, just like I do."

The Braves proceeded to tag Parsons for seven hits and four runs before he was pulled after four innings. When he returned to the clubhouse, the same sportswriter asked him how he felt about big leaguers now. "Well," admitted Parsons, "maybe they put 'em on two legs at a time."

Dave Campbell was on cloud nine after the fifth and final game of the 1967 Governor's Cup, the Triple-A championship series. He had just scored the winning run for the Toledo Mud Hens in the bottom of the tenth inning. Five minutes later, in the midst of the clubhouse celebration, manager Jack Tighe told Campbell that he would be joining the Tigers the following day.

Having just successfully completed one championship run, Campbell quickly found himself in another one as Detroit was locked in a very tight, four-team chase for the American League pennant with Boston, Minnesota, and Chicago. By this time, everyone with the Tigers was on edge, which added to Campbell's nervousness during his first big league appearance. Stepping in to pinch-hit against Washington's Frank Bertaina, he was summarily struck out.

Ken Brett also broke into the majors during the stretch run of that famous 1967 American League dogfight. Called up by the Red Sox in September, he pitched in his first game on the twenty-seventh of that month. During the final week of the season, Boston lost two players to injuries before clinching the pennant, leaving Brett as the only left-handed reliever on the club. Barely more than a week after his first major league game, Brett was pitching in the World Series.

"I was in so far over my head, I had no idea what I was doing," he recalled. "Of course, I was only nineteen years old."

In 1934, the Nebraska State League, which was completely comprised of teams with no affiliations to major league clubs, was in danger of bankruptcy when Cardinals general manager Branch Rickey offered the league the chance to stay afloat. In exchange for his choice of two players from each team, Rickey gave the league two thousand dollars. The league agreed to the proposal and Lincoln third baseman Don Gutteridge was one of the players selected by Rickey. Now a part of a major league farm system, he played for Cardinals teams in Houston and Columbus, Ohio before reaching St. Louis in September of 1936.

On September 7, Gutteridge played in his first major league game as the Cardinals took on the Pittsburgh Pirates. In the second inning of that game, he bobbled a grounder at third hit by Bill

Brubaker, then proceeded to throw it over first baseman Johnny Mize's head. The ball careened off a wall behind first base into right field, where outfielder Pepper Martin fielded it. Seeing that Brubaker was trying for third, Martin fired the ball to Gutteridge with plenty of time to spare. As he slid into third base, Brubaker kicked the ball out of Gutteridge's glove and was called safe. On a single play in his first game, Gutteridge was charged with three errors.

He trudged back to the dugout, expecting the worst from his teammates, but to the rookie's relief, they were empathetic. "Two or three of them said, 'We all make errors now and then,'" Gutteridge recalled.

Al Rosen was playing for Oklahoma City when he was told by the minor league team's owner that he was being called up to Cleveland. The Indians were in New York, but Cleveland's owner, Bill Veeck, was in Chicago and wanted Rosen to fly there first so he could meet him. When Rosen arrived in Chicago at six in the morning, Veeck was there to greet him with a one thousand-dollar check. "I was in awe. I had never seen a thousand dollars before in my entire life," Rosen remembered.

Veeck then took Rosen out for breakfast. Eating with a big league owner, having a fortune tucked in one pocket, and knowing that the major leagues were a few hours away, gave that morning a surreal cast for the young third baseman. Reality came calling soon enough, though.

In his first major league at-bat, Rosen was overwhelmed and hardly knew what to do. He came to the plate at Yankee Stadium to pinch hit and struck out against Joe Page. A few years later, Rosen was talking to Charlie Berry, who had been the umpire at home plate, and asked him if the pitches he had swung at were even strikes.

"I absolutely didn't know where I was," Rosen said of his first big league appearance. "Can you imagine? A little ol' southern boy from South Florida, first at bat in the big leagues at Yankee Stadium against the best relief pitcher in the game at that time."

Don August was promoted to the Milwaukee Brewers on June 2, 1988. Flying from Denver, he arrived in Milwaukee, but only one of his bags made it with him; the other two were lost. Fortunately, the one bag that did arrive had his baseball gear in it. After the luggage mishap, things quickly began to improve.

Brewers manager Tom Trebelhorn told him he would be starting in a few days, but that they would try to get him into a game in relief to get his feet wet. As it tuned out, August was called in that very first game with the Brewers losing to the Angels. To add to the thrill, the game was being broadcast back home in California, so he knew that his friends and family would be watching his debut. He pitched two scoreless innings, during which time the Brewers took the lead for good and gave him the victory.

In 1982, Mike Smithson was pitching for the Denver Bears, the Rangers' top farm team, in a game in Omaha, Nebraska. He was doing well in the game and had just regained the strikeout lead in the American Association when manager Rich Donnelly pulled him out of the game after the third inning. Smithson was mystified as to why he had been lifted and Donnelly had little to say. After letting Smithson stew for a while, Donnelly finally told him to pack his bags for Texas.

His first start came on August 27, 1982 at Baltimore's Memorial Stadium against Oriole star Jim Palmer. Smithson pitched a complete game, but came out on the losing end of a 3-2 decision.

Bill Lee was pitching in Pittsfield, Massachusetts when manager Billy Gardner told him not to bother going on a road trip with the Eastern League team. Later that day, Lee was contacted by the Red Sox front office and told to report to Boston. He packed his belongings into his '62 Chevy and drove into Boston, unaware that his first big league challenge would arise before setting foot in a stadium.

Boston is notorious for poor driving conditions, with narrow roads and bizarre traffic patterns. Lee assumed he was in good shape when he spotted Fenway Park's left field wall. After driving past the famous "Green Monster," he made a couple more turns to get to the parking area, only to eventually wind up across the Charles River in Cambridge.

After arriving at the park, he was informed that he would only be there for a short duration while Sparky Lyle was fulfilling an army reserve duty. But after an injury to Jim Lonborg, Lee wound up staying in the majors for good.

In his first major league game, Lee walked the first two hitters on full counts under some strange circumstances. The first hitter wrenched his back during a swing and had to be replaced by a pinch-hitter. The second batter hit a double, but the umpire was slow to turn around on it and ruled it a foul. After the ensuing argument ended, he continued his at-bat before being walked. The third batter hit a sharp ground ball to third that George Scott went deep on and turned into a spectacular double play. Lee finally struck out the next batter and was out of the inning.

In the seventh inning on September 13, 1979, Baltimore manager Earl Weaver sent Tom Chism into the game as a defensive substitute at first base. Chism still vividly remembers what it felt like to step onto major league field for the first time.

"Shaky. I looked up into the stands and it seemed like there were sixty thousand people there. I looked at the batter and was thinking, 'Please don't hit it to me.'"

The regular season of 1998 couldn't have started any better for A.J. Hinch. Oakland manager Art Howe had told the former Stanford and Olympic Team catcher that he had made the big league roster near the end of Spring Training. In his first game, he batted like a seasoned veteran. Unfortunately, many seasoned veterans were going 0-for-4 at the plate against Pedro Martinez. Two days later, he got his first major league hit against another Cy Young Award winner, David Cone.

By 1974, Sixto Lezcano had played at every level in the minor leagues as well as winter ball in his native Puerto Rico. He was doing well in the Pacific Coast League when he was called up to Milwaukee.

"I was anxious or hyper and crazy to show what I could do with the big boys," he recalled of his first day in the majors.

In his first game, against the Baltimore Orioles, he went 3-for-5, getting his first hit against Dave McNally. His third hit of the game was the biggest, though, as he drove in the winning run in the twelfth inning.

At the close of the 1993 Triple-A season, Pawtucket Red Sox pitcher Nate Minchey's name wasn't on the list of big league September call-ups. Disappointed, Minchey and his wife packed their belongings into their car and drove toward home in Texas. Along the way, they stopped to visit some friends in Arkansas for two days. Once they finally arrived home on a Thursday, Minchey's mother told him that Boston had been trying to contact him for the previous two days. When he called the team, he was told to catch a flight immediately as he was slated to start the following Sunday in Cleveland in place of the injured starter, Danny Darwin.

Minchey's entire family came up to Cleveland to watch his debut. When asked how many tickets he wanted on the pass list for the game, he requested forty. Fortunately, both teams were out of the pennant race, so there were plenty of seats available.

He got off to a rough start, walking the Indians leadoff hitter, Kenny Lofton, with his first four pitches. Lofton promptly stole second base on the fifth pitch. Carlos Baerga then hit the sixth pitch into right field to score Lofton. Then Minchey settled down, although he was still shaking a bit on the inside, as the Red Sox cruised to an 11-1 win.

"Each inning, I told myself, 'Just one more inning and that will surely be it,'" he recalled. "Before I knew it, the ninth inning came and I had a complete game."

By 1995, Chris Nichting had endured four surgeries since being drafted by the Dodgers seven years before. While pitching for the Texas Rangers' Triple-A farm team in Oklahoma City that May, he wasn't anticipating any move to the majors in the near future. One day, while in the clubhouse to pick up his check, the clubhouse manager told him before Oklahoma City manager Greg Biagini could get the chance.

"For me, it was almost like my work finally came to fruition, not so much like, 'Wow! I'm finally getting my chance,'" said Nichting of his feelings at the time.

After getting his cup of coffee that year, he returned to life as a minor league journeyman. In 1996, he had undergone yet another operation. He then resumed playing in the farm systems of the Rangers, Yankees, and Indians. Although the majors were becoming a distant memory, he still felt he could pitch at the top level. Mark Brandenburg, a teammate from Texas, advised him, "Play until you can't play anymore."

The big leagues finally beckoned again in August of 2000 as the Indians were battling for the division title. Having had an earlier taste of the majors, the satisfaction of getting called up this time was even greater for Nichting.

John Wehner was also familiar with repeated trips up to the major leagues. Wehner first broke into the majors with Pittsburgh on July 17, 1991. The Pirates were also the team Wehner grew up rooting for. When stepping into the clubhouse for the first time, he couldn't believe he was finally walking among his heroes.

"I was in awe," recalled Wehner. "These were guys I idolized in high school."

Through most of his career, he split his seasons between Triple-A and the National League. But the thrill of getting the big league call never lost its edge with Wehner. "It's sweet from the first to the last time," he explained.

In need of another pitcher, the Yankees traded minor league outfielder Jim Greengrass to the Cincinnati Reds for hurler Ewell

Blackwell late in the 1952 season. After the trade, Greengrass was immediately called up to the Reds. Greengrass eventually met Blackwell eight years later and still recalls their conversation.

"I said, 'Hey, Blackie, I just want to thank you for getting me to the big leagues.' And he said, 'Now Jim, I've been looking for you to thank you for getting me to the World Series!'"

Greengrass' first major league game came on September 9 when he was sent in to pinch-hit against the Boston Braves. Braves ace Warren Spahn was on the mound and Del Rice was the catcher. Greengrass stepped to the plate against the crafty left-hander, ready to prove he belonged there, but his nerves had other ideas.

Without warning, his right leg began jumping. Greengrass called time and stepped out of the batter's box to try to relax his leg. But the nerves flared up again three more times just before the pitch was thrown. After the fourth time, umpire Jocko Conlan walked around Rice and began brushing some nonexistent dirt from the home plate. Turning to Greengrass, he said, "For Christ's sake, kid, let him throw the ball or we're gonna be here all night!" When the first pitch, a ball up high, was finally thrown, all of the nervousness left Greengrass.

"It was like someone had turned off a faucet," he said, describing the experience.

After fouling off the next two pitches, Greengrass was called out on an inside slider that was out of the strike zone. When he tried to protest the call, Conlan, a future Hall of Fame umpire, said to him, "You're not spending any more time up here. You've been here all night, now."

In the spring of 1947, Mel Parnell was one of six pitchers (four veterans and two rookies) competing for the final two roster spots on the Boston Red Sox. When Boston manager Joe Cronin eventually chose Parnell and fellow rookie Harry Dorish, there was some resentment by the veterans toward rookies. Parnell explained the situation.

"The old veterans were all friends. They hated to see a rookie come in and knock out one of their friends. It took a little while for us to get warmed up with the rest of the team. For the first month or so, it was pretty much that way, but then we became accepted and we were just like the old veterans after that."

Parnell lost his first game, 3-2, to the Washington Senators on a passed ball by catcher Frankie Hayes. The young pitcher was still mindful of his rookie status.

"I wasn't going to say anything to him because he was an old veteran," Parnell recounted.

His first win came against Detroit, 4-1. Parnell's victory also snapped the nine-game winning streak of Tigers hurler and future Hall of Famer, Hal Newhauser.

John Romonosky was promoted to Columbus, the Cardinals Triple-A club, in 1953 and proceeded to win three consecutive games. The streak turned sour, though, as he lost the next two, both of them by close scores and with him pitching all nine innings in each. While thinking of what may happen to him next in Triple-A, he was informed by Columbus' general manager, George Sisler, that he was going to join the Cardinals on the road in Philadelphia.

On his first day with the Cardinals, he was witness to a pitchers' duel between two 20-game winners, the Phillies' Robin Roberts and the Cardinals' Harvey Haddix. The biggest thrill came days later in his on-field debut against the Milwaukee Braves.

"Coming from southern Illinois—Cardinal territory—a Cardinal fan, always listening to Harry Caray broadcasting the Cardinal games, we never missed a game," said Romonosky. "I never realized that years later I would hear that same man, Harry Caray, calling my name, 'Now pitching for the St. Louis Cardinals, John Romonosky,'"

Romonosky pitched well despite surrendering a home run to slugger Joe Adcock. While he struck out the Braves' star third baseman Eddie Mathews once, he considered himself lucky in another at-bat to hold Mathews to a double after attempting to get a fastball by the future Hall of Famer. In the bottom of the sixth, Stan Musial tied the score at three runs apiece by launching a two-run homer.

In 1953, the major league teams were still traveling by train, not by a chartered airliner. With no way of delaying a scheduled departure, the game was called (to be completed later) with the score still tied after seven innings to allow the Cardinals to catch their train.

Jim Bolger wound up doing things in reverse order. Immediately after being signed by the Reds out of high school in 1950, he was taken with the team on a road trip. His first major league at-bat came in a pinch-hitting situation at Wrigley Field; the result was a ground out. After the road trip, the Reds sent him to Charleston, West Virginia to start his minor league career. He would later spend more time in the majors with the Reds, Cubs, Indians, and Phillies.

In 1970, Kansas City was looking for a left-handed starter for their pitching rotation. They had three candidates on their Triple-A team in Omaha—Bill Butler, who had pitched in Kansas City the previous year, and Paul Splittorff and Lance Clemens, neither of whom had any major league experience.

Omaha skipper Jack McKeon thought Splittorff should get the nod. But Kansas City manager Bob Lemon, himself a former pitching star, thought that Splittorff didn't throw hard enough. With no consensus for the best candidate, Kansas City's general manager, Cedrick Tallis, came to Omaha to watch the three pitch. Splittorff got the win in a 2-1 nailbiter. Butler was shelled early in his start and Clemens was thrown out of his game.

So began Splittorff's major league career. He would win 166 games for the Royals over the span of fifteen seasons.

When Blake Stein was called up to Oakland in 1998, he may have been the last one on the team to know. On a day that he was scheduled to start for Triple-A Edmonton, his catcher, Izzy Molina, called him to ask if he had been called up to the majors. Molina's suspicions had been aroused when he learned that his own roommate was going to start in place of Stein. Rumors began to spread that he was going to Oakland until, hours later, manager Mike Quade gave Stein the official word.

Pat Ahearne was pitching well in Triple-A Toledo and began to hear talk among his teammates that he was about to be called up to Detroit. Ahearne, though, avoided any such rumors despite his eagerness to play in the majors.

"It's kind of like you don't want to say anything to jinx it," he said.

One morning, he received a phone call in his apartment. It was a radio sports talk show host asking him how he thought he'd be able to contribute to the Tigers ball club.

Not sure what to make of this, Ahearne told the host that he was still pitching for Toledo. The host, now just as perplexed as Ahearne, apologized for disturbing him and hung up. Shortly thereafter, Ahearne arrived at the field for pre-game practice, only to be told that he would be starting against the Yankees the next night at Tiger Stadium.

"It was the kind of thing, like, 'Get on the phone and call everybody you know.'"

Unlike Ahearne, Dave Stapleton didn't have to make many phone calls. His parents had traveled from Alabama to Pawtucket, Rhode Island to watch him play in Triple-A during the 1980 season. That same day, he was told to report to Boston. After receiving the news, the Stapletons extended their trip by one more hour to the north to watch their son make his major league debut.

Tom Grieve was not expecting his call-up while playing Triple-A ball in July of 1967. After playing a night game in Denver, he caught a red-eye flight to New York to join the Washington Senators in a doubleheader against the Yankees. He arrived in New York at 11:30 a.m. and arrived at Yankee Stadium shortly before the start of the first game.

He wasn't expecting to play that day as the players had finished their practice by the time he got on the field a half hour before the game. No coach told him he was playing, but he noticed his name on the line-up card posted in the dugout—batting second.

Panic set in. With no sleep the previous night, he ran some wind sprints in the outfield and played some catch just before game time. There was no time for batting practice.

In his first at-bat, against Fritz Peterson on the mound, he grounded out to the shortstop.

"It didn't matter," said Grieve. "I just wanted to hit the ball and not strike out."

When Bobby Thomson made his major league debut with the New York Giants on September 9, 1946, he had to fight a major league case of nerves. While in the outfield, he had trouble with his very first play.

"Playing in front of twenty thousand people, I had trouble moving my legs," he recalled. "I was so scared. There was a fly ball I should have eaten up, but I couldn't get my damn legs to move."

In a profession where practical jokes have been elevated to a demented sort of art form, players receiving the call sometimes act with a bit of suspicion. Bill Monboquette was playing for the Minneapolis Millers, the Triple-A team for the Red Sox, in 1958 when he received a phone call informing him that he had been called up to Boston. If the caller was expecting an elated response from the pitcher, he was surely disappointed, and probably a bit confused.

"I hung up on them four or five times because I thought someone was playing games with me," explained Monbouquette, who would go on to pitch for eleven seasons in the majors and appear on three All-Star teams.

Prior to the 1969 season, Jack DiLauro was traded from the Tigers to the Mets, never having made it to Detroit after six successful seasons in their farm system. He left Spring Training with the Mets' Triple-A club, the Tidewater Tides, and got off to a quick start, winning his first two games. While on the road in Richmond, he got a call at five in the morning from manager Clyde McCullough telling him to be in the hotel restaurant in a half hour—he was going to the big leagues. DiLauro, thinking it was a joke to get him out of bed that early, "agreed" to be there then hung up the phone and went back to sleep.

A half hour later, the phone rang again.

"Hey, DiLauro! Get your ass down here now or you're going to lose your opportunity!"

DiLauro, now very annoyed, retorted, "Who in the hell is this?"

"This is the skip, man," came the reply. "This is Clyde. Get down here now!"

DiLauro realized that it really was his manager on the phone. He went down to the restaurant and had some coffee with McCullough. As his manager began giving him the information, he still thought he was being played with. After all of the frustration with the Tigers, there was no way he could actually be going to the majors this soon with the Mets.

McCullough finally convinced his pitcher that he was going to the Mets. Nolan Ryan had pulled a groin muscle and DiLauro was known to be able to start or relieve and get lefthanders out. The next problem was that DiLauro had no clothes to wear to the majors, as big league players were required to wear jackets and ties on the road and minor leaguers were not.

DiLauro rented a car to drive back to Norfolk, collected his clothes, missed his first flight and finally arrived in New York. He hailed a cab and told the driver to take him to the players' entrance at Shea Stadium. True to form in how the day was going, the cabbie refused to believe DiLauro was the new pitcher for the Mets until they got close to the stadium.

The game was well underway when DiLauro got to the clubhouse. After getting into his uniform, he went to bullpen to meet some teammates and watch the rest of the game. Wanting to see what the stadium looked like, he walked out from underneath the overhang in the bullpen.

As soon as he walked into the lights, thirty to forty thousand fans began roaring. Stunned, DiLauro could only stand and gawk as the fans rose to their feet in a thunder of applause, apparently in response to his appearance. With little else to do, he tipped his hat and bowed to his adoring public.

But fame is such a fleeting thing. As it turned out, Phil Niekro had been throwing a no-hitter against the Mets, but a New York batter had just broken it up with a base hit as DiLauro was stepping into the light, thus drawing the crowd's ovation.

Two years later, another Mets pitcher, Jon Matlack, made his debut. It was shortly before the All-Star break when he broke in at Cincinnati's Riverfront Stadium. He left the game when he was pinch-hit for, the Mets down 2-1. The Mets proceeded to score two runs that inning, giving him a shot at the win. To give him some innings before the break, Tom Seaver was brought in to finish the game and Matlack went to the showers feeling that this game was in the bag. But Fate intervened in form of Tony Perez, who hit his second home run of the game and kept Matlack out of the win column.

Jay Johnstone was off to a hot start in 1966, hitting over .400 in Double-A El Paso. After the first ten games, he was called up to Seattle, then the Angels' Triple-A club, when outfielders Al Spangler and Bubba Morton were injured when they collided into each other during a play.

He was continuing with his torrid hitting in Seattle when the Angels lost Rick Reichardt when he had to undergo emergency surgery. Seeing no reason to keep Johnstone's bat in the minors, the Angels brought him to The Show. Johnstone recalled his first impression of the big leagues, when he stepped into the new ballpark in Anaheim.

"I looked at that grass and saw it was all cut criss-cross, the infield was red clay, and there was, like, fifty lights on each light stand. You talk about heaven!"

Johnstone went one for four in his first game, with his first major league hit coming off of Cleveland's Gary Bell.

In 1990, Indians farmhand Jeff Manto received the news that he was going to the majors from his manager in Colorado Springs, who apparently was unimpressed by the promotion.

Said Manto, "He came and told me, 'I don't know why, but you're going to the big leagues.'"

Upon arriving in Cleveland, Manto soon discovered that playing in a major league-sized park didn't necessarily mean that one played before a major league-sized crowd. Teammate Tom Brookens assured him that the fans would show up. But only 8,500 showed up, scattered throughout the stands in the old, cavernous Cleveland Stadium, to watch Manto make his debut with the woeful Indians.

After pitching in the minors for four seasons, Mark Eichhorn made his debut with the Toronto Blue Jays as they were playing in Baltimore. Eichhorn's nerves were in overdrive. On the day of his start, he was too nervous to eat. When it came time to warm up, he blew through his routine and was ready to go after five minutes.

The first batter he faced was Al Bumbry, a veteran with a slew of mind games to play against his nervous rookie adversary. Just as Eichhorn was about to throw his first major league pitch, Bumbry, with exceptional timing, stepped out of the batter's box and called for a time-out and asked the umpire to check the ball for any tampering. When the umpire requested the ball, a shaking Eichhorn bounced the ball halfway to the plate as he threw to the catcher.

Finally, the moment of reckoning came. No more hitters stepping out of the box. No more ball inspections. Now was the moment for Eichhorn to become a major league pitcher. He wound up and threw his first major league pitch. It was official— he was now a major leaguer. He was also instantly stuck with the lead-off batter on third base as Bumbry drilled the pitch off the centerfield wall for a triple.

Standing on the bag at third, Bumbry looked over to Eichhorn and grinned.

"Welcome to the big leagues, kid," he yelled.

In 1954, Guy Morton was called up by the Red Sox and stayed with the team for the last four weeks of the season. He only appeared in one game, striking out in his only at-bat. Although he would play pro ball for years to come, that single at-bat marked the total for his major league career.

"But I enjoyed it," laughed Morton.

Thirty-seven years later, Eric Wedge made his debut with the Red Sox. Having spent a great deal of the 1991 injured, he went down to Florida to get some work done in instructional league after the regular minor season was over. Two days after reporting to Florida, he was called up to Boston, where the Sox were fighting for the A.L. East crown.

In his only at-bat of his first major league season, he hit a single while pinch-hitting for Jack Clark.

Although he would play a few more seasons in the majors, it was his first experience of Fenway Park that still remained clear after he hung up his catcher's mask for the last time.

"Stepping on the field there in Fenway, which has so much tradition—it just demands respect. You're in a state of euphoria when you step on that field. It's unbelievable."

Like the players, umpires, too, dream of the day they might get the call. John Kibler was one of three umpires vying for a major league slot during Spring Training in 1963. Doug Harvey, one of the other candidates, got the job while Kibler and fellow umpire Bill Williams were assigned to the International League.

When Kibler returned home following the conclusion of the Triple-A season, he found a telegram on his door directing him to report to Chicago for a Cubs game as soon as possible. He left the following morning, but was late in arriving due to flight delays. Upon reaching Wrigley Field in the first inning, he got dressed and was out on the field at the top of the second inning.

As the game progressed, fellow umpire Shag Crawford briefed him on the ground rules of the park. Following the game, the crew drove to Milwaukee where Kibler worked behind the plate for the first time in the majors.

Tales from the Rookie Seasons

After Jack DiLauro's second day with the Mets, manager Gil Hodges called a meeting. Hodges, normally very mild-mannered, was upset at his team's recent play and began tearing into the players. At one point, he kicked a laundry basket up into the air, sending dirty underwear flying all over the locker room. As gravity took over, a jock strap landed on top of coach Yogi Berra's head.

Unaware of the mishap that had befallen his coach, Hodges continued his rant. Berra, apparently unsure of what to do, simply stood still, not daring to move lest he attract Hodges' attention and wrath.

As Hodges turned to walk back to his office, he saw Berra standing solemnly at attention, his head graced with the dirty jock and a look of awkward discomfort on his face. The manager stood there for a moment, staring at his coach.

A heavy silence descended in the clubhouse as no one was sure what Hodges would do next.

But the sight of Berra was too much for the manager and he couldn't help but to burst out laughing. After he had closed his office door, the players followed suit, breaking the tension in the clubhouse. It may have been the turning point in the season that resulted in the first World Series championship for the Mets.

"It was never the same team after that," said DiLauro.

It would be five years between major league stints for John Romonosky. After spending six weeks with the Cardinals in 1953, the minor league veteran was still classified as a rookie in the major leagues. In 1958, he was called up again, this time by the Washington Senators.

After appearing in games against the Athletics and Indians,

he took the mound in Fenway Park to face the legendary Ted Williams.

"I always wanted to be able to tell my grandchildren that I struck out Ted Williams," said Romonosky.

But the hurler soon learned about the difference between established hitters and rookie pitchers in the major leagues. After quickly getting two strikes on Williams, he began to work the corner of the plate, hoping to sneak the third strike by Teddy Ballgame. His first attempt was ruled a ball by the umpire. After his second attempt, which he clearly felt had crossed the plate, was also called a ball, he grew frustrated and challenged the umpire.

"Where the heck was that pitch?" Romonosky yelled.

The umpire removed his mask and walked halfway out to the mound to confront the pitcher. Looking straight into Romonosky's glare, the umpire calmly responded.

"Young man, I want to tell you something. You see those thirty-five thousand people up there?" asked the ump, pointing to the crowd. "They didn't come to see you pitch. They came to see Williams hit. Now get your butt out there and throw the ball!"

Williams would go on to own Romonosky that summer, hitting two home runs off of him. In comparison, Romonosky fared better against Mickey Mantle, whom he held to two mere singles while pitching five scoreless innings against the Yankees—the only two hits he allowed in the game.

As mentioned in Chapter 2, Jay Johnstone was well known in the majors for his oddball nature. His first experiences in his rookie year no doubt helped to hone his eccentricities. Several veterans on the Angels were on hand to help the rookie out in this regard.

He lockered next to Dean Chance. "Here I am, a rookie," he recalled. "And on my right, is Dean Chance telling me about every deal he could get me. This guy made more deals than Monty Hall [the host of *Let's Make a Deal*] ever thought of making."

It didn't stop in the locker room. His first big league

roommate on the road was Jimmy Piersall, another well-known eccentric. The first time Johnstone walked into the hotel room, Piersall yelled, "Stop right there!"

Johnstone immediately complied.

"Let's get one thing straight," Piersall continued. "I'm the captain of this room. What I watch on TV, you watch on TV. When I go to bed, you go to bed. When I get up, you get up."

Johnstone, fresh out of active duty with the Marines, had no problems with these orders.

"By the way," Piersall went on. "I like a little chocolate ice cream each night before I go to bed, so if you can get me some, I'd appreciate it if you put it in that little refrigerator over there."

Reporters asked Angels manager Bill Rigney why he roomed a promising young rookie with the aging, eccentric veteran Jimmy Piersall.

Rigney responded, "I didn't want to screw up *two* rooms."

"Maybe he knew something then that I never knew," said Johnstone.

CHAPTER 28

The Season Closes

I'm proud to say that it's my profession.
It's what I do.

—*Jim Pankovits, roving instructor*

In 2002, Mike Mohler was playing in his thirteenth professional season. A pitcher with over three hundred appearances in the majors, he spent his thirty-fourth birthday with the Rochester Red Wings, Baltimore's Triple-A farm team. A few days later, he was signing autographs prior to a game when he stopped to look at a baseball card from his early playing days that a fan had given him to sign. Thirty-four years of age may be young by most standards, but a baseball career can put a different perspective on time.

Grinning (and to the amusement of some nearby, younger teammates), he said, "You know you've been around a long time when you have cards that show you wearing a 'uni' [uniform] they're now wearing for 'Turn Back the Clock' Night."

Summer is nearly over. The grass, once the light green of spring, has darkened over the season and now lies in the shadows that have grown long by game time. The paint on

306

the outfield signs has blistered and begun to peel in the unrelenting sun of July and August. For the players, it's time to look back upon the season to see if this is where they thought they'd be. Some have league playoffs still to look forward to. Others wonder if September will find them in the big leagues—a dream fulfilled.

For all there is to consider in wait for next year, there is also the thought that this season is the last. The young player may have reached the peak of his talents in the minors. With no hope of making the majors, it is time to retire while still in his early twenties. Perhaps there is the chance of coaching or scouting, or perhaps it is time to leave the field for good.

The veteran looks at his options. There may have been some time in the majors during his career, or maybe he has stalled repeatedly in Triple-A. With a family to support and a long-shot chance of a return to the majors, is he ready to gamble on another season?

Steve Fireovid pitched for the Padres in 1981 and 1983, the Phillies in 1984, the White Sox in 1985, and the Mariners in 1986. In 1992, he returned to the majors with the Texas Rangers. Although he's appreciative of the opportunity he had to play, Fireovid admits he's one of the rare players who played longer than he really wanted to. But at the time, he couldn't find a career outside of baseball that interested him. Even during those later years of his career, the aesthetics of the game still appealed to him.

"I enjoyed the romantic side of the game," he said. "Making the perfect pitch at the right time, pushing my body to the limit to get the most out of it."

Most players, though, are given little choice in their retirement. Professional baseball is no charity, and with a fresh crop of players arriving each year, there is precious little time for a player to prove himself before he finds himself cut from the roster. But there are those who are left with the choice for themselves. What makes them finally leave their playing days behind, or choose to grind it out for another year?

Waiting for Another Spring

In 1996, Steve Bourgeois pitched in fifteen games for the San Francisco Giants. It was his last time in the majors. Since then, he has played in Triple-A and Mexico and back to Triple-A again. Despite an uncertain future, he still aims for a big league return.

"As long as I have a uniform on," he said in 2000, "I have a chance."

Another member of the "Rookie Class of 1996" who has since returned to the minors, outfielder Jon Zuber, also believes that he has more baseball seasons ahead of him—and more time in the majors.

"The thing that keeps me going is that inside, when I step out on the field, I think that I can help the team win. And I think at the major league level, I have something to offer a team if I could get the opportunity."

Adam Hyzdu was seemingly on the inside track to major league stardom. In 1990, the San Francisco Giants selected the eighteen-year-old outfielder as their first round choice (and the fifteenth overall pick) in the amateur draft. But as the seasons went by, he acquired the label of that of a minor league journeyman.

Ten years later, he was playing for Altoona in the Double-A Eastern League. In fact, he had only spent one complete season above Double-A ball despite his solid batting. Gone was the teenage prospect. In 2000, Hyzdu was a husband and father balancing the needs of his family and the dream of playing major league baseball.

"Every year it gets harder," he said of his career and his off-field demands.

Jason Baker's return to baseball as an outfielder was over before the end of the 2000 season. By August, he had returned to the mound full time. Although he had some regrets about giving up his bat, he still was very much aware of his fortune in being able to stay in the game.

"It's just fun playing. I enjoy being with the guys. I know some day it's all going to go. I'm going to do a regular job so I'm going to enjoy this while I can."

In more than a decade of professional baseball, Nate Minchey has traveled many roads from the bus rides of the Midwest League to the bullet trains of Japan. He's been traded, called to the majors, sent back to the minors, and released. After staring at life after baseball numerous times, he greets each new season with great appreciation.

"I've quit, retired, and checked out at least ten times in my career," he said. I spent five years in A-ball, so there were many nights I was going to quit. After a bad game, I would look out the window of the team bus on the way back to the hotel and think about possible career moves as each business went by. It would be like, 'Could I deliver pizza? Could I pump gas? Could I sell auto parts?'"

Minchey found himself with an injured arm and without a team at the end of the 1996 season. By February the following year, his agent was still unable to get him a contract. Minchey himself began to make phone calls, but with no success. As he and his wife began discussing plans for their future lives, a last-ditch call to a friend with the Colorado Rockies came through with an invitation to Spring Training. He made the team on the last day of training camp. His performance that year was enough to get him an offer from Japan.

"That's how close I was to being out of the game. Every day after that is just gravy."

End of the Road

It's the end of the 2000 season and the Albuquerque Dukes are involved in yet another league playoff. But even as the players take the field, the other club personnel must prepare for a future without the Dukes. Aside from some of the players and coaches, no team personnel will be going to the new Dodgers affiliate in Portland for 2001.

Media Relations Director John Miller was still undecided about his career after the close of the 2000 season. "I'd stay in baseball if the right opportunity were there," he explains. "I feel I've been in it long enough. I don't have to be desperate like I used to be—that I would go to the ends of the earth to do this anymore. I've grown to like Albuquerque in the short time I've been here. Maybe I'll stay here."

Phil Dauphin was cut by the Montreal Expos during Spring Training in 1996 while attempting a comeback following a knee injury. This is a common occurrence in the spring for veterans trying to get a roster spot, but falling just short of the team's needs.

"When you get cut in the minors during Spring Training, you find out when you show up and see that your locker has been cleaned out," said Dauphin. "Nobody wants to say anything to you because they know it could be them next."

Shortly after his release, he was signed by the Angels. The plan was for him to play in Lake Elsinore (Class A) just long enough to make sure the knee was fine before being moved up. The night before he was to report to Lake Elsinore, he was in a traffic accident and hurt his back. Afraid of being released, he did not tell team officials and tried to tough it out. But after struggling through the season, he decided to retire.

"Injury or no injury, it was time to get out. During the national anthem before games, I would get this nervous, butterflies-in-the-stomach feeling. Now it was gone. I knew this was it—time to shut it down."

At least the season ended on a high note as the team won the California League title, the second championship of his minor league career. He gave that championship ring to his mother and still wears the ring he won with the Iowa Cubs.

Dauphin had played for seven years in the minor leagues for

the Cubs, Reds, Braves, Expos, and Angels, but never got a cup of coffee in the majors. It's a bittersweet feeling, having come close. But he also remains aware of how special his experience in baseball was.

"I always thought when I get done, I'd want to know that I did everything I could to get to the big leagues. I feel like I did. It's a little bit tougher because at least I was on the big league rosters of two teams, which a lot of guys don't get a chance to do. I felt like, 'God, I was so close!'

"But then I can tell people that I went to Spring Training and had a locker next to Randy Myers. Man, it was amazing! Getting dressed next to all these guys I had seen on TV—Grace, Sandberg, and Randy Myers. Having a Cubs batting practice jersey with my name on it."

George Virgilio was both a teammate and a roommate of Phil Dauphins for three years in the minor leagues. Like Dauphin, he played for several organizations (Braves, Expos, and Orioles), but never made it to the major leagues. Along with his farm system experience, he spent a year playing in Italy and another with the New Jersey Jackals of the independent Northeast League. He also spent winters playing in Hawaii, Puerto Rico, and the Dominican Republic.

He retired in 1998, despite offers to play for other teams. "I still have chances to go back, but it's time to turn the page," he said in 2000. Late in 2000, he became an associate scout for the Houston Astros. Although content to put his playing days behind him, he still wanted to remain in the game.

"Some people go to school for an education and get a degree in something. My 'degree in something' is in baseball, in a sense. I've been to a certain part of the game that a lot of people can't get to, and I can pass that on. It's not necessarily that I want to be a scout, but it's a foot in the door."

Guy Morton played in the minors for another six seasons after his single at-bat with the Red Sox before returning to school to complete his degree. In those six years, he often made the league's All-Star team (and was, in fact, voted to the Carolina League's first team of their All-Time All-Star Team ahead of Johnny Bench, who made it to the second team). However, he was often hindered by a recurring injury of an Achilles tendon. During his time in college, he became involved with coaching scholastic baseball. However, by 1961, he had a wife and three children to support.

The actual decision to finally leave the game was based on practicality. He knew the chances of a thirty-year-old minor league journeyman returning to the majors were slim, especially in the days when only sixteen major league teams existed. Heeding a different calling away from the diamond, he became a church pastor and still remains in the ministry today.

"I knew I was going to wake up and not have a job out there in the future," he explained. "That's the tragedy of playing minor league ball. You'll stick with it so long, believing that you're going to make the majors. Before long, you're thirty years old, your friends have finished college, have their own practices and careers—and there you are and you haven't even finished your degree. Suddenly you have to wake up to that. I had to wake up to that, too."

Despite spending the last forty-plus years away from the game, he still realizes how special that time was. The days he spent playing with teammates like Ted Williams, Bobby Doerr, Harmon Killebrew, and Hank Aaron remain clear in his mind.

"I love the game. Memories like that are more than money can buy—getting to know these people; a lot of great pitchers I caught."

John Wehner's boyhood dream of playing for the Pittsburgh Pirates came true in 1991. After a World Series-winning stint with the Florida Marlins, he returned to his beloved Pirates. In 2000, he etched his own name in team history when he hit the final home run in the history of Pittsburgh's Three Rivers Stadium. After playing for the Pirates in their new ballpark in 2001, Wehner retired.

Kelly Gruber enjoyed a successful career in the majors for ten years. The two-time All-Star third baseman also won a World Series in 1992 with the Toronto Blue Jays. But spinal injuries cut his playing days short after he played in eighteen games for the California Angels in 1993.

Despite the grueling pain in his back, he was still hungry for more playing time. Following surgery to fuse several vertebrae in his neck, he attempted a comeback with the Baltimore Orioles in 1997.

"I went back primarily to make sure I was done," Gruber said of his decision to return to the field.

After spending a few months with the Rochester Red Wings, the Orioles' Triple-A team, he was sure that he was, indeed, done.

"I wasn't playing up to my capabilities. It wasn't fun for me anymore."

With that, he retired permanently with the knowledge that he had given the game his best effort and left behind no lingering questions.

Mike Smithson pitched in the majors for eight years. After being released by the Angels in the spring of 1990, he retired. He currently coaches baseball at his old high school in Centerville, Tennessee.

After injuring his leg in 1954, Jim Greengrass played another two seasons in the majors, but the leg never completely healed. He continued to play another six seasons in the Pacific Coast League with the hope of returning to the major leagues, but his hope never came to fruition and he retired from baseball at age thirty-six.

"I never regretted any of it," he said of his years in the game. "I had a good time and had ups and downs like everyone else."

The end of John Romonosky's pitching career began, strangely enough, with eight shutout innings. Although primarily a relief pitcher for the Senators, he was used to start a game during a double-header in 1959. After throwing seven scoreless innings, he began to tire, but was reluctant to tell his manager for fear of losing his spot on the big league roster.

He pitched a scoreless eighth inning, but eight innings was a lot for someone whose arm was conditioned for shorter durations, and the stress began to show. The first three batters in the ninth each doubled with long line drives to the outfield wall, scoring two runs. Finally, Washington manager Cookie Lavagetto pulled his makeshift starter from the game.

A couple of days later, Romonosky's shoulder began to hurt. After being diagnosed with an inflamed tendon, he was given a cortisone shot. Rather than having him take up a roster spot while waiting for his shoulder to heal, the team sent him to their Double-A team in Chattanooga (they had no Triple-A team at the time) for what was supposed to be a temporary stay.

However, once a pitching spot was open in Washington, the Senators called up a young southpaw instead of Romonosky. This lefthander, Jim Kaat, would go on to pitch for twenty-five years in the major leagues, winning 283 games and 16 Gold Glove awards. Despite his frustration with the injury he felt was from misuse by his manager, Romonosky, to this day, has no hard feelings over being passed up for the other pitcher.

"They brought up the right guy," Romonosky said, over forty years later. "He was a real nice fellow, too. We used to play miniature golf together."

Romonosky would play in the minors for two more years, pitching in the Yankees farm system in 1960 and for the Twins Double-A team, Nashville, in 1961. With the demise of the Southern Association, to which Nashville belonged, following the 1961 season, Romonosky was one of many minor leaguers out of work. He considered playing in the Mexican League for a few more years, but having experienced the climate and the living conditions there before, finally decided to retire.

After his fourth season, Steve Dawes was informed that he had been traded to the Cardinals to be a player-coach in their farm system. Although initially excited, he decided to call it a career after weighing a coach's pay and schedule against other things he could be doing outside of baseball. "I didn't want to hang around just to be hanging around," he said of his decision to leave the game.

John Herrnstein decided to hang up his uniform when the Atlanta Braves informed him that he would start the 1967 season in Richmond, their Triple-A team. Over thirty years later, he still stands by his decision. "The minor leagues were fine on the way up, but not on the way down."

It was a few hours before the final game of the 2000 Frontier League season and Chillicothe pitcher Nathan Gardner was looking back over his career. He first came to the Paints in 1997 after graduating college and getting bypassed in the amateur draft. A year later, he was signed by the Reds and spent two years in their farm system before being released. He returned to Chillicothe for one more season.

After the game was over, he was returning home to Charleston, West Virginia with his playing days behind him. Perhaps he would get into coaching at some point in the future, but for now he was out of baseball. Did he have any regrets about never making the majors?

"No, it's been a lot of fun. I got to see a lot of places I never would have seen if I wasn't in baseball. I met a lot of great people."

On August 10, 1952, Ron Neccai (he of the twenty-seven-strikeout game in the minors) made his major league debut with the Pittsburgh Pirates. A rotator cuff injury the following spring effectively ended his career. After a brief comeback attempt in the Pacific Coast League in 1955, he retired for good.

"I had a great time," he recounted. "I'm not unhappy about losing my career to an injury. I would like to have played more, but I'm one guy who can say, 'I gave the game a nickel and made a fortune out of it.'"

Transition

Baseball life continues, sometimes as planned and other times taking unexpected turns. The interviews for this book took place in 2000 and 2001. Here is where some of the interviewees were in 2003.

Chris Bourjos retired in 1983 due to leg problems. In 1984, he began working for the Toronto Blue Jays as a scout, mostly observing major leaguers for trade information. During a brief tenure scouting amateurs, he signed Chris Weinke, who never made it as a major leaguer but later won the Heisman Trophy as a quarterback for Florida State. Bourjos also signed Blue Jays pitching ace Roy Halladay. In 2003, he joined the scouting department of the Montreal Expos.

After the 1971 season, Joe Nossek retired from playing baseball. The following year, the Milwaukee Brewers hired him to manage the Danville Warriors, their affiliate in the Midwest League. In what would be his only year of managing in the minors, he led the Warriors to the league title. In 1973, he was tabbed to be the Brewers' third base coach. He is currently a coach for the Chicago White Sox.

The 2000 season marked an end for Bryan Eversgerd's pitching career after twelve seasons. It did not mean the end of his baseball career, though, as 2001 saw him coaching the young pitchers of the Potomac Cannons, a Class-A Cardinals team.

"I think what keeps me going is the competition," said Eversgerd. "Plus the fact that I've made a living at a game I love to play. I feel fortunate to do this."

Trey Hillman returned to manage the Columbus Clippers in 2001, his eleventh as a manager in the Yankees organization. During the following off-season, he accepted a position as Director of Player Development for the Texas Rangers. After spending a year in the front office, he returned to the dugout, this time in Japan, to manage the Nippon Ham Fighters of the Pacific League.

Chris Poulsen played another two years for the Chillicothe Paints before retiring after the 2002 season.

After his major league resurrection with the Indians in 2000, Chris Nichting pitched for the Cincinnati Reds and Colorado Rockies in 2001 and 2002. Looking back on his more than ten years in the minors and handful of seasons in the big leagues, he wishes he had bought a camera back when he started in 1988 to take pictures of every ballpark he played in.

"How amazing would it be just to have a collage of fields, both inside and outside. Some of them don't even exist anymore."

Bill Valentine became an American League umpire in 1963. His career ended in 1968 when he was fired after helping form the umpire's union. Although he wishes he could have been in baseball for a longer amount of time, he has no regrets about helping his fellow umpires during a time when pay was low and benefits, including a break during the season, were few.

In 1985, Jay Johnstone retired after playing the major leagues for twenty years with the Angels, White Sox, Phillies, Yankees, Padres Cubs, and Dodgers and winning two World Series rings. Johnstone still keeps in contact with Jimmy Piersall, the veteran he roomed with on the road during his rookie year.

"He taught me a lot about baseball," Johnstone said. "But he taught me even more about life."

Following his 2000 stint with the Columbus Clippers, Jon Zuber went to Japan, playing for the Yokohama Bay Stars of the Central League. In 2002, he returned to the United States, playing in the Reds organization at Triple-A Indianapolis before retiring.

Johnny Pesky remains a baseball lifer. After a ten-year career with the Red Sox, Tigers, and Senators that included an All-Star selection in 1946, he went into the coaching ranks in both the minor and major leagues. He also managed the Red Sox in 1963 and 1964 and again for a five-game interim in 1980. He still works as a roving instructor in the minors.

J.M. Gold's career has been plagued by arm problems requiring major surgery. The pitcher, who was selected by the Brewers out of high school in the first round of the 1998 draft, pitched for the High Desert Mavericks of the Single-A California League in 2003.

Jamie Keefe was named the manager of the Chillicothe Paints in 2001 and is now in his third season at the helm of the team.

Gene Bennett still works in the Cincinnati Reds front office. After over fifty years, he has many former teammates whom he remains in touch with who have also gone on to become major league coaches, managers, and team officials.

R.A. Dickey made his major league debut with the Texas Rangers on April 22, 2001. He still pitches for the Rangers.

Chad Akers, who had returned to affiliated ball in 1999 after three-plus seasons in the independent Northern and Atlantic Leagues, completed his second full season in Triple-A Tacoma with a solid .297 batting average in 2001. During Spring Training the following year, he was injured. His playing career remains in limbo.

Following his unexpected managerial stint with Dubois County in 2000, Fran Riordan continued in his role as player-manager the following season with the Richmond Roosters. In his first full season at the helm of a team, he guided the Roosters to the Frontier League championship while also being chosen as the first baseman on the league's annual All-Star team. He returned to the Roosters in 2002, leading them to another league title (the first back-to-back champions in Frontier League history) while repeating his All-Star honors at first base. He also became the Frontier League's career hits leader during his second stint with the Roosters when he got his 404th base hit at, coincidently, Dubois County.

Due to the league's age restrictions, he retired after the 2002 season. His number was retired by the Roosters. He played for the North Shore Spirit of the Northeast League in 2003.

After his major league career with the Reds, Cardinals, and Phillies, Chuck Harmon scouted for the Indians and Braves. He also continued his involvement in basketball as a scout for the Indiana Pacers during their ABA years. He has been inducted into the Indiana High School Halls of Fame for baseball and basketball as well as the University of Toledo Hall of Fame for those two sports. A Little League baseball field in his hometown of Washington, Indiana has been named in his honor. He currently resides in Cincinnati and gives talks to students about his experiences.

Even decades after he retired, Harmon has trouble sometimes letting it sink in that he had played major league baseball. "I'm seventy-six and still can't believe I was playing with Willie Mays. But I've got evidence," he said in 2000.

Johnstown outfielder Ben Crowley returned to the Johnnies for his third and fourth seasons in 2001 and 2002. He also continues to coach at Catholic University during their winter workout camp.

John Kibler umpired in the National League from 1963 until his retirement in 1989. During his tenure, he officiated in four All-Star Games and four World Series.

Four years after Rick Cerone brought professional baseball

back to his hometown of Newark, New Jersey, he gave the city a new baseball milestone. The Bears defeated the Blueport Bluefish in the championship finals to win the 2002 Atlantic League crown, the city's first professional baseball title since 1946.

Two weeks after his interview for this book, Adam Hyzdu was called up to the major leagues by the Pittsburgh Pirates. After eleven seasons in the minors, he finally made it to The Show. He continues to play for the Pirates.

Pat Ahearne continues to pitch in professional baseball. After leading the Eastern League with a 2.61 ERA in 1999, he pitched for the Mariners' Triple-A team in Tacoma in 2000 and led the league in wins with thirteen. He signed with the Florida Marlins as a free agent later that year and played for Triple-A Calgary in 2001. He returned to Blueport of the Atlantic League for the first part of the 2002 season before being signed by the Detroit Tigers. After completing the season with the Toledo Mud Hens, Detroit's top farm team, he went to South America to play for Caracas in the Venezuelan Winter League. He pitched in the Tigers farm system again in 2003.

Following the 2000 season, the Cleveland Indians promoted Akron manager Eric Wedge to their Triple-A team in Buffalo. Wedge led the Bisons to the International League playoffs for the next two seasons and was named the Minor League Manager of the Year by *The Sporting News* in 2002. In 2003, Wedge returned to the major leagues—this time as the manager of the Indians.

After retiring from baseball, John Romonosky joined the Franklin County Sheriff's department in Columbus, Ohio. He began working special off-duty hours at Jets Stadium, home of Pittsburgh's Triple-A team. Word quickly got around to the managers there that one of the deputies was an ex-major league pitcher. Desperate for someone who could consistently put the ball in the strike zone during batting practice (as this job usually fell to the coaches), they paid him to throw to their hitters. For another seventeen years Romonosky would have a locker in a minor baseball stadium as the batting practice pitcher. He still lives in the Columbus area.

At the end of the 2000 season, Jason Baker was offered a scouting job with the Tampa Bay Devil Rays organization. Still seeking to remain a player after spending five seasons in the minors and another in independent ball, he switched independent leagues, signing with the Albany Alligators of the All-American Association. After appearing in a few games for the Alligators in 2001, he retired.

Umpire Durwood Merrill retired after the 1999 season. In his twenty-three years in the majors, he officiated in two All-Star Games and the 1988 World Series. After his retirement, he continued to work with the Hooks Christian Service, a volunteer organization he co-founded to provide assistance for the poor in rural Texas. He passed away at age sixty-four on January 11, 2003.

Dave Campbell spent eight years in the major leagues, playing all four infield positions as well as outfield for the Tigers, Padres, Astros, and Cardinals. Today, he is a baseball analyst for ESPN television.

Former Chillicothe Paints manager Roger Hanners passed away at age seventy in January 2002. Hanners led the Paints to three divisional titles and a wild card playoff berth during his tenure. The Frontier League has since named its manager of the year award after him.

Former big league hurler Nate Minchey continues to pitch in Japan. In 2001, he changed teams, playing for the Chiba Lotte Marines and leading the Pacific League in earned run average. He was also named the league's Pitcher of the Month in September of 2002.

Broadcaster Andy Young left baseball after the 2001 season. The demands of a growing family (he and his wife had just had their first child) were a big factor in his decision, as well as his concerns as to whether he would ever land a major league job. He currently teaches English at Kennebunk High School. As for what the future holds for him, he recalls a comment from Paul McCurtain, a minor league pitcher whom he once interviewed.

"He [McCurtain] was talking about his baseball career and said, 'I'm still a work in progress,'" said Young. "You could apply that to life. That's what we all still are today."

Bill Lee retired from the major leagues following a fourteen-year career with the Red Sox and Expos, during which the colorful pitcher became known as "Spaceman." His playing days continued sporadically with, among other venues, the Senior Professional League and a barnstorming tour of Cuba sponsored by the Hooters restaurant chain. In 1988, he ran for president of the United States as a candidate of the Rhinoceros Party, an organization devoted to mocking politics.

Lee's son, Andrew, also pitched professionally in the minors and independent leagues.

Dave Bresnahan became a stockbroker and financial advisor. Still enthralled with the game, he is also a season ticket holder for the Arizona Diamondbacks. He was sitting in his front row seats with his nine-year-old son as the Diamondbacks won the 2001 World Series.

After playing for three teams in two years in the Atlanta farm system, David Dalton was released by the Braves. He returned to his old team in independent ball, Chillicothe, for the 2001 season. In 2002, he was signed to a contract with Fortitudo Bologna of the Italian League.

Marty Brennaman still broadcasts games for the Cincinnati Reds. In 2000, he was honored with the Ford C. Frick Award, which is given annually by the Baseball Hall of Fame to a broadcaster in recognition of their excellence in their profession and for their contributions to the sport.

The Ties that Bind

Players are drafted and teams are assembled based on an organizations needs. Players of all backgrounds, from all over the country and beyond, from high school and college, are brought together to make a team. The seasons of sharing living space, long bus rides, the victories and defeats on the field, and the agonies and insecurities off the field forge friendships that are unforgettable. Some continue long after the last out is made in a career; others fall by the wayside as the people move on in their own directions.

After over ten years in baseball, Bryan Eversgerd and his wife count the friendships every December. Their Christmas card list has grown to over two hundred addresses.

"If I haven't seen a guy for five or six years and then I see him and talk to him, it's like we pick up right where we left off," said George Virgilio. "The camaraderie with the guys always seems to be there."

"You make some of your best and greatest friends in the minor leagues because you live with them day and night and you go through bad times and good times with them," said Fred Scherman. More than thirty years after their playing days ended, minor league roommates Scherman and Mike Kilkenny still maintain their friendship.

After the exact numbers from a long ago season begin to blur, and the recollection of a specific play fades in with all of the rest, the memories of friendships and the people remain clear. For Jim Pankovits, it stretches across the country—from the trailer in Covington, Virginia to the campfires built with other teammates on the beaches of Hawaii. He also remembers Bruce Bochy wearing a black armband on his uniform when Elvis died in 1977.

When former big league pitcher Ron Negray was asked if what the most memorable part of his career was, he reflected not on his own achievements, but on the players he knew.

"I played with seven Hall of Famers and against about seventeen," he said. "I played with a lot of players that went to the majors. Some became good players and some became good managers. Sparky Anderson, Roger Craig, Chuck Tanner, Tom Lasorda, Don Zimmer—these were my roommates also."

In 1950, John Romonosky played briefly for the Winston-Salem Cardinals in the Class-B Carolina League, managed by George Kissell. Forty-nine years later, Romonosky attended a major league game in Cincinnati in which the St. Louis Cardinals were the visiting team. George Kissell was still with the Cardinals, now as a minor league field coordinator, and was with the team at Cincinnati's Cinergy Field. When his ex-pitcher caught his attention, Kissell immediately recognized him despite the years that had passed. The two proceeded to reminisce about the 1950 Winston-Salem squad, which included a little second baseman named Earl Weaver.

"It was unbelievable that a man can remember every player of that year and those which he managed years before and years afterward," said Romonosky.

"It's the close-knit ties with the other players that I miss the most," says John Herrnstein in his office. A few mementos on a shelf are the only physical evidence there of a career that ended over thirty years ago. But the friendships and shared experiences of this game transcend the trappings of old photographs and yellowing baseballs with signatures in faded ink.

Final Outs

To this day, Phil Dauphin has difficulty describing baseball life to those who haven't been there. "I told my wife a couple times that there's stuff that's so off the wall that was just considered normal at the time. You come across so many characters, and it makes for such a good time. Then you step back and say, 'I can't believe we did that!'"

Sixto Lezacano has played on a myriad of fields from the sandlots of Puerto Rico to the grand stage of the World Series. During his twelve years of playing in the major leagues, he was never sent back down to the minors. Returning to the minors as a coach, he has seen many players end their careers in the anonymity of the bush leagues and a successful few progress to big leagues. For all of them, he offers this message from the heart.

"To all the minor league players that never made it to The Show, my congratulations for being brave enough to give all you had. And for those who contemplate this step as their next step, to remember that the meaning of 'failure' is 'not trying' and to try hard remembering that they are professional role models, too."

BIBLIOGRAPHY

Chadwick, Bruce, *Baseball's Hometown Teams—The Story of the Minor Leagues*; New York: Abbeville Press, 1994.

Groeschen, Tom, "Red's First African-American not Big News in 1954", *The Cincinnati Enquirer;* Cincinnati, Oh: Gannett Co., Inc., March 31, 1997.

Johnson, Lloyd and Miles Wolff, *The Encyclopedia of Minor League Baseball—Second Edition;* Durham, N.C.: Baseball America, Inc., 1997

Obojski, Robert, *Bush League: A Colorful, Factual Account of Minor League Baseball from 1877 to the Present;* New York: MacMillan Publishing Co., 1975.

Scandura, Mike, "The Longest Game Revisited: A Fifth Year Anniversary", *Pawtucket Red Sox Yearbook;* Pawtucket, R.I.: Pawtucket Red Sox, 1986.

Smith, Allen H. et. al., *Three Men on Third: A Book of Baseball Anecdotes, Oddities, and Curiosities;* New York: Breakaway Books, 2000.

Thorn, John; Peter Palmer, Michael Gershman, David Pietrusza, Matthew Silverman, Sean Lahman, *Total Baseball—Sixth Edition;* New York: Total Sports, 1999.

Reports and Box Scores by Unlisted Contributors Compiled from the Following Publications:

Baseball America; Durham, N.C.: Baseball America, Inc., 1998-2003.

The Columbus Dispatch; Columbus, Oh: Columbus Dispatch Printing Co., 1920-2000.

The Sporting News; St. Louis: The Sporting News Publishing Company, 1920-2000.

INTERVIEWEES

Bob Addis
Pat Ahearne
Chad Akers
Rick Asadoorian
Don August
Dennis Bair
Jason Baker
David Barnes
Larry Barnett
Joe Bauman
Gene Bennett
Joe Bick
Jim Bolger
Chris Booker
Bob Borkowski
Steve Bourjeois
Chris Bourjos
Alejandro Bracho
Marty Brennaman
Dave Bresnahan
Ken Brett
Rick Burleson
Dave Campbell
Rick Cerone
Harry Chenault

Tom Chism
Nick Clark
Mike Climer
Dave Collins
Ben Crowley
George Culver
David Dalton
Phil Dauphin
Justin Davis
Steve Dawes
Leah Deffenbaugh
Steve Deffenbaugh
Steve Demeter
Chris Dickerson
R.A. Dickey
Jack DiLauro
Bob Doerr
Marty Dunn
Mark Eichhorn
Harry Eisenstat
Chris Enochs
Bryan Eversgerd
Rodney Fender
Neil Fiala
Steve Fireovid

Cliff Fralick
Woody Fullencamp
Al Gallagher
Nathan Gardner
Jay Gehrke
Jerry Don Gleaton
J.M. Gold
Marty Good
Jim Greengrass
Tom Grieve
Shane Griffen
Steve Grilli
Gary Groll
Kelly Gruber
Don Gutteridge
Chris Hanners
Roger Hanners
Chuck Harmon
Jeff Heaverlo
John Herrnstein
Mike Hershberger
Robert Hewes
Holly Hill
Trey Hillman
A.J. Hinch
Cal Hogue
Rex Hudler
Adam Hydzu
Jay Johnstone
Bryan Joseph
Jamie Keefe
Kelly Keefe
John Kibler
Ralph Kiner
Jimmy Kowalski
Dave Koza

Josh Lamberg
Dominic Latkovski
Tom Lawless
Bill Lee
Tye Levy
Sixto Lezcano
Brad Lidge
Steve Luebber
Jeff Manto
Babe Martin
Jim Martz
Gordon Massa
Jon Matlack
Matt McLaughlin
Max McLeary
Durwood Merrill
John Miller
Nate Minchey
Jim Miner
Bill Monbouquette
Joe M. Morgan
Guy Morton
Ron Neccai
Ron Negray
Rocky Nelson
Scott Nelson
Chris Nichting
Joe Nossek
Jim Pankovits
Mel Parnell
Tom Parsons
John Pesky
Chris Poulsen
Cameron Reimers
Hank Riebe
Fran Riordan

Mike Roarke
Bob Robertson
Mike Robertson
Brooks Robinson
Kathy Robson
Garry Roggenburk
John Romonosky
Al Rosen
Reid Ryan
Joe Santry
Hank Sauer
Jim Saul
Fred Scherman
Ken Schnacke
Takuro Seki
Matt Sheets
Joe Short
Mike Smithson
Paul Splittorff
Dave Stapleton
Blake Stein
John Stewart
Mike Tamburro
Tommy Tanzer
Bobby Thomson
Brian Tollberg
Josh Turner
Bill Valentine
Mike Veeck
George Virgilio
Chico Walker
David Walling
Eric Wedge
John Wehner
John Wend
Jim White

Joel White
Bryan Wickline
Dallas Williams
Kevin Wolski
Andy Young
Jon Zuber

BVG